The Responsibility of Intellectuals

REVOLUTIONARY STUDIES
Series Editor: PAUL LE BLANC

The Responsibility of Intellectuals:
Selected Essays on Marxist Traditions in Cultural Commitment

ALAN M. WALD

HUMANITIES PRESS
New Jersey ▼ London

This collection first published 1992 by Humanities Press International, Inc., Atlantic Highlands, New Jersey 07716, and 3 Henrietta Street, Covent Garden, London WC2E 8LU

Library of Congress Cataloging-in-Publication Data

Wald, Alan M., 1946
    The responsibility of intellectuals : selected essays on Marxist traditions in cultural commitment / Alan M. Wald.
        p.   cm. — (Revolutionary studies)
    Includes index.
    ISBN 0–391–03735–8
    1. Radicalism—United States.   2. Intellectuals—United States. 3. Communism and intellectuals—United States. 4. Communism and culture—United States.   I. Title.   II. Series.
HN90.R3W35   1992
305.5'52—dc20   91–37649
                                 CIP

A catalog record for this book is available from the British Library

Printed in Mexico

To Dorothy and Quentin,
with love and gratitude

. . . writing, like other practices, is in an important sense always aligned: that is to say, that it variously expresses, explicitly or implicitly, specifically selected experience from a specific point of view.

Commitment, strictly, is conscious alignment, or conscious change of alignment.

. . . Thus to recognize alignment is to learn, if we choose, the hard and total specificities of commitment.

Raymond Williams, *Marxism and Literature* (1977)

Contents

PART IV. COMMITMENT

Acknowledgments

I am grateful to the following publications for permission to reprint essays in this volume:

Pembroke Magazine for "Sculptor on the Left," Spring 1987.

Michigan Quarterly Review for "The New York Literary Left," Winter 1989.

Monthly Review for "From Margin to Center," June 1990.

Smyrna Press for "Trotskyism in the Sixties," 1991.

The Nation magazine/The Nation Company, Inc., for "Remembering the Answers," December 26, 1981; and "C. P. Ups and Downs," June 12, 1982.

Radical America for "The Legacy of Howard Fast," January–February 1983; and "An Activist/Scholar Remembers," March 1987.

Minnesota Review for "Tethered to the Past," Fall 1978; "Radical Pedagogy," Spring–Fall 1988; and "Down the Academic Memory Hole," Spring 1991.

Boston Review for "Reading, Writing, and Red-Baiting," October 1986.

Guardian for "A Radical Writer Rediscovered," December 26, 1984; and "To Live without Hypocrisy," August 16, 1989.

Labour/Le Travail for "Marxism in the United States," Fall 1989.

MELUS for "The Culture of 'Internal Colonialism,'" Fall 1981; and "Theorizing Cultural Difference," Summer 1987.

Humanities in Society for "Hegemony and Literary Tradition in America," Fall 1982.

Against the Current for "In Tribute to *Burger's Daughter*," May–June 1986; "Racism and Academe," May–June 1988; "Free Speech and the Campus Anti-Racist Movement," May–June 1991; and "Chicano Radicalism," July–August 1991.

Radical Historians Newsletter for "Jacoby's Complaint," May 1988.

A Tribute to George Breitman, ed. Naomi Allen and Sarah Lovell (New York: F.I.T., 1987), for "Remembering George Breitman."

"Victor Serge and the New York Anti-Stalinist Left" was written in 1987 for a special issue of an Italian journal on Serge that never appeared; a French-language version was published in *Cahiers Leon Trotsky* (Grenoble), September 1988.

"Continuity in Working-Class Culture" was prepared in the early 1980s for a special issue of the journal *Sez*, which folded before publication.

Some portions of the Introduction have been adapted from Alan Wald's contribution to "Why Socialism Now?", *Jewish Currents*, July–August 1990.

Introduction

The History of a Literary Radical: From Old Left to New

The single most important and treasured fact of my political, intellectual, and personal life to date is that I had the good fortune to be a college student during the 1960s. The bulk of the scholarly work embodied in this selection of essays, and the axis of the political activism that has complemented my writing, are critical extensions of the theory and practice absorbed and lived in that decade.

My radicalization probably began in 1962 at the time of the Cuban Missile Crisis. As a junior at Walter Johnson High School in Bethesda, Maryland, I was startled by the news that several seniors had refused to cooperate in an air raid drill. The student body had been ordered by our teachers to practice an orderly retreat to the basement of the school building for "protection" in case a nuclear bomb was dropped by the Soviet Union on the United States' capital, seven miles from my school.

One of these older students, who by example taught me to challenge questionable societal values even when legitimatized by authority figures such as teachers, went on to attend Antioch College in Yellow Springs, Ohio. Some time later, I saw a newspaper photograph of "Antiochians" being hosed down by police as they demonstrated against a local barber who refused to cut African-Americans' hair. I knew instantly where I wanted to go to college.

After a first year devoted to creative writing, sexual initiation and some mild drug experimentation, I joined the local chapter of Students for a Democratic Society (SDS) in the fall of 1965. In January 1966, as part of Antioch's work-study program, I moved to Cleveland where I was affiliated with SDS's Economic Research and Action Project (ERAP), led by Paul Potter, Kathy Boudin, and others on the city's West Side. While studying at Fircroft College in Birmingham, England, in the fall of 1967 on an exchange program, I became convinced that I needed the structure and stability of a socialist organization to develop myself politically. Shortly after returning to Antioch in December 1967, I became a "candidate" member of the Young Socialist Alliance (YSA) whose Antioch members had until then worked effectively and in a nonsectarian manner inside the local SDS chapter.

In general, my experience during the 1960s gave me a notion of politics qualitatively different from what I had previously understood. I learned firsthand how "liberalism," the doctrine in which I had been schooled by my family and which seemed a pragmatic extension of my middle-class Jewish background, can ideologically assist domination. Whether by design or default, liberalism's proponents allow abstract worthy sentiments to obscure the real levers of power and the mechanisms of social change.

I also saw how mass movements, the motive force of any structural transformation of society, were built; how radical movements were sometimes derailed (especially by being channeled into the Democratic Party); and how the competition of political programs worked their way out within such movements. I learned about the interconnectedness of world affairs, something captured vividly in a pamphlet published at Antioch called *Detroit Is Vietnam* by a young professor, James D. Cockcroft, in the wake of the 1968 rebellion in Detroit's African-American community. From the political and personal struggles I experienced during the 1960s, I forged an alternative set of values that I have retained to this day.

However, it is important to emphasize that, while my encounter with the 1960s was first and foremost an activist experience, I also recall the decade as having been enhanced by a far greater intellectual depth than has been attributed to it by some of the recently published accounts. One popular image of the 1960s is that of mindless youths in a hedonistic rebellion, rejecting the "Old Left" in a fit of arrogance. My experience tended in the opposite direction. Indeed, it was only in the context of 1960s activism that I learned about the "Old Left" and the legacy of the struggles of working people, women, people of color, and radical intellectuals in the United States and around the world, something that had been shut out by my traditional education.

I remember vividly an SDS meeting at Antioch at which a member read aloud passages from Joseph Freeman's 1938 *An American Testament*, pointing out ways in which Freeman's experiences were parallel to our own. I eagerly took courses in which we studied writings by Randolph Bourne, John Reed, Richard Wright, and Lincoln Steffens. When I assumed an Antioch student government post as "Assistant Community Manager in Charge of Publications," we staff members launched a successful literary-political journal called *The Antioch Masses*, in honor of the most famous pre–World War I radical magazine.

Another significant Antioch SDS project was our successful effort in 1966 to get Carl Oglesby, former national president of SDS, hired by the college

as "Activist Scholar in Residence," With Oglesby's inspiration, I partici-
pated in seminars with readings that shuttled from Frantz Fanon and
Herbert Marcuse to Herman Melville and the Marquis de Sade. It was on
Oglesby's bookshelf in his cluttered office in the basement of Antioch's
Horace Mann Building that I first saw Isaac Deutscher's magnificent three-
volume biography of Leon Trotsky.

First in SDS, and later in a more organized fashion in the much better-
organized YSA, I participated in a steady series of study groups and other
educational activities. Even at Antioch, where all education was touted as
"relevant," the kind of study that took place in these groups—organized by
ourselves and aimed at helping us to more effectively change the world—
was by far the most vital and memorable educational experience I had there.
The combination of intellectual work and political practice at Antioch made
me much more curious about the world than all of the high school and
formal college class instruction I had ever taken. Moreover, it was in these
study groups that I first began to read feminist writings as well as literature
by and about people of color.

While in Cleveland as a member of ERAP I participated in a radical
theater that performed adaptations of Bertolt Brecht plays (the names of
characters and settings were changed, but not Brecht's politics) for the
white Appalachian community free of charge in a storefront. At Antioch
the SDS newsletter published poems on war and other political-personal
themes written by myself and others. The Antioch YSA attracted me
because a number of leading activists were drama majors, while others
possessed a contagious enthusiasm for history and philosophy. In short, the
intellectual-cultural dimension of the 1960s was crucial to my own formative experience and helped to shape my vision of the kind of socialist politics
that were necessary to emancipate society.

Most important for this volume of essays, the 1960s convinced me of the
need to continue and critically advance the traditions of left-wing activist-
scholars and cultural workers. In the United States, the various left traditions reached significant proportions in the 1930s, but their proponents had
then to face the terrible political tests of World War II, the blows of the
McCarthyite witch-hunt and disillusionment with the Soviet "experi-
ment." When the legacy of committed intellectuals was initially revived in
the 1960s, its New Left version seemed to be a step forward because it had
been purged of an earlier blind allegiance to the Soviet Union, although the
Maoist wing of the movement perhaps even more blindly adhered to China.
Moreover, the new incarnation of the tradition was rapidly responding to
many liberatory strains of thought—feminism, the nationalism of the oppressed, lesbian and gay rights—that were at best incipient in its earlier phases.

In retrospect, however, the 1960s manifestation of commitment was also retrogressive in the failure of its leading participants to construct a serious, internally democratic, coherent socialist organization with a pro-working-class perspective that could have embodied the experiences of the past and synthesized those of the present. By the end of the decade a polarization had begun. On the one hand, there were groups of self-proclaimed "Leninist parties" that evolved at different rates into tight-knit, dogmatic political sects. On the other hand, there was a general retreat from militancy accompanied by a simplistic rejection of caricatures of classical Leninism. By 1990 most of the left groups had become hermetically sealed cults, reduced to practical impotency. From the ex-radical apostates came tragic-comic declarations of allegiance to "post-Marxism."

Although this collection of essays mainly reflects the stages of my scholarship devoted to recouping what remains relevant of the Communist, Socialist, and Trotskyist cultural legacies in the United States, there are at least two important ways in which the underlying vision of socialism they embody was acquired during the 1960s.

From the early New Left of SDS and from various antiwar, antidraft, and civil rights organizations, I gained an appreciation of the indispensability of culture, community, antiracism, and gender equality to the socialist project, as well as a hatred of authoritarianism and a distrust of liberal palliatives.

From the Black Power movement I learned that those who have been the targets of oppression must lead the struggle against it. As a student and teacher of literature, I also learned from the cultural movements of African Americans, Latinos, Native American Indians, Asian Americans, and women about the disempowerment inherent in the uncritical assimilation of a patriarchal and Eurocentric culture. Participation in activities in support of the right of Palestinians to self-determination made me realize my strong sense of Jewish identity in a manner harmonious with the morality that had been instilled in me in my youth.

During the 1970s and 1980s, as a graduate student and professor in my late twenties and thirties, the rudimentary orientation described above was enriched and modulated in at least three other ways through continued political activism and complementary research into the history of the cultural left in the United States.

From the Trotskyist movement I acquired an understanding of how and why revolutions might degenerate because of certain material conditions and mistaken policies that subverted the revolutions' original goals. I also learned of the necessity of an internationalist perspective that places the human needs of oppressed people above loyalty to any particular state, party, ideology, nationality, or ethnicity, and I learned about the antidemo-cratic nature of one-party states and the substitution of an elite vanguard for the will of the general population.

From my encounters with individuals who participated in the Communist movement, I learned of the extraordinary heroism, selflessness, and dedication that is an indelible part of the U.S. working-class tradition. From those Communists profoundly shaken by the Khrushchev revelations of 1956, but who refused to renege on their commitment to fundamental social change, I learned how the admission of important mistakes can enrich and dignify the movement as a whole.

The impact of events of the past few years in Eastern Europe, China, Central America, South Africa, and the Middle East has rendered more complex but not fundamentally undermined my understanding of socialism as a system self-managed by democratic control of the economy by the associated producers. The strategy for achieving socialism still entails the encouragement of the working class and subaltern groups to struggle in organized self-activity for reforms in a manner resulting in a revolutionary democratic transformation of the state. Such a strategy needs to be adjusted to national conditions, including the needs of people of color, women, and various other oppressed groups.

While my fields of research bring me into contact with a plethora of writings by apostate Marxists, I have yet to encounter a perspective other than socialism that has the capacity to eliminate not only the horrors of capitalism and imperialism, but also to resolve the potentially explosive problems of the crumbling Stalinist states such as the Soviet Union and those in Eastern Europe. While I have never felt comfortable saying that I "believe" in socialism, I am convinced more than ever that socialism remains the only rational choice for an informed humanity. It is to a socialist future that the cultural interventions included in this volume are dedicated.

Those familiar with twentieth-century radical thought in the United States will probably recognize the texts invoked by the titles of this volume and its introduction. "The Responsibility of Intellectuals" refers to a landmark essay by Noam Chomsky that appeared in the *New York Review of Books* on 23 February 1967. With a passion, eloquence, and clarity that has haunted me ever since, Chomsky urged his colleagues to pledge their skills, resources, and the general advantages of their lives as middle-class academics to halting U.S. aggression in Vietnam.

The conjoining of "Marxism" and "Culture" in the volume's subtitle should immediately summon the name of Raymond Williams, without doubt the Marxist thinker who most significantly problematized the term "culture" in our time, and who was a harbinger of the explosion of Marxist theory in the humanities that now goes under the name of "Cultural Studies." The Introduction's title, "The History of a Literary Radical," is from an essay that itself became the title for a 1920 collection of writings by Randolph Bourne, an intellectual and opponent of World War I who didn't hesitate to stand alone while his mentors and colleagues adapted to the pro-war fashion of the times.

When I first began to assemble my essays for publication, I found that I had material that could easily fill a thousand pages, far too much for a single volume. I began by eliminating writings according to broad criteria. I chose not to include essays that were to any degree incorporated into or drawn from my first three books, *James T. Farrell: The Revolutionary Socialist Years* (1978); *The Revolutionary Imagination: The Poetry and Politics of John Wheelwright and Sherry Mangan* (1983); and *The New York Intellectuals: The Rise and Decline of the Anti-Stalinist Left from the 1930s to the 1980s* (1987). I next eliminated political and cultural writings on subjects upon which I had not conducted very much original research but had relied mainly on secondary sources—primarily political essays on topics such as the Nicaraguan Revolution, critical Leninism, and theories of postcapitalist societies. I then eliminated all of my shorter book reviews, which appeared in scores of publications ranging from the *New York Times* and *Washington Post* to specialized academic journals and radical newspapers.

I tried to group the remaining material into four broad categories that encompass the bulk of my writing.

"Trotskyism and Anti-Stalinism" was the focus of most of my primary research until the mid-1980s. The essays here are collateral to or complement my major research projects. Politically, they reflect my view that "anti-Stalinism" as a political posture had progressive political potential only so long as it was linked to a positive vision of revolutionary socialism (which for me includes some of the key elements of Trotskyism). While I regard the achievements of this trend in areas such as imaginative literature to be relatively minor, I nevertheless argue that the early stages of the cultural politics of this tradition embody a highly significant component of the socialist legacy that may partly serve as a guide to the future and most certainly affords instructive lessons into the past.

"Communism and Culture" includes essays that largely predate my present research on the lives of neglected and/or noncanonical Communist literary figures. For the most part these essays focus on critiques of the official Communist Party policies that should be understood largely as rationalizations of the needs of the Soviet ruling elite. However, several of the later pieces point to my new interest in augmenting this political critique with a richer assessment of the diverse cultural practice of individual pro-Communist writers, which very often contradicted or occurred independently of such policies.

"Race and Culture" combines critiques of Eurocentrism in literary studies with analyses of antiracist movements on university campuses. This is an area in which my, activist political commitments and scholarly interests have converged most usefully.

"Commitment" includes essays focused more directly on the problems of intellectuals who wish to devote their unique skills to the cause of social emancipation under the problematic conditions of the contemporary world. The subjects range from the dilemmas of the current generation of university scholars, to the troubling example of the heroic Stalinist Lionel Burger in Nadine Gordimer's novel *Burger's Daughter*, to the legacy of the working-class Trotskyist writer George Breitman.

A collection such as this will be of little interest to readers fixated exclusively on the "big names" of radical literature and politics, or to those seeking strong arguments for or against the "ranking" of various writers in a literary or political canon. While my work may occasionally focus on major intellectual figures such as Leon Trotsky or Lionel Trilling, I have been more consistently drawn to individuals and even historical moments conventionally regarded as "minor" but which seem to have considerable potential for explorations that may deepen our understanding of socialist culture. While occasionally I make comparisons among writers and may even "rank" a work above or below another, these are minor and relatively uninteresting aspects of my work. Moreover, I have no inclination to urge creative writers to devote their art to particular causes. I learned firsthand from a five-year close friendship with James T. Farrell the fallacy of creating "art on demand," correlating literary technique to a particular politics, or promoting any form of prescription in the arts no matter how idealistic or worthy the cause may be.

I am mainly interested in the textures and shapes of the lives of writers and intellectuals committed to socialism, although I am also committed to exploding mystifications of the professional ideologists of ruling elites. My aim in regard to radical cultural workers is not to hector, chastise, or "lead." Rather, in exploring episodes in Marxist cultural history, I aim to critically reconstruct models for contemplation in light of the ever-changing exigencies of the ongoing socialist project.

In striving for political clarity, I am concerned with a rigorous critique and fruitful interaction of various left traditions. I seek to promote skepticism of allegiance to any states above the people they rule, no matter how benign the rulers' mask. I am revolted by "orthodoxy" on the left, whether invoked in the name of "Leninism," "Trotskyism," or "Marxism." But I am also aware of how frequently categorical rejections of classical Marxist traditions, especially on the part of intellectuals sitting on the sidelines, have merely led their proponents back to the repetition of earlier misconceptions—to theoretical postures that are actually pre-Marxist and pre-

Leninist, and sometimes are more sectarian and elitist than the "vulgarities" that were to be transcended.

As regards race and culture, I am drawn to theories of nationalism and internal colonialism as applied to political and cultural critique and resistance. In striving to create a liberating culture within universities, our primary concern at the moment should be to seek to enrich and broaden what is called "The Western Tradition" by setting it in the broader contexts of class, gender, nationality, and ethnicity.

In those essays forming the category of "commitment," I focus upon the tripartite interaction among theory, practical application, and organizational allegiance. Here again, my aim is not to exhort the reader but to inspire critical self-reflection.

In preparing these essays for publication, some minor corrections and adjustments have been made, although in a few cases where factual errors occurred in the original text I have let them stand and added footnotes to acknowledge my fallibility. Stylistically the essays vary a bit according to the place of original publication, particularly as to the presence or absence of documentation. In a few cases I have restored passages that were cut from the published versions for reasons of space. My priority in assembling this volume was not so much to preserve the "best" of my work—since, in fact, some of what I consider the "best" among my essays has been rewoven into my three books–but to present a general record of my writing. If I were writing these essays today, I would no doubt do some things differently in accordance with developments in cultural theory from which I have learned and to some extent have helped to shape. I would probably substantially modify, or at least interrogate, the categories of mass culture, popular culture, and even modernism, which I employ at times too naively. I would more consistently strive to apply a more effective Marxist method that simultaneously engages issues of class, gender, and race. I would substitute the term "United States" for "America," and I would be more careful, consistent, and subtle about my use of the highly charged term "ideology."

Nevertheless, while I have no aversion to revising my ideas in light of new information and experiences, I stand in the main by the argument of this book. From the outset in the 1960s, I have sought a bridge among various Marxist traditions. Now, as we enter the 1990s, I believe that I have a clearer and more modulated view of the desired synthesis. If I am fortunate, these studies will rebound among the most serious of my own, as well as the newer, generation of left-wing intellectuals. As for the immediate sources of stimulation behind much of the writing, I must acknowledge the hard-nosed and often harrowing criticisms of my comrades on the editorial board of *Against the Current* magazine, where several of these pieces first appeared; the continuing vitality of the theoretical work of Ernest

Mandel, Michael Löwy, and so many of the contributors to *New Left Review* and *Socialist Register*; my activist colleagues in Concerned Faculty, the United Coalition against Racism, the Baker-Mandela Center, and the Latin American Solidarity Committee at the University of Michigan; and longtime political *companeros* such as Berta Langston, Joanna Misnik, and Patrick Quinn.

ALAN M. WALD
Ann Arbor, Michigan

PART I
Trotskyism and Anti-Stalinism

1

Sculptor on the Left: Duncan Ferguson's Search for Wholeness

A man does not get rid of what is his own, even if he throws it away.

— Goethe

1. INTRODUCTION

The range of American artists and intellectuals whose lives were profoundly affected by the political fervor of the 1930s is wider than extant literature suggests. In addition to the scores of well-known literary critics and novelists, propelled to the left were many painters, sculptors, film-makers, actors, and musicians. Moreover, not all embraced Communism; a significant number were attracted to social democracy, Trotskyism, anarchism, and other varieties of radical thought. While many followed a common pattern, becoming radicalized early in the decade and deradicalized at its end, others differed markedly in the tempo and duration of their politicized lives. The life of the sculptor Duncan Pomeroy Ferguson (1901–1974), although in some respects idiosyncratic, reflects certain aspects of the impact of the Depression on American artists not considered in previous studies.

Ferguson was a student of Robert Laurent, a major figure in the modern rebellion against the "official" art forms given the imprimatur of the National Academy and the National Sculpture Society. Laurent and Ferguson were among the first sculptors to introduce direct carving in wood and stone into twentieth century American art; their work was characterized by respect for the medium and a simplification that eschewed elegant decorative elements. Ferguson, in particular, was noted for his cold but well-crafted nudes, and his tactile and amusing small animals. At the height of his fame in the mid-1930s, the Harvard-educated Ferguson accepted a teaching position in the Department of Fine Arts at Louisiana State University

3

(L.S.U.). He was part of the "Yankee invasion" of new faculty made possible by Governor Huey P. Long's expansion of state education.[1]

Ferguson carried to Baton Rouge some of the ambience of Greenwich Village, where he had previously lived and sculpted. In the staid Southern environment, his uncompromising and individualistic demeanor helped form his exotic and perhaps even outlandish persona, a persona accentuated by his electric blue eyes, wildly bushy reddish brown mustache, and rakish gait. A growing number of students and faculty found him an original, brilliant conversationalist as he held forth in his deeply resonant voice. He also held views characteristic of Bohemian artists of the time, including the notion that the intellectual life should be a disciplined, exclusively male activity, and the conviction that sentiment and human relationships—such as having children—that might steal time and energy from the creative process should be avoided.

Feted by the campus newspaper, courted by such prominent colleagues as Robert Penn Warren and Cleanth Brooks, Ferguson seemed well on his way to a distinguished career as an artist and teacher. Yet before the decade was over he experienced a crisis in his art—a loss of his sense of self, subject, and audience—followed by a dramatic conversion to Marxism. With the same theatrical excess that characterized his earlier devotion to Bohemianism, he announced that true revolutionaries must break entirely from their past, dispense with all luxury, and psychologically "kill their family."[2] In 1941, at the age of forty, he resigned his position as chairman of the department and journeyed back north to begin reshaping his life as a member of the industrial working class. He shaved his mustache, set his sculpting aside, and began a new career as a Trotskyist militant.

Ferguson's political commitment never waned, but within a decade he had moderated his rebellion against his family and earlier life. For some years he placed politics decisively before art. Then he began to search for a synthesis of the two, a quest that eventually dominated his thought. Of this obsession he wrote in his personal notebook: "I don't compare with Goethe in any way except this: my search for wholeness."[3] The last years of his life were spent in an effort to resolve his artistic crisis and to make a comeback that perpetually eluded his grasp due to ill-health, poverty, and a tumultuous personal life that rendered him unable to cement a lasting marital relationship.

During the ordeal of his struggle with terminal cancer, he expressed much bitterness over the incompleteness of his life. But in the course of a pilgrimage that he began in the late 1930s, he left behind a rich experience that ought to be examined by those who wish to understand how the interaction of art and Marxist politics profoundly shaped an earlier generation of American radicals.

2. THE CRUCIBLE OF FAMILY, 1901–1926

Duncan Ferguson was born in Shanghai on 1 January 1901. His father, the dominant figure in his life, was also one of the most influential Westerners in modern Chinese history. Like most Fergusons of Scottish descent, Dr. John Calvin Ferguson (1866–1945) was a descendant of Fergus I, an early king of Scotland. He was the great grandson of Peter Ferguson, who immigrated to southern Canada in the 1820s; the grandson of Duncan Ferguson, a farmer in Ontario; and the son of John Ferguson, a Methodist minister. His extraordinary intellectual powers, drive, and singleness of purpose were evident from his youth. At the age of thirteen he met Mary Wilson, also the child of a Methodist minister, deciding virtually from the onset that they eventually would marry. He declared his intention to follow his father in the Methodist ministry and, after graduating from Albert College in Ontario, took a degree in theology from Boston University in 1886. Some years later he earned a doctorate from the same institution.

Recognizing at once the unusual abilities of the young minister, the Board of Missions of the Methodist Episcopal Church sent Dr. Ferguson and his new wife, Mary, to China in 1887 to establish Nanking University, of which he became the first president. Nine years later the need to support a growing family forced Dr. Ferguson to leave this mission-run institution to accept an appointment (1897–1902) by the Chinese government as president of Nanyang College (later the National Ch'iao Tung University) in Shanghai. Dr. Ferguson's devotion to learning the Chinese language and culture impressed the officials he met. Under their tutelage, he began collecting works of art as a hobby, eventually achieving world renown as the author of authoritative books and articles on Chinese art. Dr. Ferguson became the only non-Chinese to sit with the committees of scholars who examined the art treasures in the imperial palaces after the imperial dynasty was deposed in 1911. He was also a consultant on Chinese art to leading museums in the United States. In addition, from 1899 to 1929, Dr. Ferguson owned and published the Shanghai daily newspaper *Sin Wan Pao*, which became the largest Chinese-language newspaper in the country. From 1907 to 1911 he published the *Shanghai Times*, an English-language newspaper, as well.

Near the turn of the century Dr. Ferguson's career extended into the area of Chinese government service. From 1898 to 1911 he served as foreign advisor to the viceroys of Nanking, and from 1900 to 1910 to those of Wuchang. In 1902 he was appointed secretary to the Chinese Ministry of Commerce, frequently representing the Chinese government on missions abroad. In 1915 he was made Counsellor to the Foreign Office. From 1917 to 1929 he served as advisor to successive presidents of the Chinese

Republic, and, later, to the government of Chiang Kai-shek. Dr. Ferguson was interned in Peking during the Japanese occupation. His wife had died in 1938, after some years of invalidism. In 1943 he returned to the United States, living in New York for the last years of his life.

Eight of the Ferguson children grew to maturity. The last-born were Duncan and Peter, who remained close throughout their childhood and were thought by the family to be brilliant. In 1901, because of anti-foreign sentiments following the Boxer Rebellion, the family went to Switzerland a few months after Duncan's birth, returning to Shanghai in 1903. Later that year Peter was born. In 1907 Dr. Ferguson bought a house in Newton, Massachusetts, which was the family house in the United States until 1919. Until 1910, the family was based in Newton with Dr. Ferguson making frequent visits from China in the course of his various government responsibilities. That year, with the two eldest sons at Harvard, the rest of the family returned to China, remaining in Peking until 1914 when they returned to Newton for the education that was not then available in China. For Duncan and Peter this proved to be enrollment at the Newton Country Day School. This was a preparatory school with advanced academic standards from which in due course they both went to Harvard, Duncan in the class of 1922 and Peter in the class of 1923.[4]

Duncan arrived at the Country Day School in 1914. He had attractive smooth features and an English accent, and soon it was acknowledged that he was the brightest student in the class. He was very rational, business-like, and decisive; but a part of him was also attracted to the highly individualistic Joe Lee, the son of a pioneer innovator in education. One day Duncan might be absorbed in Christian Science, and the next he was propounding a new theory about breathing techniques. Religious devotions, including prayers and the memorization of extensive passages of scripture, formed a natural part of the Ferguson home environment, but when Duncan entered Harvard he declared himself without religious preference.[5]

His academic record at Harvard suggested that his family's highest expectations were about to be realized. He won a scholarship every year, made the Dean's list, was inducted into Phi Beta Kappa, and graduated summa cum laude. During World War I he enlisted in the Harvard unit of the U.S. Marine Corps and was stationed for a few months at the Plattsburgh Training Camp in upstate New York. Practical-minded at the beginning of his academic career, he had entered Harvard as an economics major but was soon consumed by a love of the arts. In early 1920 he transferred to a concentration in English literature. He also became addicted to classical music. He was almost a straight-A student and by his senior year he was so far ahead of his classmates that he was able to spend the entire year reviewing the whole of classical music, as well as playing the piano and singing in the choir. At the time he dreamed of becoming a great composer, until he realized that a slight hearing defect would prevent him from achieving this goal. In politics he evolved from a conventional supporter of Woodrow Wilson to a pacifist, a great admirer of Christ as an exemplary human being. He also opposed the Palmer Raids and considered voting for Eugene Debs as a protest against an unjust economic system.[6]

At Harvard he met Mary Manley, the younger sister of a classmate, and they were soon engaged. Following Duncan's visit to China in the summer of 1921 they vowed never again to be separated. They were married in the spring of 1922 after he had received a teaching appointment in the English Department at Brown University. His intention was to support himself as an instructor while writing biographies and histories of art, but within a short time he discovered in himself a tremendous longing to become a sculptor. He became aware of this desire when he started to mold things in his hands—soap from his sink and mud from the shore of a lake he visited during the summer. While teaching at Brown in 1922–23, he began to study clay modeling and plaster casting with Albert Henry Atkins at the Rhode Island School of Design. In the fall of 1923 he left Brown and took a position in the Fine Arts Department at Harvard.

At that time something quite unexpected occurred: Duncan attempted suicide by walking theatrically into the Charles River and shooting himself above the heart. He was hospitalized for two months (which compelled him to resign his position) and remained under the care of a psychiatrist for some time.[7] The breakdown was related both to his rebellion against his strong-willed father and his transformation into an artist. He had left home a somewhat prosaic person, quite the opposite of his brother Peter, a philosophy major at Harvard who had a speculative and roaming mind, but had now evolved into a very different sort of personality, highly aesthetic and emotional, even though he retained his decisive, argumentative demeanor.[8]

Dr. Ferguson responded to his son's breakdown by calling it a "scandalous catastrophe," as if his illness could be judged morally, not medically. Duncan's wife rose to his defense: "Only I know through what suffering Duncan has passed to become a man. It appears to me that there is hardly a sorrow which he has not endured. Loneliness, misunderstanding, privation, and the agony of creative genius coming to birth. Proud, fine, sensitive beyond what you may imagine, he is a wonderful man and a loyal friend to me."[9] By the spring of 1926, however, the marriage between Mary and Duncan was over. Their relationship had been complicated from the start: Mary had a sharp tongue and a mother who seemed to have adored Duncan more than her daughter. Another angry letter from Dr. Ferguson epitomized the conventional values his father held that seemed so oppressive to his son, despite warm memories of family love: "What foolish children you are! You know that I hate such silliness. . . . you must not think of permanent separation which means the scandal of divorce and remarriage."[10] He implored Duncan not to break Mary's heart. Mary wrote back that, in fact, it was she who had left Duncan for another man.[11]

Duncan's breakdown in 1924 was his only one, although in his later life he exhibited suicidal behavior and threatened suicide.[12] The "creative genius" Mary's letter referred to was undoubtedly a positive force offsetting despair as he sought to forge an identity independent of his father; the canalization of his energies into a disciplined craft provided a means of coping with recurring episodes of depression. Duncan had always combatted psychological pain with self-discipline; as a student he boasted of his powers of concentration and will, even claiming some success as a hypnotist. Sculpting served as a rigorous means of conquering the uncertain world around him. With painstaking skill he made it conform to his own interior vision. He became convinced of his own genius as an artist, and declared himself a seeker of truth in the tradition of Blake, Goethe, and Yeats. To him, art was not merely a profession, but a spiritual encounter with nature itself, a sacred act. Decades later he recalled how in 1925, a year before his divorce, he and Mary had been vacationing on an island in Silver Lake, New Hampshire. Spotting a beautiful oak tree, he took an axe, cut it down, and began spontaneously to carve. It became "Woman and Child," his first large-scale work in wood, depicting a natural woman from her head to just above her hips, carrying a baby on her back with his legs wrapped around her waist.[13]

Just before his separation from Mary, Duncan spent a brief period teaching at Simmons College in Boston. He then moved to New York City where he studied with Robert Laurent at the Master Institute of Unified Arts. Laurent proved very attractive to the son of an authority on Chinese art, for, although Laurent was conversant with the Cubists, Futurists, and other avant-garde artists, he was especially influenced by non-Western art of the South Seas and the Orient. He did many bas-relief carvings in wood, numerous heads directly in stone, and on one occasion an aluminum nude for a public display that caused a near riot. Like Duncan, he conceived of a sculptor as being entirely different from a decorator or illustrator, and his work revealed a true love of plastic form. While much of his work was innovative, the poised dignity and massive volume of some of Laurent's sculptures have also been characterized as expressing "a kind of twentieth century classicism."[14] It was under Laurent's tutelage that Duncan sought to integrate the beauty of the human figure with the pure beauty of sculptural form, creating a large number of works remarkable for their classical serenity and great individuality.

3. FROM BOHEMIA TO REVOLUTION, 1926–1941

Between 1925 and 1935 Duncan became established as a sculptor of distinction. He lived mainly in New York City, in the Bohemian fashion of the day, and spent his summers at Cape Neddick, Maine, the site of an art colony presided over by Laurent. His Greenwich Village accommodations were poor; for a while he lived in the cellar of a Chinese bakery surviving on a daily bowl of soup. Checks came regularly from Dr. Ferguson, who was soon amazed by and appreciative of his son's genius, but this money was spent almost exclusively on art materials and other expenses connected with Duncan's work. Dr. Ferguson understood that Duncan's spartan personal life and his irresponsible handling of financial matters—resulting in hundreds of dollars of unpaid debts—were a by-product of his singleminded devotion to artistic perfection. But he was frustrated by Duncan's refusal to follow his advice and by his long periods of silence. At times there was a near break in family relations that was primarily Duncan's doing. Although his behavior caused his father much grief, Dr. Ferguson and other family members did everything possible to leave the door open to a future rapprochement. But Duncan was resentful of his rigid, domineering personality, and was determined to make his own way on his own terms.

Duncan's sculptures now seem tame in comparison with the abstract expressionism that later came to dominate American art, but he was originally received as part of the avant-garde. When he began his career in New England, the *Boston Transcript* called him "a progressive among Boston sculptors," remarking that it was "more unusual to have a 'radical' among sculptors than among painters." This was in spite of the fact that much of his work recalled that of Aristotle Maillol, a creator of noble and serene figures who avoided the dramatic poses characteristic of Rodin, and Gaston Lachaise, whose female nudes were rendered with graceful, swelling forms. Among Duncan's oeuvre were only a few abstract pieces. For example, his first one-man show in Boston featured a spindle-like shape surmounting a globular one. Intended as a study in form, one viewer described it as an aristocratic potato masher.[15]

What was "progressive" and "radical" in Duncan's early work may have derived from the versatility that allowed one to see in his sculpture the convergence of widely differing currents of thought and experience. For example, the simplicity of line and form in his work, and its directness and quiet intensity, may have been influenced by his Chinese cultural background. Some critics saw in his art an "oriental detachment and economy of form, plus a certain caressable quality that characterizes small Chinese animal sculpture."[16] Yet there was nothing in his work that was imitative or archaic. It contemporaneously expressed the immediate response of the sculptor to the world around him.

In New York, Duncan displayed his work at the Whitney Studio Club, the Brooklyn Museum, the Grand Central Galleries, the Museum of Modern Art, and the Whitney Museum. His work was purchased for the permanent collections of the Newark Museum, the Whitney Museum, the Hamilton Field Foundation, the Museum of Modern Art, and the private collection of Mrs. John D. Rockefeller. The zenith of his success during his New York period was a 1929 one-man art show at Edith Halpert's Downtown Gallery on West 13th Street.

The *New York Sun* raved that Duncan's show made the art galleries of New York seem like "real" galleries for the first time in a long while, and hailed him as a "new genius."[17] The *New York Times* called his work "so distinguished that it can be talked of only in the plainest words, in accordance with William Morris's direction to refrain from ornament when dealing with art."[18] *Art News* observed that "Mr. Ferguson's one-man show undoubtedly marks a noble addition to the ranks of good American sculptors. There is a strength and maturity about his finest work that is surprising in an artist still under thirty."[19]

Duncan had worked with many different materials before the 1929 show, including alabaster, plaster, wood, and marble. But a large number of pieces in the show were done in clay for bronze casting with various patinas, reflecting his view that critics and patrons frequently overemphasized the aesthetic pleasures of the media while neglecting the fundamental qualities of the sculptural form itself.[20]

Duncan had already acquired a certain fame, but it mainly stemmed from exhibits of his sculptured heads and sensitively stylized animals. Hence the critics were surprised by the directness and power of the large male nude that dominated the 1929 show.

"Male Nude" depicted a life-size man at ease, hands clasped behind his back, with the poise and grace of an athlete. His muscles were firm and rippling beneath spare flesh. The compactly built body had energy and beauty traveling in sure modulations from the shoulders to the feet that firmly gripped the ground. "Male Nude" was not a study in anatomy or musculature, but rather served as an exposition of the human form in fluid classical terms. It was a remarkable example of unrestrained power in easy repose, a distinctive Ferguson creation.

Also on display were several of Duncan's cats, which were his specialty. "The Sleeping Cat," life-size, was done in plaster. "Anatole," a Persian cat, was an alabaster likeness of one of Duncan's pets. It evidenced both charm and humor. A Siamese cat had reddish buff body color with ears, face, and paws tapering gradually to a deep amber, and a slight dull bluish glaze to its

L.S.U. show of Ferguson's work in 1937.
"Male Nude" is on the far left.

eyes. All the cats were sculpted so that the contour guided the hand, rendering it difficult to stroke the animal in the reverse direction. The cats were always in repose, compounding the sculptor's work, since animals are in life less expressive at rest than when walking or attacking prey.

Among other pieces on display were the heads of "Esther" (a former girlfriend) and "Mimi" (the wife of Robert Laurent), both impressive for their linear simplicity. "Sleep" was an alabaster head that was striking in the serenity of its subject. "Torso," in teakwood, was notable for its subtle fusing of one fluent plane with another and for the intellectual discipline of its entire construction.

In addition to the works featured in his one-man show, Duncan during this period also prepared life-size figures for a display in the Museum of the City of New York. They were carved from linden and dressed to illustrate how a card party in New York might have looked in pre-Revolutionary days. He also designed the door trim and overhead panel in the exhibition room of the Daylight Gallery of the Downtown Gallery. The sculptors Laurent and William Zorach contributed other features to the room.[21]

During the early Depression several important events occurred in Duncan's personal life, forcing him to reconsider the risky career he had chosen as an independent artist. First was his marriage to Alice Decker, an art student he had met in 1929 or 1930. Tall, dark, beautiful, and charming, Alice came from a well-to-do family. As a sculptor she specialized in carving small animals. In the summer of 1931 Duncan and Alice traveled steerage on the *Leviathan* to London where they were married, then toured Europe. Alice's mother, however, was distressed about Duncan's small income. His cottage in Maine had no heat, and his living quarters in New York were so unsatisfactory that Alice's father insisted on paying the rent for a new apartment on Waverly Place.[22]

A year later came the death of his brother Peter, who had been closely bonded to Duncan by the childhood they had shared, and by the emotional depression both had endured during their college days. Taken under the wing of Alfred North Whitehead at Harvard, Peter had prepared for a career in philosophy. However, at the last minute he switched to psychology, accepting a teaching post at Bowdoin College. Striding across the campus with his blond head held high, Peter was a popular figure. Students and faculty were stunned when he fell gravely ill during a flu epidemic in 1932, and he died of pneumonia at the age of twenty-eight. His death came as a great blow to Duncan and may well have induced in him a feeling of survivor's guilt from which he never fully recovered. A year later he carved "Portrait of My Brother," one of his most beloved heads. It was sculpted largely from memory, with the help of a few photographs. The finely cut features of Peter's head and the expression of the face bring the viewer's eyes back to it again and again. One eyebrow was slightly higher than the other, a characteristic expression. Thirty years later, Duncan still wondered whether the entire course of his life might have been different had Peter lived.[23]

Finally, the deepening of the Depression after 1931 made it increasingly difficult for Duncan to make ends meet on his irregular income from sales of his work. This situation also made him acutely conscious of the commercial orientation of many galleries and of the pressure on artists to adapt to whatever was in fashion. During 1933 and 1934 he began to work for various projects of the Works Progress Administration while Alice was employed as a social worker in a psychiatric hospital. He began applying for teaching jobs and after a while accepted an invitation to join the Louisiana State University faculty for the 1935–36 academic year as an Instructor of Sculpture, Wood Carving, and Stone Cutting. The following year he was promoted to Assistant Professor. In 1939, following a four-month leave to teach at Bennington College, he became an Associate Professor and Acting Head of the Department. In 1940 he was awarded tenure.[24]

The impact of the Depression on Duncan turned his art in a more public direction. Prior to the early 1930s, his work had been largely confined to

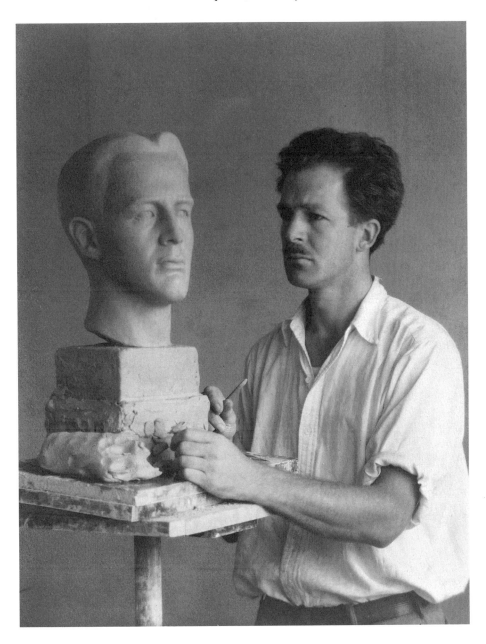

Duncan Ferguson in 1933 sculpting a head
of his recently deceased brother, Peter.

free-standing sculpture, carved in wood or stone, or modeled in bronze. After moving to Louisiana, Duncan received a series of commissions that occupied him with architectural sculpture throughout the state. In this new work he found he could reach large numbers of ordinary people whom he could educate as well as touch aesthetically with his craft.

For example, one of his commissions involved the execution of the first high relief topographical map of Louisiana which was placed in the main lobby of the new State Exhibits Building in Shreveport, in a pit three feet below floor level, lighted from recesses beneath the floor. Duncan researched the project by examining maps of the U.S Geological Survey and the Mississippi River Commission. With four of his students—Dagny Andreassen, Jules Struppeck, and John and Lois Mahier—he built a plaster model one-third the size of the finished map. The finished version featured models of the state capital, the Huey P. Long Mississippi River Bridge at New Orleans, and oil derricks indicating the main oil fields in the state.[25]

He also sculpted a terra-cotta relief panel for the lobby of a new post office at Leesville. Called "The Letter," it was commissioned by the Fine Arts Division of the U.S. Treasury Department. The clays for the panel were mined by his students, who fired them in the L.S.U. kiln. The panel itself was four feet square in modestly high relief. "The Letter" simply depicted a farmer leaning on his hoe, watching his wife read a letter; the figures are set against a background of furrows in a plowed field. A viewer, however, might see a story behind the scene. The expression and demeanor of the figures suggest that the farmer had been at work when his wife came to him with the letter, probably from someone close to them, and read it to him while he rested leaning on his hoe. The panel captures the moment that she had finished reading the letter and the two were deep in thought, perhaps reminiscing about the loved one who had sent it. The man stands, resting his chin on his hands which clasp the top of the hoe handle. His eyes look out unseeing into the distance, while the woman, seated, has let the letter fall loosely in her hands, which lie relaxed upon her knees. It is a moment of communion between them and the person from whom the letter has come.[26]

Another major project was the preparation of nineteen panels and four cast stone plaques for the new Agricultural Center at L.S.U., a job commissioned by the W.P.A. Since Duncan had only two-and-a-half months in which to complete the work, he used what he called the "Atelier" method. This was a Renaissance practice in which students learned their art by working on a project from beginning to end under the direction of a master artist. Duncan's students collaborated with him from the first preliminary drawing to the final casts. The stone casts were sent to a bronze factory where they were set in bronze. They served as decorations to the building.

"The Letter," 1939.

The sculpting of the decorations followed the mode of the building itself: the style was simple and direct with a minimum of ornament. In order to depict the agricultural bounty of Louisiana, Duncan arranged the panel series in five sets of three each in two pairs. The five sets grouped two vegetable or plant subjects with an animal subject; one pair contrasted agricultural labor with scientific labor, while the other counterposed a tractor with a mule and plow. Of the four plaques, one depicted the head of a cow, another the head of a horse, a third showed crossed hands holding agricultural tools, and the last cotton and cane. The plaques were in high relief, with their designs projecting from the surface of the building.[27]

Duncan also designed panels for the new state office building constructed in Baton Rouge, and a figure for a fountain at the Louisiana State Polytechnic Institute in Rustin. In March 1937 he held an exhibition of his sculpture at the L.S.U. Art Gallery, featuring twenty-seven past and recent pieces. In November of that year he organized an exhibition which elucidated in clearly understandable form several of the creative problems and technical processes involved in the architectural sculpture being done at the L.S.U. Art Center. He also displayed his work in New Orleans in the company of a number of other artists who called themselves the New Southern Group.[28]

The Fine Arts Department at L.S.U. had been established in 1934. The enrollment of sculpture students reached thirty during Duncan's tenure. Part of his attraction was an innovative teaching method that emphasized creative work more than history or didactic instruction. The first year was divided into thirds, giving equal attention to clay modeling, stone cutting, and wood carving. Duncan also demanded that his students thoroughly master the mechanical aspects of sculpting. For example, they built their own armatures to support their clay figures.

Duncan continued to teach his students the method of direct carving that he, Laurent, William Zorach, and a few others championed in opposition to the Renaissance practice of carving models first, which had become so widespread in the eighteenth and nineteenth centuries that direct carving became virtually a lost art. He believed that the possibilities of what can be done with clay were so limitless that students would not be able to develop adequate discipline. He was convinced that beginning students needed the restraint that came from a resistant material such as stone.[29] Among his most outstanding students were Jules Struppeck, who won a competition for sculptural decorations in the auditorium of a New Orleans hospital, and Lois Mahier, who wrote a thesis on the color properties of Louisiana clays.[30]

Duncan's marriage to Alice began to deteriorate during 1935 and 1936, continuing a pattern that plagued him for the remainder of his life. Some of their friends thought that artistic rivalry was the source of the conflict. On one occasion Duncan went so far as to accuse Alice of stealing his ideas. But perhaps more decisive was a serious car accident in December 1935 that left Alice permanently affected with double vision. Duncan had been driving the car and she may have blamed him. In the summer of 1936 they traveled to see Duncan's parents in Peking. Alice consulted a neurologist while Duncan worked on a fine head of his father. But that fall when they returned to the United States, Alice moved to New York, leaving L.S.U. and Duncan forever.[31]

In the meantime, Duncan began to pursue Demila Sanders, a young journalism student assigned by the school newspaper to cover the display of

Duncan working on bust of Dr. Ferguson in Peking, 1936, accompanied by Alice Decker and Mary Ferguson.

his work in the University Art Gallery. Under the pretext of wanting to discuss some errors in her news article with her, he invited Demila to his office; to her surprise, he offered her a choice from among his sculptures. Demila was perplexed by Duncan's attention, for she felt that she was so beneath him culturally and intellectually. She was also frightened of him, for his wild mustache and spontaneous behavior made him seem at times like a madman. When she resisted, he memorized her daily schedule and waited for her outside her classes. Encountering her on campus, he presented her with books and flowers. When she refused his gifts, he left them at her feet. Eventually he won her and bought her a bicycle so that she could ride from her dorm to his cottage in the woods on the outskirts of campus to spend nights with him.[32]

Demila was attracted mainly by Duncan's brilliance. She was unnerved by his unorthodox appearance, but, in fact, he was quite attractive. In his late thirties, he was a man of average proportions, 5′ 7″ and 140 pounds, whose Scottish ancestry was accentuated by a reddish tinge to his sandy brown hair. His eyebrows were light brown with one or two hairs always askew. His legs were well-shaped from hiking and his torso well-developed from sculpting, giving him a virile appearance. He also had a distinctive laugh; a bit sly, but also enticing in a way that made others laugh at whatever had amused him.

The Ferguson family had a distinctive countenance that enabled relatives to recognize each other even though they had never met; it was especially noticeable in Dr. Ferguson, Duncan, and Peter. Duncan had many other characteristics of his father. They both looked and acted "important." When he described his father's devotion to principle and his intimidating presence, Duncan gave the impression that he would like to have the same said of him. Yet when Dr. Ferguson came to the L.S.U. campus with Duncan's older sister Mary in 1938, there was no question as to who was the dominant figure. Dr. Ferguson was quite a bit taller and sturdier than Duncan, with a remarkably compelling gaze. Even at seventy-two he stood perfectly erect and walked with a long stride. Duncan seemed but a slighter version of this impressively handsome, distinguished gentleman.[33] Ironically, Dr. Ferguson's strong-headedness, which was one of the reasons Duncan resented him, was a feature that the son reproduced most fully—for in his relation to Demila, Duncan acted precisely as his father had toward him in trying to shape her life and destiny.

Unlike Duncan's previous wives and lovers, Demila came from a poor sharecropping background; she had been the first in her family to receive an education. He aspired to transform her, Pygmalion-like, into a cultivated woman who would be a proper companion and servant for an artist and professor. He insisted that she have a bun appended to her short hair, apply make-up, and wear gloves and a hat. Then he taught her how to use his linens and family silverware. Finally, when she pleaded that she wanted to spend a year in New York trying to break into journalism, he arranged for her to be chaperoned by his friends, Fran Warren and John Hackett, who were assigned to teach her to walk properly, appreciate classical music, and absorb the other accoutrements of culture.[34]

Warm and charming with other women, Duncan became domineering and insensitive with his own wives and lovers. Not only did he refuse to engage in intellectual or personal discussion with Demila, he forced her to participate in his trials of self-discipline. In the summer of 1939, for example, Duncan and Demila visited the White Mountains of New Hampshire. Wishing to relive some adventurous times spent there during his Harvard days, Duncan began hiking up 6,000-foot Mount Washington dragging Demila behind. They both were wearing tennis shoes and their feet were bloody by the time they reached the top. Duncan refused to take the cog railway back down and, after becoming lost in the dark on the mountainside, they arrived home aching and exhausted. The next morning Duncan insisted that they climb another, fortunately smaller, mountain.[35]

As it turned out, the year that Demila went to New York City, 1939–40, was to be the most decisive one in Duncan's mature life. For some time he had become uncertain about the direction his art should be taking. This uncertainty may have been partly rooted in the commercialism and opportunism he had encountered in the New York art world. He sensed that if he did not conform to new trends in art, he might be passed by, thus losing his audience. Work with his students at L.S.U. and his W.P.A. projects raised further questions concerning his relationship to society as an individual artist. He may also have been compelled to dramatically alter his life because of guilt and self-hatred for both failing his father (even though on one level he clearly rejected his father's values) and surviving his brother Peter. For whatever reason, he suddenly became receptive to the radical political ideas that had been for some time animating large numbers of Americans in response to the Depression.

In 1939, the L.S.U. faculty had become bitterly divided over a variety of political and academic issues, and Duncan, who held generally left-wing sympathies but had been repelled by the Communists he had met in New York, became attracted to the radical faction. In July he joined eighteen faculty members in issuing a statement denouncing external political pressures and influences at the university, and called for faculty control of hiring, scholarship, salaries, promotion, academic publications, and grades.[36] At this time there appeared on the L.S.U. campus a well-known social psychologist named Richard Louis Schanck.

Schanck, in addition to being a shrewd operator who supervised research projects on rural society at L.S.U. while dispensing credit to students who never came near the campus, was a self-annointed Trotskyist. He quickly came to strongly influence Duncan's political thinking. Schanck was a man whose very walk and appearance testified to a monomania for saving people. His dark brown eyes, set under thick black eyebrows, were variously described as piercing, hounding, mesmerizing, and compelling. He had a smooth baby face. His black hair stuck out from his head. He always wore an overcoat, and walked as if he were marching into a gale. He was only average size, but appeared larger because of the tremendous force of his personality. He often spoke with anguish, his voice seemingly rent with tears. His mode of political activism was purely cloak and dagger. He convinced Duncan to contribute financially to bring a pair of Trotskyist organizers, Paul and Ray Rasmussen of the Socialist Workers Party, to the L.S.U. campus. Together the four began to recruit Duncan's art students to revolutionary Marxism.

When Demila returned to L.S.U. that spring, she was puzzled by the group of unfamiliar people waiting on the railroad platform with Duncan—Schanck, the Rasmussens, and several others. While she had been in New York becoming cultured, he had been radically transformed under Schanck's influence into a middle-class artist's conception of what a "Bolshevik" should be like. Duncan immediately informed her that they must break all ties with the past, excise all warm feelings about their families, renounce their valuable possessions, and dispense with any vestiges of bourgeois morality that had been retained. He began lecturing her about subjectivity and introspection, insisting that she refrain from using "I" in letters and conversation. He even described her as "petty-bourgeois" because her sharecropping family had managed to obtain a small plot of land. When Schanck, who seemed to possess a compulsion to play God with other people's lives, learned that Duncan was sexually possessive, he announced that "A political person does not act that way." He then concocted a scheme to rid Duncan of this reactionary attitude: Schanck spent a weekend with Demila in Duncan's New Orleans studio. Perhaps he really did have Duncan's best interests at heart, for while with Demila he never laid a hand on her. Despite Schanck's scheming, certain of Duncan's traits never changed. After agreeing that a double standard was bourgeois and that one's sexual relations should be a wholly private affair, Duncan insisted on prescribing to Demila those men with whom she could and could not sleep.[37]

He also continued to mask his inner thoughts. When Demila asked him for an explanation of his turn to Trotskyism, Duncan spoke only of the time that he ran away from his sixth birthday party in China because his parents had refused to invite the children of their Chinese servants. He also referred to a paper on Trotsky he had once written, as if this early interest forshadowed his later choice.[38]

Divorced from Alice, Duncan proceeded to marry Demila. The New Orleans ceremony was witnessed by Schanck, the Rasmussens, and the new-fledged cadre of art students. Afterwards they all trooped back to Duncan's studio in the French Quarter to talk about Trotskyism until the wee hours, finally falling asleep on the half-dozen cots that had been set up in the studio.[39]

After his political transformation, Duncan found being a member of the L.S.U. faculty unbearable. His reasoning was simple: since workers form the only class capable of bringing about real social change, a real revolutionary must become a worker. He broke off relations with everyone who was not sympathetic to his newly acquired views, including Robert Penn Warren, to whom he had been very close, and the gentle scholar Cleanth Brooks. In the spring of 1941 he and Schanck resigned their faculty positions and traveled north to Gambier, Ohio, where Schanck owned a house. From there they drove to Akron daily to meet with rubber workers, among whom the Trotskyists had a following. Duncan continued his efforts to erase his past. One night he forced Demila to take all their love letters—there were hundreds of them, since they had corresponded at least once a day while she was in New York—to a field and burned them in a huge bonfire.[40]

Duncan and DeMila Ferguson, Coyoacan, Mexico, 1943.

While Duncan and Demila made preparations to move to New York City to become active members of the Socialist Workers Party, Schanck continued his political activity in Ohio. His behavior, however, became increasingly bizarre and eventually he was totally disowned by the Trotskyists. Several years later he was accused of stealing a ballot box during an election in a local of the Rubber Workers Union in Akron. "Doc Schanck," as he was then known, was observed burying the box in the woods by union officials and police. He was sentenced to jail and served time, which made wonderful copy for a Communist Party pamphlet called *Inside Job! The Story of Trotskyite Intrigue in the Labor Movement*. Schanck later returned to teaching and became chairman of the Sociology Department at Bethany College. In 1954 he published a short book called *The Permanent Revolution in Science*, dedicated to Leon Trotsky.

4. JOURNEY TO OBLIVION, 1941–1974

In the fall of 1941, Demila moved to New York City. There she met with Socialist Workers Party leaders James P. Cannon, Albert Goldman, and Felix Morrow, who told her that the Rasmussens had already placed her and Duncan's names on the party's membership roll without their knowledge. Shortly thereafter Duncan arrived and they took a loft at 46 West 21st Street. It was a large place where Duncan intended to sculpt as a background to his political activities. However, his plans never materialized. Not only did Marxism fail to resolve the crisis in his art that had begun in the late 1930s, just before his radicalization, but politics also began to absorb all his time so that he sculpted only on rare occasions. As a result, the Ferguson loft became transformed into an informal social center for members of the Trotskyist movement in New York in the 1940s. Duncan and Demila regularly entertained party friends and contacts there and also, since it held over a hundred people, it was used for large fundraising events.

News of Duncan's resignation from the L.S.U. faculty must have followed him to New York, for he soon received an offer to become chairman of the Art Department at Queens College where he was supposed to have a free hand in designing a program in accord with his own philosophy. Duncan immediately requested to meet with James P. Cannon, the chairman of the Socialist Workers Party; two other leaders, John G. Wright and Vincent R. Dunne, also attended the meeting. In response to Duncan's questions as to whether he should accept the Queens College offer, Cannon told him that his own preference would be for Duncan to take the job; among other benefits, it would lend the party added prestige and allow it to reach individuals with whom it might not otherwise come in contact. But Cannon also emphasized that Duncan's decision had to be a personal one, because the party never ordered its members to take or leave certain jobs. As it turned out, Duncan had already made up his mind: He had decided to become a working-class political leader. He couldn't stand the thought of being an intellectual in a working-class party and he was firmly opposed to taking any job that would tie him to the past. Furthermore, it was wartime and able-bodied males were presented with the options of being drafted or taking a job in essential industry. So he rejected the offer, instead enrolling at the Delehanty Trade School where his skilled hands enabled him to complete the course in just a few months. Then, with the assistance of Milton Alvin, a Trotskyist C.I.O. organizer, he found employment at Crucible Steel across the river in New Jersey, the site of an important organizing drive. Duncan worked there as a lathe operator with over ten thousand other workers. Although his aristocratic bearing and voice made him conspicuous, he eventually became a shop steward. He also won the respect of fellow party members who elected him a delegate to the next national convention of the party.[41]

In 1943 the party proposed that Duncan undertake a special assignment. He was asked to move to Coyoacan, Mexico, to care for Leon Trotsky's widow, Natalia Sedova. Demila was invited to accompany him. Duncan's main task was to assist in all household duties, but also, because he and Natalia both spoke French, he was assigned to attempt to win Natalia politically from Grandizio Munis, a Trotskyist veteran of the Spanish Civil War who had developed differences with the Socialist Workers Party and appeared to be gaining influence over Natalia. They left for Mexico by train in January 1944.

The Mexican sojourn was difficult. Duncan and Demila slept on a wooden board in a hut without heat. Because Natalia insisted on breakfasting in private and before anyone else, she instructed Duncan and Demila to do yard work for an hour or so before breakfast, without the usual coffee and orange juice they had been used to. Among his other duties, Duncan was Natalia's chauffeur. Natalia seemed to respect Duncan, but it was obvious that she was already closely bonded to Munis. Although Duncan never complained about the conditions in Coyoacan, Demila protested that she was treated as a servant rather than a political comrade. After only eleven months she left Mexico in December 1944. In May 1945, Duncan rejoined her in New York.[42]

Duncan had hoped that the Mexican assignment would be followed by another major responsibility, perhaps as the fraternal representative of the Socialist Workers Party to the Fourth International headquartered in Europe. But no such assignment was forthcoming, possibly because he was still regarded by Socialist Workers Party leaders as being too inexperienced.[43] However, he was quite active in the New York branch of the party, serving regularly on the city executive committee, and writing sometimes under his party pseudonym, "Duncan Conway."[44]

On several occasions during the latter part of the 1940s he carried out full-time party assignments. He worked for the Civil Rights Defense Committee, which had been formed to defend Trotskyists and militant members of the Teamsters Union convicted under the Smith Act during World War II. For several years he ran Pioneer Publishers, the Trotskyist publishing house. He also did some translating for the party, including a book by Daniel Guerin on Afro-Americans. For five years he worked as a house carpenter for the N.E.S. Company in White Plains, New York. Among the few pieces of sculpture he completed during the 1940s were a bust of James P. Cannon (1943), which he did as a tribute to the American political figure he most admired, and one of Leon Trotsky (1945), which he provocatively entered in an art contest run by Stalinists.[45]

When Duncan worked full-time for the party, Demila often had to take jobs—first as a typist, then as a factory worker—to pay the rent and buy food. She also had to cook, clean, entertain, and carry out her own political work. Every Sunday of their life together she served Duncan breakfast in bed, but he never reciprocated. Duncan's toughness—his view that any display of tenderness was a weakness—grew increasingly aggravating. Soon after their marriage, he told Demila that "if you get sick, don't expect me to take care of you"; on the train to Mexico he announced that "if you have problems, don't expect me to solve them." On more than one occasion he made it plain that, should his party duties ever conflict with his marriage, the party would come before Demila, just as it came before art. He also occasionally resorted to violence when his will was thwarted or his jealousy provoked.[46]

Tensions in their marriage intensified in the mid-1940s. Demila took a new job that required lifting heavy boxes. One morning as she got out of bed her uterus prolapsed. Duncan curtly told her to get to a doctor and left for his full-time party assignment. After entering a hospital she threatened to leave him, which prompted a dramatic change in his behavior. For the first time in their relationship he began talking about his personal feelings and waiting upon her attentively. After the operation he gave her doctor one of his sculptures, a form of payment for medical bills that he would continue in later years. However, after she returned home his old behavior pattern resumed and Demila, like his previous wives, Mary and Alice, had no choice but to leave him. She really didn't want to leave, but she couldn't stand living with him any longer.[47]

About this time Duncan's father fell ill. He spent a year-and-a-half in New York City, before moving to a sanitarium in up-state New York for the final six months. Dr. Ferguson continued to reach out to his son, even

Head of Leon Trotsky (1945).

buying copies of the Trotskyist newspaper, the *Militant*, on the street to read to learn about Duncan's ideas, and then leaving them around his apartment for Duncan to see when he visited. Shortly before his death the family gathered in Dr. Ferguson's room. Duncan stood on one side of the bed and his older brother Charles, a Wall Street businessman, on the other, each holding one of their father's hands. Dr. Ferguson smiled up at them and said, "When I can have my capitalist son on one side and my Marxist son on the other, it's not such a bad world after all, is it?"[48]

After a period of depression following Demila's departure, Duncan soon began a relationship with Laura Slobe. Laura was an artist who had joined the Socialist Workers Party in Chicago in 1942. A few years later she moved to New York where she began drawing political cartoons for the *Militant* under the name Laura Gray, although she regarded this work as secondary to her painting and sculpture. Pretty and charming, she, like Duncan, suffered severe conflicts over her inability to discover a means of expressing herself artistically within the revolutionary movement. Her situation was further complicated by ill health: tuberculosis and the loss of one lung had left her sickly. As with Duncan's previous romances, Duncan's affair with Laura began with great promise, especially given their common political and artistic interests. However, in 1949 a temporary rupture in their relationship occurred and Duncan went South for a few weeks to visit friends from his L.S.U. days and to get his drinking and temper under control. While there he engaged in some intensive but largely unsuccessful self-analysis of his own behavior and motives. In one letter he wrote that "for good or bad, I have for some reason always had to reject all my experiences, leave everything behind me, denying myself and my past to such an extent that my memory—of everything—has been completely atrophied."[49] Later, after twenty years of reading Freud and mulling over his problems, Duncan characterized the "total rejection and denial of my past" that occurred when he became a Trotskyist in 1940 as a form of "guilt" and "masochism."[50] But attempts at self-reform were to no avail and after a few years Laura left him. Duncan later regarded the relationship as one of the high points in his life. He genuinely believed that Laura was a brilliant painter, and when she died in 1958 at the age of forty-nine he became quite despondent.[51]

The first indication that Duncan might be reconsidering the wholly subordinate place he had assigned to art in his life as a revolutionary militant came in 1954, at the height of the McCarthyite witch-hunt. On 30 January 1954, the New York Council of the Arts, Sciences, and Professions held a conference on "The Artist and Professional in the Age of McCarthy." Duncan attended the gathering, which probably marked the first association he had had with artists and intellectuals outside the Trotskyist movement since 1941. There he delivered a statement that was later published in the *Militant* newspaper and as a Socialist Workers Party pamphlet. His remarks were politically clear but they offered little that was original regarding the role of the artist in capitalist society.

He began his remarks by presenting the traditional socialist argument that artists and intellectuals must ally with the organized working class since it was the only force that can effectively combat reaction and help create a better world. He restated the Socialist Workers Party view that "McCarthyism is the American form of fascism, and it is already on the march!" After defining artists as "truth-seekers," he criticized those speakers at the conference who had characterized McCarthyism as merely repressive, thereby offering the false assurance that this new reactionary movement could be defeated by liberal Democratic Party politicians. On 19 February 1954, he gave a public talk for the party called "The Artist and Professional Vs. McCarthyism: Their Stake in the Anti-McCarthy Fight." In the talk he reiterated and elaborated these same points, and recounted the story of John Milton's turn from poetry to a twenty-year engagement with revolutionary politics.[52]

By the mid-1950s Duncan's mental and physical condition had worsened. An attack of crippling rheumatoid arthritis that began in 1951, possibly caused by stress, was by 1953 causing him great pain and swelling of the joints of his hands, wrists, elbows, shoulders, and back. No longer able to hold a hammer, he had to abandon his $100-a-week job as a carpenter. It also became virtually impossible to play the piano and difficult to sculpt. He did not want to take a full-time party assignment—he wrote in his personal notebook that this was partly due to "guilt" and a desire to avoid "externally imposed restrictions"—so he lived on money provided by his family including $800 a year in dividends from stock left to him by his father, proceeds from the occasional sale of a piece from his father's art collection that had been divided among the children, and occasional small gifts from his sisters.[53] He was desperately lonely for a permanent companion, although, when he turned on his charm, he never had difficulty finding women to sleep with, on occasion several at the same time.[54]

The years 1955 and 1956 proved to be particularly depressing. Despairing about the course of his life and consumed by continuing "guilt about party failures," he was often too depressed to attend party meetings. When he made an effort to sculpt he ended up fiddling with his tools, or else escaping to the solace of his hi-fi set. Mozart, Dvorak, Wagner, and Charles Ives were among his favorites. He felt he was succumbing to what he called "passive living"—spending his time reading and observing, rather than taking any initiatives to do anything. The summers which he spent gardening at Mountain Spring Camp, run by the Trotskyists, remained among his few pleasures. It was there in 1955 that he did the last of his busts of political figures, a likeness of Carl Skogland, one of the founders of the Socialist Workers Party and a central leader of the 1934 Minneapolis Teamsters strike who had been sent to prison during World War II on trumped up charges of violating the notorious Smith Act.

By this time Duncan's personality had also changed notably. In his notebook he recorded Blake's statement in *The Four Zoas* that "Attempting to be more than man we become less." Where he originally had dissociated himself from his relatives, he now began to treasure his family connections. He became particularly devoted to his sisters, Florence, Helen, and Mary, and began a voluminous correspondence with old friends. Increasingly he was drawn back to memories of his earlier life, to what he called "the old Duncan." He began to feel as if he were haunted by a döppelganger—a ghostly double of himself from an earlier time. Eventually, he became obsessed with the theme of the döppelganger in Western culture, hunting down references to it in art and literature. He developed the thesis that it was connected to Freud's concept of the superego, and traced its appearance in works by Heine, Schubert, and Yeats.[55]

In the winter of 1957, Duncan impulsively moved to Los Angeles to stay with Joseph and Reba Hansen. He hoped that a new environment, and the company of old party friends, would provide him with a fresh perspective on his problems. What struck him most was what he believed to be the worthless and unproductive life he had been living. He was seized by an overwhelming desire to change fundamentally his situation. Then, all at once, the conflict he had previously experienced between art and politics became resolved for him in a new way. He wrote a letter to one of his former students at L.S.U. explaining that he was at last putting his life back together on the basis that "the most important political work I can do is sculpting." He considered this revelation as "one of those major turning points where everything becomes simple and clear."[56]

Elated by his new outlook, he returned East for another summer at Mountain Spring camp. There he joyously told Laura Gray that he had finally learned "to synthesize my sculpture and politics."[57] At the camp he became infatuated with a party member from Cleveland, making up his mind rather precipitously to leave New York and live with her. Shortly after moving to Cleveland, it became clear that he had misunderstood the nature of their relationship. His momentary delusion, however, had served to break him free of New York and his studio, which he characterized as "a prison because it was the place of non-sculpturing."[58]

In Cleveland, his friend Sam Pollock helped him find an exciting new workplace—a huge rectangular room, fifteen by thirty feet, with a twelve-foot ceiling, hot and cold running water, constant heat, a smooth hardwood floor, and north wall windows that admitted so much light that they had to be shaded, all at a rent of only $25 a month. In his new studio he found that he could sculpt nine or ten hours every day. He became committed to making an artistic comeback. To his sisters he reported that Cleveland was much colder than New York, but "now I don't *need* to get sick."[59] To the Trotskyist Evelyn Reed he reflected that "the important thing, for me, is that I am back to sculpting, which is where I should be since it is the thing I know best and am most capable at and through which I can make my most important contribution."[60] He hoped to be able to live from the sale of his work, although he was forced to sell some of his stocks for much-needed cash.

In the summer of 1958 he returned to New York to cast a bronze. There, at an exhibit of work by the sculptor Sir Jacob Epstein, he met Cleo Bell for the second time. Cleo had been a student of Jules Struppeck, Duncan's disciple at L.S.U. who later taught at Tulane University. Duncan had been introduced to Cleo the previous year when, during his return trip from Los Angeles to New York, he had stopped at Tulane where he attended Struppeck's classes as a visiting dignitary. Duncan persuaded Cleo to leave her art co-operative in Portchester, New York, and come to live with him in Cleveland as his wife. In December they took a trip South during which they examined Duncan's architectural sculpture in Baton Rouge, which they found was still in good condition.

Since neither Duncan nor Cleo had any money, their new relationship began with numerous handicaps. As with Duncan's previous wives, Cleo soon discovered that she had assumed a tremendous burden. She worked eighteen hours a week as a lab technician in a doctor's office, throwing pottery in her spare time. Duncan sculpted full time, but did not reach the level of productivity or realize the income that he had anticipated. At first he thought he might find an audience in the union movement, and he had hoped that Sam Pollock, a union official, would help him obtain commissions to do a series of busts of other union officials. But only two materialized. In April 1959 he wrote: "Discouraging and depressing, this business of trying to make a living by working hard and seriously at something that is apparently not socially desirable or worth being paid for. But on the other hand, it is not a new discovery for me, and it is my own choice. . . ."[61]

However, his career took a small step forward when he was offered a teaching position at Karamu (which means "a place of meeting" in Swahili), an interracial cultural center that had been established in 1915. Karamu sought to provide leadership in the arts in the Cleveland area, while also serving as a neighborhood settlement house. Duncan became its first teacher of sculpting, thus rounding out Karamu's program of classes in ceramics, drawing, print-making, music, theatre, and dance. Eventually he worked out an arrangement that paid about $1300 for twelve months of teaching a weekly two-hour evening class for adults (he later taught children as well), and performing two hours of maintenance work each week including firing sculpture pieces, dismantling sculpture stands, organizing armature materials, and repairing coils, switches, and control devices on electric kilns. The Karamu job created a certain status for Duncan in the art community; it allowed him to have access to kilns and other resources. At the same time, Cleo began teaching pottery, wheel-throwing, and ceramics at Karamu, augmenting their small income with part-time work at other art centers in the Cleveland area. As soon as Cleo had saved enough money, she sent to New York for Duncan's piano as a gift. Duncan played only rarely, but did some choral singing as he had during his Harvard days.

The evolution of Duncan's personality that began in New York continued in Cleveland, although he treated Cleo no differently than any of his other wives, all of whom he had largely excluded from his intellectual life. He grew increasingly sentimental and became so emotional about deaths of party friends that on one occasion he was asked to not attend a memorial meeting.[62] His political attitudes also changed, although not fundamentally. When James P. Cannon had been the national leader of the Socialist Workers Party, Duncan had been a loyal disciple. He condemned Cannon's factional opponents as "traitors" to the party, and fervently participated in party debates. But after Cannon retired to Los Angeles, Duncan, on several occasions, criticized organizational measures party leaders sometimes took against members of oppositions within the party. Even though Duncan was appointed to the party Control Commission, which was supposed to safeguard party norms, he avoided attending some National Committee plenums where the "internal party situation" was discussed.[63] Duncan refrained from becoming deeply involved in these controversies. In the summer of 1967 he described in his diary how one of his oldest friends among the leaders of the party had grown "cold" to him because of a position he had taken on an internal dispute. He wrote that he "must get out of it. I want no part of this area of politics. Sculpture is far more important."[64] In Cleveland Duncan did little more than attend Socialist Workers Party branch meetings, and occasionally irritated branch leaders by his sarcastic criticisms.[65]

In Cleveland he advanced to a new and final stage in his effort to unify his political and artistic lives. Although his periodic attempts to write on art and politics had suffered from writer's block, he began giving some public talks on "The Artist's Relation to the Revolutionary Movement," drawing upon his experiences over the previous quarter of a century. He presented one during the summer of 1965 at a Midwest Educational Conference sponsored by the Socialist Workers Party and the Young Socialist Alliance. His tape recorded remarks began with a self-description that would have startled those familiar with the manner in which he once placed politics before art: "I'm speaking to you as a practicing artist. . . . I consider myself primarily a practicing artist. I also consider myself, for better or for worse, a consistent revolutionist." He proceeded to elaborate the fundamental ideas of Trotsky on the nature of art—including Trotsky's argument that a socialist or human culture was preferable to a "proletarian" one, and Trotsky's observation about the inadequacy of Marxism as a method of judging artistic content or technique. His presentation became increasingly personal and autobiographical as he strayed from his prepared text and answered questions from the audience.

At one point he quoted Emerson, "Art is a jealous mistress," to underscore the contradiction between the amount of time and effort demanded to produce art (he also extended his argument to other forms of professional work), and the amount of time and effort demanded by a revolutionary party in order to carry out its political tasks. Duncan insisted that there should be a role for the artist in a revolutionary movement, however dialectical that role might be: "First, the artist has to know and fully understand why, if he wants to play a role in the fight against capitalism and for a socialist form of society, why he can only fully play that role in the revolutionary movement. That is one side of it." The party, however, must accommodate the special situation "somewhat better than it has always handled it in the past."

He further elaborated that "What is involved is not that the artist in the revolutionary party asks for or wants any special privileges or any special position. But there is a problem of just plain, simple, factual distribution of time. The artist is not an artist unless he spends a major part of his time producing art. A major part of his time, because it is too difficult an area to conquer without spending a major part of his time. But the problem is that a major part of your time must go to party work—that is what membership means." He concluded, therefore, that a revolutionary artist must struggle to find a suitable role in a party.

Admitting that the problem was scarcely the most important one facing the revolutionary movement, he nonetheless insisted that it should not be minimized or dismissed. In support of his position, he emphatically quoted James P. Cannon that "The revolutionary workers and artists need each other," and that "the artist has a special contribution" to make to the workers' movement. He proposed that the issue be correctly understood "so that it is possible for an artist to come into the party, and continue producing as an artist," adding that: "This I can speak of autobiographically, because I have known that conflict for some thirty years; and I have never resolved it. I don't think it will ever be resolved short of the lack of need of a revolutionary party because the revolution has been made. And the conflict is going to remain there for any artist who comes into the party. It is going to be a very rough road for him. All I say—let's not make it any rougher than necessary."

He made it clear that party leaders had not interfered directly with his work as an artist: "The party did not say 'do this' or 'do that' rather than sculpture because it is more important." However, he cited examples of two other artists, Laura Gray and a talented composer, who he believed were told by some members to work in factories. "Neither did," he noted. "They had better sense. But this is what they were told to do, and as loyal party members perhaps should, although I think perhaps not. I think they were right to reject party discipline at a point where it was so obviously wrong." He concluded by appealing to what he felt was the socialist humanist foundation of the revolutionary movement: "Our movement is made up of human beings; and the party is no good if it crushes the vitality of its membership, and certainly does its best never to crush or dampen the strength and vitality of any individual as an individual; we hope not to. . . . This is all I have to say."[66]

1961 photograph of Duncan Ferguson with bust of Cleo (1959).

Accompanying this distinctly new view of the role of the revolutionary artist came a new productive phase in his own work. He completed a remarkable bust of Cleo, and other heads of women derived from it that were much more expressive than his earlier work. He also completed several other portraits and abstract pieces, and had additional works in progress. In September 1969, Karamu informed him that they wanted to organize a large retrospective of his sculptures to be held in October or November 1970. He was to assume responsibility for putting it together and to prepare a statement of his aesthetic point of view, at a salary of $140 a month paid over the next fifteen months. Duncan wrote his sister Florence that the prospect of the retrospective "scared" him because he had "already too much experience with shattered hopes."[67] Still, he was excited by the idea of a final show. He began at once to send out inquiries in an attempt to locate his various works. He also collected materials about artists he admired from which to construct his aesthetic statement—clippings on Picasso, Auden, Daumier, Duchamp, Rimbaud, Leonardo da Vinci, as well as essays by Hilton Kramer. He studied recent Marxist analyses such as Ernst Fischer's *The Necessity of Art* and Arnold Hauser's *Social History of Art*.

Unfortunately, difficulties in his personal life prevented the realization of this last effort. Although his arthritis had almost vanished after he settled in Cleveland, he suffered a large stroke in the mid-1960s followed by small ones. These caused various neurological problems including: paralysis in his right leg and in the fingers of his right hand, blurring of speech, short-term memory loss, a jumbled sense of time, and general confusion. He sometimes couldn't walk without a cane, and he had to visit the hospital frequently for physical therapy. In addition, he had to engage in complicated negotiations in order to receive medical treatment as a charity case. Whenever possible, he left Cleveland for a few months in the winter to spend time at the desert house of Milton and Tybie Alvin in southern California In 1970 he had extensive surgery on his hand, for which he paid with a sculpture of the doctor's wife. He found it increasingly difficult to get to the Karamu studio, and when he did go he could sometimes work for only one-half to three-quarters of an hour. Fractured bones, diverticulosis, and ulcers were among many health problems that plagued him.

His life deteriorated in other ways. His relationship with Cleo had followed the same trajectory as had his previous marriages, and by the mid-1960s they had frequent, sometimes violent, quarrels. In 1965 a love affair he had been secretly conducting in New York ended tragically when the woman, who had been under the care of a psychiatrist, committed suicide by putting her head in a gas oven. For Duncan her death was "an emotional blow that ripped my heart open" and each year thereafter he suffered extreme depression on the anniversary of the event.[68] His drinking, confined mainly to scotch and beer, increased at times to the point where it sometimes began early in the day, although at other times he could stop entirely for a stretch of weeks and months. But it usually took only a few drinks to turn Duncan belligerent. Instead of saying, "I beg to differ," he would blurt out: "That's sheer tripe and Stalinist trash as anyone with the brain of a marmoset can see."[69] After this happened a few times at the homes of friends, the Fergusons became rather isolated socially. He regarded Rod Holt, an electronics genius he had met a short time after arriving in Cleveland, as his only friend in the city. With Holt he discussed novels, plays, music, science, Freudian psychoanalysis, art, and all the other topics he refused to share with his female companions. Eventually Cleo was forced to leave Duncan in order to preserve her own sanity.[70]

As early as July 1968 he recorded in his personal notebook that he had "an overwhelming need to talk about my problems" because he was "living a suicidal life" in which he would "rather sleep than anything else." In August 1969 he wrote his sister Florence that "my present life is generally a lonely and cheerless one," and on 1 January 1971, he recorded in his notebook that he was "near suicide." When he became so depressed that he could not even read, he would take several teaspoons of chloral hydrate "to destroy the hours." A month later he wrote a party friend that "working on an important piece of sculpture would make me feel better than anything else I can think of."[71] But by the end of 1971 he knew that his time was running out. The Karamu retrospective had been cancelled because of his inability to make the necessary arrangements. He simply couldn't care for himself and the Socialist Workers Party began assigning young members to live with him. In December he wrote that he was constantly "nagged by things that have to be done that never will be done."[72]

In 1973 Duncan discovered that he had advanced lung cancer. He underwent cobalt treatments and moved to the West Coast. In southern California he tried to fight the disease by exercising, but it was too late. A part of him was irreparably demoralized. He filled his notebook with reflections on his disordered life and a record of his despairing dreams. There was, however, no change of his basic beliefs. He would have agreed with the traditional Marxist view of the purpose of existence as stated by his Trotskyist friend George Novack in an essay on "Socialism and the Meaning of Life": "So far as our hooded vision can presently see, the overwhelming goals of humanity are to get rid of class society and go on to create all those conditions that can promote to the utmost the flowering of its collective creativity. . . ."[73] He maintained to the end that Marxism was the only philosophy that could make sense out of the forces shaping our lives, and thus, to the rational mind, the only liberating philosophy. However, it would not be an accurate description of Duncan's final days to minimize the bitterness that overwhelmed him on an immediate, personal level. For some time he had been "filled with a sense of almost total frustration of my life in its final years."[74] When Demila came to see him in a nursing home in Santa Monica, he repeated over and over again that "I've had a miserable life."[75]

He received some comfort from a stream of devoted party friends who came to his bedside, and there were, too, the memories of his artistic achievements. Late in December 1973 he inquired from his hospital bed

Duncan Ferguson in 1973, just before his death.

about the location of his bust of James P. Cannon, then eighty-four years old, who would outlive Duncan by only a few months. The last words in his diary expressed his joy at receiving a package and opening it to see the "head of Jim." Shortly afterwards he slipped into a coma and died on 29 April 1974.[76]

The name of Duncan Ferguson does not appear in any recent histories of American sculpture. His works now sit shrouded in the basements of the Whitney and other museums that once displayed them. To some, Ferguson's search for wholeness in his political and artistic lives may seem but a footnote to contemporary cultural history. Yet his struggle and fate were shared by a number of artists and intellectuals who had been transformed by the social struggles of the 1930s. His troubled life also embodies important issues still faced by artistic and intellectual rebels who seek to fuse their cultural practice with political radicalism. In that sense he left a lifetime of activities well worth consideration. Also left is a personality aura that will live as long as those who knew him have memory.

Notes and Acknowledgments

Research funds for this study were made available through the Rackham School of the University of Michigan and the Robert H. Langston Foundation. I am grateful to George Novack and Patrick Quinn for their careful editorial assistance, and to Mary Ferguson for her generous cooperation in every phase of the project. The following friends of Duncan Ferguson cooperated in personal interviews, many of them tape recorded: Cleo Ferguson, Milton Genecin, Tybie Genecin, Barbara Gray, Al Hansen, Reba Hansen, Rod Holt, Demila Jenner, Almeda Kirsch, Berta Langston, Joe Lee, Ethel Lobman, George Perle, and Jean Tussey. In addition, the following people provided information by mail: Cleanth Brooks, Dorothy Breitman, George Breitman, Farrell Dobbs, Alex B. Daspit, Caroline Durrieux, D. B. Fricke, Boyer Gonzales, Robert Heilman, Fred Hochberg, Charles Hyneman, William Lewis III, Frank Lovell, Lois Mahier, Howard Mitchum, Shirley Pasholk, Harry Ring, Roscoe J. Saville, Davidson Sommers, Eliot Stanley, John Staggs, Eric Voegelin, Robert Penn Warren, George Weissman, and Ralph Wickiser. The Ferguson papers are in the possession of Rod Holt, his literary executor, who has given me permission to quote from letters, notebooks, and diaries.

1. Eliot Hungerford Stanley, "The Tiger Stays for Dinner: L.S.U. in the Era of Huey P. Long: State Politics and Academic Concern in a Southern State University (1928–42)," Harvard Honors Essay, 1963, p. 45. See also Robert B. Heilman, "Baton Rouge and L.S.U. Forty Years After," Sewanee Review 87, no. 1 (Winter 1980): 126–43.
2. Author's interview with Demila Jenner, 17 July 1981.
3. Ferguson's personal notebook, undated.
4. Author's interview with Mary Ferguson, 6 May 1981.
5. Author's interview with Joe Lee, 26 August 1982; Harvard College Records Office.

6. Harvard College Records Office; letters from Duncan Ferguson to Florence Ferguson, 3 August 1919 and 2 March 1920.

7. Harvard College Records Office; author's interviews with Mary Ferguson, 6 May 1981; Demila Jenner, 17 July 1981; and Al Hansen, 10 July 1981.

8. Author's interview with Joe Lee, 26 August 1982.

9. Letter from Mary Manley to Dr. Ferguson, 22 June 1926.

10. Letter from Dr. Ferguson to Mary Manley, 10 May 1926.

11. Letter from Mary Manley to Dr. Ferguson, 22 June 1920.

12. Author's interviews with Milton and Tybie Genecin, 23 July 1981; and Rod Holt, 13 July 1981.

13. Ferguson's personal notebook, undated.

14. Wayne Craven, *Sculpture in America* (New York: Thomas Crowell and Company, 1968), 575.

15. Boston Transcript, undated clipping from the Ferguson papers.

16. Ibid.

17. *New York Sun*, 9 March 1929, p. 8.

18. *New York Times*, 10 March 1929, p. 8.

19. *Art News*, 16 March 1929, p. 9.

20. Foreword to brochure for the Downtown Gallery Exhibition.

21. *New York Times*, 19 February 1935, p. L25.

22. Author's interview with Mary Ferguson, 6 May 1981.

23. Ferguson's personal notebook, undated.

24. Letter from D. B. Fricke to Alan Wald, 11 February 1980.

25. *The Progress*, 11 March 1938, p. 14.

26. *Morning Advocate*, 3 September 1939, p. 2.

27. *The Reveille*, 12 November 1937, p. 3.

28. *Morning Advocate*, 14 March 1937, p. 2.

29. *The Progress*, 11 March 1938, p. 14.

30. *Daily Reveille*, 2 March 1938, p. 6.

31. Author's interview with Mary Ferguson, 6 May 1981.

32. Author's interview with Demila Jenner, 17 July 1981.

33. Ibid.

34. Ibid.

35. Ibid.

36. Stanley, "The Tiger Stays for Dinner," p. 84.

37. Author's interview with Demila Jenner, 17 July 1981.

38. Ibid.

39. Ibid.

40. Ibid.

41. Author's interview with Milton Genecin, 23 July 1981.

42. Author's interview with Demila Jenner, 17 July 1981.

43. Ibid.

44. Author's interview with Milton Genecin, 23 July 1981.

45. Ibid.

46. Author's interview with Demila Jenner, 17 July 1981.

47. Ibid.

48. Author's interview with Mary Ferguson, 6 May 1981.

49. Letter from Duncan Ferguson to Laura Slobe, dated only 1949.

50. Diary entry for 9 June 1967.

51. Author's interview with Demila Jenner, 17 July 1981.

52. Ferguson's notes for lecture on "The Artist and Professional Vs. McCarthyism," in Ferguson papers.
53. Ferguson's personal notebook, undated.
54. Author's interview with Demila Jenner, 17 July 1981.
55. Ferguson's personal notebook, undated.
56. Ibid.
57. Letter from Duncan Ferguson to Howard Mitchum, 13 October 1957.
58. Diary entry for 7 September 1957.
59. Letter from Duncan Ferguson to Florence and Mary Ferguson, 7 September 1957.
60. Letter from Duncan Ferguson to Evelyn Reed, 2 November 1957.
61. Diary entry for 27 April 1959.
62. Author's interview with Milton Genecin, 23 July 1981.
63. Diary entry for 27–29 December 1963.
64. Diary entry for 18 July 1956.
65. Author's interview with Jean Tussey, 3 August 1982.
66. Tape recording of Ferguson's lecture on "The Artist and the Revolutionary Movement," in Ferguson papers.
67. Letter from Duncan Ferguson to Florence Ferguson, 29 September 1959.
68. Diary entry for 3 July 1968.
69. Letter from Rod Holt to Alan Wald, 16 September 1982.
70. Author's interview with Rod Holt, 13 July 1981.
72. Diary entry for 3 December 1981.
73. George Novack, *Humanism and Socialism* (New York: Pathfinder, 1983), 148.
74. Ferguson's personal notebook, undated.
75. Author's interview with Demila Jenner, 17 July 1981.
76. Diary entry for 3 December 1973.

2

Victor Serge and the New York Anti-Stalinist Left, 1937–47

We must enroll ourselves in the school of reality, knowing that the movements of tomorrow will invent more than they will borrow from the past.
Victor Serge in a letter to Dwight Macdonald, 2 November 1941

Almost four decades after his death in 1947, Victor Serge's reputation in the United States is just now beginning to blossom. Translated into English during the 1960s and 1970s primarily by Richard Greeman, Serge's most important novels have only recently begun to attract the attention they warrant.[1] Favorable reviews have appeared since 1970 in leading publications such as the *New York Times Book Review*, the *New York Review of Books*, and the *New Republic*. In 1983, Serge's work was the subject of a feature article in the *Village Voice*, and in 1986 Serge was the topic of a panel discussion at the Socialist Scholars Conference in New York City.[2]

Serge previously was known primarily for his political writings, and especially for his journalism. Moreover, he was read and promoted almost exclusively by very small Trotskyist groups headquartered in New York City and by a small circle of New York writers originally influenced by Trotskyism. At the time Serge first encountered the intellectuals who comprised this "anti-Stalinist Left," he found that they held in common with him the view that a genuine Marxist opposition to the policies of the Soviet ruling elite was inauthentic unless it embraced a complementary stand against capitalism and for revolutionary socialism. As Daniel Singer, author of *The Road to Gdansk* (1982), observed four decades later: "To bury Stalinism really means to revive the idea of socialism and to begin its construction all over again, a prospect as deadly for the aged leaders of 'really existing socialism' as it is for the old capitalist masters."[3]

Within a decade, however, the prevailing anti-Stalinism of most of the

39

New York writers overwhelmed their other concerns, including their advocacy of socialism. Arguing that developing an independent revolutionary socialist movement was impossible, they consciously chose to ally with the "West" as the lesser of two evils locked in struggle in the "Cold War." The "West," of course, was their euphemism for imperialism, which had now become an acceptable ally against what they called "Red Fascism." Many of these writers rose to influential places in academe and publishing, and subsequently became known as the "New York intellectuals."[4]

From his Paris exile in the late 1930s, until his fatal heart attack in Mexico on 18 November 1947, Serge engaged in a sustained personal correspondence with several individuals from this milieu. He was closest to Dwight and Nancy Macdonald, but among the others with whom he corresponded were Sidney Hook, Max Eastman, William Phillips, and Irving Howe. He also contributed frequently to the New York publications *Partisan Review*, *Politics*, *Socialist Call*, and especially the *New Leader*, for which Serge served as the Mexico correspondent during the final years of his life. When news of his death came, the *New Leader* and the *Call* sponsored a public memorial meeting in New York City at the Rand School of Social Science on 23 December 1947.[5]

A few fugitive pieces by Serge also appeared in the *New International*, until 1940 the Trotskyist theoretical journal of the Socialist Workers Party, and in *New Essays*, a "council communist" publication edited by Paul Mattick.[6] Posthumously, in 1948–49, sections of Serge's *Year One of the Russian Revolution* were published in installments in the *New International*, which had by then become the journal of Max Shachtman's Workers Party.[7] The Workers Party had separated from the Socialist Workers Party in the spring of 1940 and was distinguished by its view that the Soviet Union was a "bureaucratic collectivist" society. In contrast, Leon Trotsky had argued that the Soviet ruling system was a degenerated form of the dictatorship of the proletariat in which workers' political power had been usurped. Between 1949 and 1950 the *New International* also printed seven excerpts from Serge's journals, which today remain the only English translations of this material.[8] In 1947, his name was listed as an international contributor to *Modern Review*, a Menshevik-oriented socialist journal largely funded by the International Ladies Garment Workers Union. Although a memorial tribute to Serge was published in its pages, he apparently contributed no articles to this journal.[9]

Serge's connections with the New York anti-Stalinist left were substantial. When seen as combined with and in some ways complementing his participation in European political exile circles in Mexico, his association with the anti-Stalinist New York intellectuals constituted a major political preoccupation. From his Mexican home Serge studied and vigorously participated in the New Yorkers' debates about the future of socialism, the meaning of World War II, and the political character of the Soviet Union. Articles he published in Mexico were translated into English and those that appeared in the U.S. press were conversely rendered in Spanish. The political views Serge formulated in lengthy letters to Dwight Macdonald were also expressed in the debates that animated "Socialism and Liberty," the organization of left-wing refugees Serge had founded in Mexico, and in its newspaper, *Il Mundo*. The major theme that preoccupied Serge and his New York counterparts was one that remains central to our own times: how does one construct a revolutionary socialist movement given the caricature of socialism that Stalinism has imposed upon the Soviet Union?

A review of Serge's relations with the New York anti-Stalinist Left will help to fill in a crucial chapter in Serge's biography, one not covered in *Memoirs of a Revolutionary*, which brings Serge's story to a close at the time of his arrival in Mexico in 1941. It may also enrich an understanding of the important debate over the legacy of Stalinism, a central task if one wishes to prevent the repetition of past mistakes. But one cannot approach the subject with the expectation of receiving clear, unambiguous, and final answers.

Serge's own political evolution has already been the subject of considerable controversy. Peter Sedgwick felt compelled to add an appendix to his 1963 translation of *Memoirs of a Revolutionary*, in which Sedgwick struggled, perhaps unsatisfactorily, to explain Serge's startling 1947 declaration in a personal letter to Charles de Gaulle of his support to the reactionary *Rassemblement du People Francais*.[10] In 1982, Richard Greeman published an essay on "Victor Serge and Leon Trotsky, Relations 1936–40," in which Greeman made the surprising assertion that the sharp differences that developed between the two were not substantive but were primarily due to misunderstandings.[11] Following Sedgwick's tragic suicide in 1983, a previously unpublished manuscript was discovered in which he claimed that Serge's early writings sharply contradicted his ideas about bolshevism as articulated in his acclaimed memoirs.[12] A final assessment cannot be reached until a scholar publishes a thorough political biography that assesses Serge's post–World War II writings in Europe, Mexico, and the United States.

Like the conundrums of Serge's career, assessments of the American anti-Stalinist Left have suffered considerable confusion and misunderstanding, and its legacy has continued to be an ambiguous terrain contested by revolutionary Marxists and social democrats, as well as by liberals and neoconservatives. In general, the New York group in the years between the Moscow Trials and the Cold War was undergoing a profound process of deradicalization, migrating from a quasi-Trotskyist support of Leninism to a championing of various forms of social democracy. Eventually, most came to espouse an anticommunist liberalism. Such was the route followed by Sidney Hook, Lionel Trilling, Diana Trilling, Clement Greenberg, and William Phillips.

But others made the transition at different paces and in different ways. Dwight Macdonald, for example, remained an independent Trotskyist until 1946, when he became an anarcho-pacificist. James Burnham was transformed overnight from a leading theoretician of the U.S. Trotskyist movement to a follower of Vilfredo Pareto and eventually ended up along with Max Eastman and John Dos Passos on the editorial board of the reactionary *National Review*. Meyer Schapiro, Lewis Coser, and Irving Howe (the last two were much younger than most of the others) remained ardent if idiosyncratic Trotskyists until the late 1940s, before quietly shifting toward the radical hue of social democracy promoted by *Dissent* in the early 1950s.[13]

What most of them had in common was a progressive repudiation of any form of Leninism; this particular political apostasy became the *sine qua non* for survival in the intellectual world in the McCarthy era. Thus most evolved from authentic anti-Stalinists, that is, revolutionary communists opposed to Stalin's theory and practice, to ersatz anti-Stalinists, that is, anticommunists opposed to bolshevism in all its forms (as the progenitor of totalitarianism), but who continued to call themselves "anti-Stalinists" for self-serving reasons. In the latter phase many succumbed in varying degrees to a vulgar anticommunist ideology that associates all movements for fundamental social change with the crimes of the Stalin regime.[14]

Victor Serge, however, never repudiated Leninism, although he cogently argued that some of Lenin's practices had inadvertently assisted the rise of Stalinism. Serge also held the unsettling view that the degeneration process that led to Stalinism began less than a year after the Bolsheviks seized power, with the establishment of the secret police. In general, however, he steadfastly defended the October Revolution, and the Bolshevik seizure of power from the Provisional Government that had preceded it. But during the mid-1940s Serge's association with the Menshevik-oriented *New Leader* had become so intimate that on 27 February 1945 Macdonald wrote him in despair:

> Our political views, my dear Victor, seem to be diverging rapidly. . . .
> I'm . . . very sorry to see you becoming a regular contributor to the *New Leader*, which is an extremely rightwing labor paper, of a low intellectual level, and which has become the organ of exhausted and bourgeoisified former leftists like Max Eastman . . . and Sidney Hook. . . . the *New Leader* has no political ideas or principles except anti-Stalinism. The only reason I can see for someone like yourself, with your past record and your fine moral and intellectual sensitivity to the real needs and interests of the masses, to accept such a political milieu is that anti-Stalinism is becoming your own basic political principle.[15]

Serge's relationship with the U.S. Left was initially due to his connections with Trotsky's Left Opposition. In 1937, while the Trotskyists were a faction in the Socialist Party, they promoted two works by Serge detailing the degeneration of the Russian Revolution and contrasting the practices of Stalin with those of Lenin and Trotsky. One was a pamphlet translated by Ralph Manheim and published by Pioneer Publishers, the Trotskyist publishing house, called *From Lenin to Stalin*. In fact, the first attention Serge's writings received in the U.S. press was a review of the pamphlet by the novelist and Trotskyist sympathizer James T. Farrell that appeared in *Beacon*.[16]

The other work was a 298-page book, *Russia after Twenty Years* (in England it was published as *Destiny of a Revolution*), translated by Max Shachtman and published by Hillman-Curl, Inc. In both publications the political analysis of the causes of Stalinism and the necessary remedies to eliminate or prevent it were virtually identical with those offered by Leon Trotsky in *The Revolution Betrayed: What Is the Soviet Union and Where Is It Going?*, published the same year. The U.S. Trotskyists no doubt regarded Serge as one of their own.

The reviewers, of course, interpreted *Russia after Twenty Years* according to their own political inclinations. In a lengthy and thoughtful critique in the *New International*, Maurice Spector, the founder of Canadian Trotskyism, judged Serge's theorization of the degenerative process to be far more cogent than the interpretations suggested by Eugene Lyons and others in recent books.[17] In the *Nation* Edmund Wilson, a great admirer of Trotsky, praised *Russia after Twenty Years* as "one of the most important works that have yet been published on the Soviet Union"; Wilson also seemed to endorse Serge's (and Trotsky's) view that the socioeconomic gains of the Russian Revolution remained, in spite of its horrendous political degeneration.[18] Eugene Lyons, himself already having moved sharply from a procommunist stance to pure and simple anti-Stalinism, praised Serge in the *Saturday Review* without mentioning that such a distinction was central to Serge's argument.[19] In contrast, Matthew Josephson, a supporter of the U.S. Communist Party writing in the *New Republic*, described Serge's book as a work of "Trotskyist partisanship," adding that it contained "a terrible catalogue of the fates which have befallen all his friends and fellow plotters" by an author "unabashed in his hope for new violence."[20]

But Serge's friendly collaboration with the U.S. Trotskyists was short-lived. In fact, in 1936 he had left Trotsky's International Left Opposition, a precursor of the Fourth International, to join the Spanish Workers Party of Marxist Unification (POUM), which the Trotskyists regarded as a centrist party. Although Serge proclaimed his intention to remain on good terms with his former comrades, conflicts with them steadily increased. In July

1938 Serge published a letter in the *New International* that praised the journal but also insinuated that Trotsky had used Stalinist methods of debate by amalgamating Serge's views on the 1921 Kronstadt uprising with the anti-Bolshevik views of Mensheviks and others. Serge had criticized the Bolsheviks for failing to make every effort to negotiate with the Kronstadt sailors before suppressing their uprising.[21] A second communication from Serge, published in February 1939 in the *New International*, was more sympathetic to Trotsky's interpretation of Kronstadt, and also included a defense of bolshevism against the criticisms of Anton Ciliga, a leader of the Yugoslav Communists who was imprisoned by Stalin in the mid-1930s. Serge, however, proceeded in the subsequent paragraphs to present a provocative defense of the policies of the POUM.[22]

Although the journal's editors, Max Shachtman and James Burnham, responded to Serge on both occasions with tact and diplomacy, relations between the Trotskyists and Serge reached a nadir with the publication of Trotsky's June 1939 essay, "The Moralists and Sycophants against Marxism." In this vitriolic polemic, Trotsky accused Serge—possibly on the basis of inaccurate information about Serge's views—of infecting the revolutionary movement with a "moralism" that would eventually lead to "reaction."[23]

Serge's ties to the literary current that would become the New York intellectuals began in earnest in late 1938, with the publication of "Marxism in Our Time," translated by Dwight and Nancy Macdonald. This spirited yet nonsectarian defense of classical Marxism appeared in the pages of *Partisan Review*, which had broken with the Communist movement and evolved toward a quasi-Trotskyist position a year earlier. Dwight Macdonald, an editorial board member of *Partisan Review*, wrote Serge in December 1938 asking permission to publish a translation of a section of *Conquered City*. The natural affinity that was instantly evident between the two men was not accidental, for Macdonald, although he was moving toward Trotskyism and would join the Socialist Workers Party in the fall of 1939, had also questioned Trotsky's views on Kronstadt in a 1938 letter to the *New International*.[24]

With the German invasion of France in the spring of 1940, the Macdonalds threw themselves heavily into rescuing political refugees by attempting to get visas for antifascists to leave Europe for the United States and Latin America. The Macdonalds were especially concerned with individuals like Serge who had been connected with Trotskyist and other non-Stalinist revolutionary socialist tendencies, because they tended to be shunned by refugee organizations influenced by liberals and Communists. Naming their group the Fund for European Writers, the Macdonalds collaborated with the Emergency Rescue Committee, a broader organization which sent Varian Fry to Europe as its representative.[25] In Paris, Serge was still associated with the Trotskyist milieu. He collaborated, for example, with the International Federation of Independent Revolutionary Art (FIARI) which had been inspired by a manifesto signed by André Breton, Diego Rivera, and Trotsky, and was employed by the American Trotskyist journalist and correspondent for *Time* magazine, Sherry Mangan, as a research assistant. But Serge was understandably infuriated by Trotsky's critique of him in "Moralists and Sycophants," protesting that he had been profoundly misrepresented.[26]

The Macdonalds worked tirelessly to obtain a U.S. visa for Serge and his children. His wife, Lioubov Kibalchiche, was at the time confined in a psychiatric hospital in Neuilly sur Marne in France. Despite initial hopeful signs, their efforts were blocked by the decision of George Warren of the President's Advisory Committee on Political Refugees to pass the visa application on to the State Department; Warren believed the State Department would consider Serge as a potential Soviet agent.[27] Numerous intellectual supporters of the U.S. anti-Stalinist Left—James T. Farrell, Sidney Hook, Max Eastman, Meyer Schapiro, and Herbert Solow—sent letters protesting this decision.[28] While the U.S. government continued to characterize Serge as an "anti-Stalin Communist," Dwight Macdonald and the others protested that he was simply an enemy of Hitler and Stalin.[29] Finally, the Macdonalds were able to arrange for Serge and his twenty-one-year-old son Vladimir to go to Mexico via Cuba and Martinique in the summer of 1941. They were soon followed by his six-year-old daughter, Jeannine, and Laura Sejournee, a thirty-year-old Italian in the film industry who would become Serge's second wife.

Throughout the entire ordeal the Macdonalds wrote Serge almost weekly, convinced that it was crucial to continually offer him hope. They also sent considerable amounts of money. Once he was established in Mexico, Dwight assisted Serge in getting published in a variety of U.S. journals and in circulating his book manuscripts to publishers in both the United States and in England. He and Nancy translated many of Serge's writings, and it was Dwight who proposed that Serge write his memoirs and later made tireless efforts to get them into print.[30]

Serge's debut in *Partisan Review*, "Marxism in Our Time," introduced the theme for which his later political thought is primarily valued: a critique of the loss of democracy in the Soviet Union, from the point of view of defending original aims of the revolution itself. His basic view never changed. He held that the harsh policies necessary to save the revolution under siege later led to the disenfranchisement of the working class through a process of centralization of power and repression of "heresies."[31] The same theme was dramatized in the selections from *Conquered City*, translated by Gertrude Buckman, first wife of the poet

Delmore Schwartz, which appeared in *Partisan Review* two years later.[32] While somewhat more critical of the Bolshevik tradition than Trotsky— among other matters, Serge contended that the Left Opposition was incorrect in not calling for the legalization of opposition parties in its 1923 platform—Serge's basic categories and perspectives remained Trotskyist until the advent of World War II.

By the fall of 1941, some changes in Serge's views were already in evidence when he participated in a *Partisan Review* discussion that also involved James Burnham and Dwight Macdonald on the nature of fascism and World War II. Here Serge vigorously refuted the arguments for the fundamental identification of the monstrosities of Hitlerism and Stalinism, despite their superficial similarities, but he also applied in passing the term "bureaucratic collectivism" to the Soviet Union, indicating that he now held that it encompassed a new form of class society. Still, Serge also predicted, as did the Trotskyist Fourth International, that mass revolutionary upheavals would destroy all forms of global capitalism and Stalinism in the wake of the war.

More significantly, in terms of Serge's attitude toward World War II, his views as expressed in the article seemed a hybrid of those being propagated by the followers of James P. Cannon in the Socialist Workers Party and those of Sidney Hook. Max Shachtman's Workers Party, as well as Macdonald, argued for a two-stage strategy which called for a socialist transformation of the United States before waging a war against Hitler. However, the Socialist Workers Party contended that, because a revolutionary movement failed to develop before the outbreak of the war, the antifascist and anticapitalist struggle must be "telescoped"; thus its members participated nondisruptively in the war effort when they were drafted as soldiers, while the party press continued to denounce the imperialist aims of the United States and to support ongoing struggles for economic and social justice of trade unions and Afro-Americans. Hook, from a social democratic perspective, advocated outright "critical support" of the war.

Serge's writings, which were never totally clear, repudiated the two-stage strategy, but used a weaker formulation of resistance to imperialist policies than that of the Socialist Workers Party. Instead of declaring outright opposition to Allied efforts, he said, in words similar to those Hook might have used, that "the Churchill regime is fighting *in spite of itself* for the European revolution, the defeat of the Nazis being the precondition of that. . . ." He then added a statement suggesting that on some level one should withhold "critical support" to the Allies: "we have other jobs than to give aid to governments which are subjectively reactionary [such as the United States and England], that is, accomplices of the enemy, and objectively the playthings of historical necessities which they don't understand. We have our own jobs and it is only in doing these without compromise that we will contribute to the downfall of the Nazis—never in becoming conformist."[33]

Among the other pieces Serge published in *Partisan Review* were a summary of the situation of French writers in 1941, a memoir of his departure from France, and a powerful tribute to Trotsky following the latter's assassination in August 1940.[34] But it was not until publication of his 1945 essay on the postwar prospects for France that Serge revealed that he was in a significantly new stage of political evolution. The piece focused almost entirely on the dangers of Stalinism, now divested of any progressive features whatsoever. Although Serge supported the need for a revolution in France in the abstract, he virtually excluded a practical effort in that direction: "no large political movement will be able to make itself known without the support of the totalitarian Communist Party; and if it does make itself known through this party, it cannot fail to fall under its leadership."[35]

Serge's last contribution to *Partisan Review*, a contribution to a symposium on "The Future of Socialism" which he titled "The Socialist Imperative," appeared just weeks before his death. Here the case for socialism is largely made on the grounds that no other ideologies have succeeded any better. The balance sheet of the Russian Revolution, Serge argued, has ended in an "appalling deficit." Moreover, he concluded that "the seizure of power by civil war is a burden to the victors themselves, and leads to a dictatorship, opposed by its very nature to the fulfillment of socialist humanism." Workers' control has become complicated by the development of new technology, which only specialists can manage. Most importantly, Stalinism is now the main enemy. The hope for socialism rests on "aspirations toward the rational organization of society for the realization of a higher human dignity. . . ."[36]

Although formally a supporter of Lenin and a defender of the legacy of the October 1917 Bolshevik Revolution, Serge's practical politics in the 1940s wobbled between left- and right-wing social democracy. His contributions to the *Socialist Call* tended to reflect the former, and those to the *New Leader*, the latter. His first *Call* piece, on 7 May 1943, was an essay on World War II that originally had been accepted by the *New Leader*'s left-leaning editor Daniel Bell, but then had been suppressed by Bell's seniors because it overemphasized the need for socialism.[37] Serge was described in the *Call* as a former Trotskyist who was now a "champion of revolutionary democratic socialism."[38]

Subsequent Serge articles in the *Call* asked U.S. radicals to consider the persecuted dissidents in the fascist and Stalinist prisons of Europe as the hope of the future, analyzed Soviet war strategy, noted the centrality of democracy to socialism, and optimistically spoke of the Soviet people's ability to liberate themselves.[39] A stirring obituary by Lewis Coser (using the pseudonym Louis Clair), insisted that "Serge taught us that one can hate Stalinist oppression without becoming so imbued by hatred that one forgets the many evils of this world, seeing only one great evil."[40]

Coser's remark was a direct swipe at the politics expressed in the *New Leader* where Serge's essays exposing various crimes of Stalinism, both inside and outside of the Soviet Union, had become a regular feature, along with occasional pieces on the activities of Spanish socialists in exile. More than twenty such articles were published in the weekly *New Leader* between 1943 and 1947, most often appearing in 1944 and 1945. The first was a front-page description of the Stalinist attack on a memorial meeting held in Mexico for Carlo Tresca, Victor Alter, and Heinrich Ehrlich. The last was an exposé of the privileged treatment Trotsky's assassin was receiving in Mexico.[41] In the *New Leader*'s obituary for Serge, he was described in terms quite agreeable to the *New Leader*: "At his death, Mr. Serge was a confirmed democratic Socialist opposed to totalitarianism of all varieties. He often said that his dillusionment with the Bolshevik brand of totalitarianism began in 1921 with the ruthless suppression of the revolt of the Kronstadt sailors by the Bolsheviks."[42]

Although he disagreed with Dwight Macdonald's somewhat purist posture toward World War II, Serge did side with Macdonald in the latter's 1943 break with *Partisan Review*, mainly because he perceived *Partisan Review* as retreating from political discussion altogether.[43] Serge's contributions to Macdonald's new journal *Politics* began in the vein of his *Socialist Call* pieces and gradually drifted toward the tenor of his *New Leader* writings. In January 1945, for example, Serge criticized *Politics* for being too soft on "communist-totalitarian" influence in the French Resistance. Yet, Serge periodically gave the Russian Revolution its due in a manner that would have not been tolerated in the *New Leader*. For example, in a published commentary on Macdonald's famous essay, "The Responsibility of Peoples," Serge discussed the long history of pogroms in Russia, including the massacre of 200,000 Jews by Czarist and nationalist forces in the Ukraine and in White Russia during the Russian Civil War. He unabashedly concluded that: "The victory of the revolution finally put an end to these horrors."[44] Nevertheless, his last contribution to *Politics*, in the spring of 1947, denounced a piece by George Padmore on Indochina for failing to expose Ho Chi Minh as a Communist tool of the Kremlin. By such a criticism Serge implied that the national liberation struggle in Indochina was simply part of a worldwide campaign directed by Moscow to establish its totalitarian rule. Serge concluded that the struggle in Indochina "poses to all of us—liberals, socialists, radicals alike—this question: should we sympathize with colonial revolts when their real meaning is the expansion of totalitarianism?"[45]

In sum, Serge's relations with the New York anti-Stalinist Left between 1937 and 1947 were divided among its three central constituents. With the revolutionary socialists of the Socialist Workers Party and the Workers Party, Serge shared a commitment to preserving the achievements of the October Russian Revolution. His statement to Macdonald in 1941 was typical:"We must begin anew, exactly in order to preserve the essence of October 1917 and the experience that followed."[46] Serge also shared a somewhat hyperbolized version of Trotsky's erroneous prediction of the certainty of postwar social upheavals that would revolutionize Europe and cast off the totalitarian rule of Stalinism in the Soviet Union. As he wrote to Macdonald in 1942: "More and more I look at this war as a call to change the face of the world. I have the feeling that the breadth of the changes taking place and those to come will surpass anything we imagined on any level."[47] With the left-wing social democrats, however, Serge dismissed the relevance of any existing Leninist movements, considering even the Trotskyists as leftovers of a moribund moment in history.[48]

Finally, with the right-wing social democrats, with whom he became increasingly associated in 1944–45, Serge shared an acceptance of the view that participation of Communists in ostensibly democratic or national liberation struggles condemned those struggles to domination by the Kremlin, thereby justifying "critical" support of capitalism and imperialism. This was most evident in early 1945, when Serge sided with a series of *New Leader* attacks by Max Eastman and Liston Oak on Macdonald as a dupe of Greek Stalinism:

> To think that the Communists can be *outdone* or that in the present situation they can be *outflanked* by the masses is to misunderstand the power of a formidable apparatus which is *all-powerful*. I would defend the lesser evil formulation, which we've often used in a stupid and slipshod manner. In escaping Nazi-Paris, we accepted the lesser evil of Vichy France and that saved the lives of thousands of us. The fate of the genuine socialists in Athens under the Plastiras regime is not an enviable one. . . . But they will survive, or at least they have a good chance of surviving. Under a camouflaged Communist regime, they'd have no chance to survive. . . .[49]

Central to Serge's political evolution was one objective fact: the failure of postwar revolutionary upsurges to overthrow capitalism in Europe and break the yoke of Stalinism in the Soviet Union. Yet this failure does not adequately account for Serge's general migration from a Trotskyist to a "Third Camp" socialist to a nonrevolutionary "lesser evilist." After all, it was clear that the forces of imperialism had embarked on their most intensive form of world domination, and the Stalinist "monolith" would crack just two years after Serge's death, with the 1949 Tito-Stalin rift. Serge had become, one might argue, politically disoriented. In part this was due to his situation in Mexico where the Stalinist movement had grown considerably. Serge and his associates in "Socialism and Liberty" were subjected to vile personal attacks as well as physical violence. On the one hand this resulted in Serge's justified fear of Stalinist brutality, but it also generated a certain degree of paranoia. The latter was evidenced in Serge's unproven conviction that Robert Sheldon Hart, Trotsky's murdered body-guard, had actually been an agent of Stalin, and in the unsubstantiated view that Arkady Masloff, a former leader of the German Communists who died in Cuba, was actually murdered by Stalinists.[50] Moreover, he personally knew Walter Krivitsky, the Soviet military intelligence officer who defected in 1937, and was seriously affected by his death under mysterious circum-stances in 1941.[51]

Yet a careful scrutiny of Serge's correspondence indicates that he failed to fit comfortably into any orthodoxy, including that of right-wing social democracy. For example, despite surprisingly cordial letters to Max East-man, whose reactionary transformation was indisputable, Serge held back from joining Eastman's celebration of American "freedom."[52] He could write Sidney Hook in praise of Hook's debunking of "laws" of dialectical materialism yet simultaneously insist on the dialectical method's practical value.[53] In other words, even as Serge clearly moved to the right, his deep emotional ties to the Russian Revolution and his experience of Leninism under the leadership of Lenin and of the Left Opposition were sufficiently strong to cause him to pull back in one way or another from complete acquiescence to the vulgar anticommunism that was engulfing intellectual life in the United States. In reviews of *Memoirs of a Revolutionary*, after Serge's death, Stanley Plastrik and Irving Howe, onetime leaders of the Workers Party, both insistently emphasized that Serge never became a "professional anti-Bolshevik" but firmly stood on the ground of the Rus-sian Revolution to the end.[54]

What does one make of Victor Serge? First, one must recognize that, while he may not have been a Marxist theoretician or political leader of great stature, he was a man of extraordinary intelligence, integrity, and artistic sensibility. The political evolution of Victor Serge in the 1940s is not testimony to his personal weakness, but to the weight of adverse pressures during the Cold War—pressures intensified by the continuing horrors of Stalinism and the inability of Trotskyism to offer a credible alternative. Anyone who lightly dismisses the change of views of former revolution-aries such as Serge as "sellouts" naively misjudges the seriousness of the problems confronted by his generation.

On the other hand, Serge's devolution from revolutionary Marxism—from an equally intransigent opposition to both imperialism and Stalinism—was genuine and should not be disregarded by his admirers who wish to appropriate the entirety of his legacy for the contemporary revolutionary socialist movement. Serge obviously underestimated the horrors of imperialism and overestimated the omnipotence of Stalinism. Just as the world was more complex than either Lenin or Trotsky had imagined or anticipated, so too was it for Victor Serge.

Perhaps most significant is the meaning of Serge's political program as articulated during the late 1930s. He called for a rethinking of socialism, for a new socialist language and new ideas, for a new definition of freedom, and for a new emphasis on the centrality of democracy to the socialist project. Who could disagree? And yet, despite these admirable goals, it appears that Serge's practical politics did not advance beyond Leninism but in fact regressed to the kind of politics that *preceded* the very Leninism that another part of his intellect held as a valid and profound achievement for human liberation!

Serge's association with the New York anti-Stalinist Left teaches us this: If Serge aspired to sustain a revolutionary Marxist position, he may have been unjustified in his break from the International Left Opposition; "Socialism and Liberty" as well as the POUM and other groups with which he subsequently associated turned out to be equally riven with factionalism and even more impotent than the Trotskyists. The groups that descended from the International Left Opposition, one might argue, are the only Marxist organizations that have given serious consideration to the central issue that absorbed Serge until his death: a Leninist explanation of the deterioration of Leninism into Stalinism.[55]

Serge also erred in his trust in the *New Leader*. He held that the journal allowed for a plurality of views that the Trotskyist movement did not allow. Perhaps he was correct insofar as the United States and some other Trotskyist movements were concerned, but he certainly misjudged the political significance of the *New Leader*. There can be no doubt that it is a major journal of twentieth-century American culture, but it became so precisely because it was a major vehicle by which a generation of rebels against capitalism, nationalism, and imperialism became reconciled with the status quo. Would Serge have become one of these apostates? There is no certain answer. Several peripheral contributors to the *New Leader* such as Paul Goodman, Dwight Macdonald (in the early 1950s) and C. Wright Mills, turned left again under the impact of the Cuban Revolution, the Vietnam War, and the American civil rights movement. Certainly Serge would never have been comfortable in the celebration of the "American Century" that followed the 1940s as long as he continued to reject the simplistic formula that Leninism leads to Stalinism.

The general goals of Serge's program for the reconstruction of socialism are unobjectionable as ideals, but they require a much more precise content before one can determine whether the particular form in which they are being mobilized as a rallying cry will lead to an advance or a regression for the revolutionary socialist movement.

Notes and Acknowledgments

I am grateful to Daniel Bell, George Breitman, Albert Glotzer, Richard Greeman, and Susan Weissman for sharing information and materials with me, and to Vladimir Kibalchich, Yale University Library, and the Tamiment Library at New York University for use of papers. As always, I am indebted to Patrick Quinn for his careful reading of a draft of the manuscript, and for his penetrating challenges to my assumptions and evidence. Joanna Misnik and Claudine Raynaud assisted with translations from Serge's correspondence and unpublished papers in French. The translations and some of the research were made possible by a grant from the University of Michigan.

1. Greeman is not only Serge's most capable translator but also his most astute critic. See the following articles by Greeman: "Victor Serge and the Revolutionary Tradition in Literature," *Triquarterly* 8 (Winter 1967): 39–60; "The Laws Are Burning: Literary and Revolutionary Realism in Victor Serge," *Yale French Studies* 39 (1967): 146–59; "Victor Serge's *The Case of Comrade Tulayev*," *Minnesota Review* 15 (Fall 1980): 61–79; "Messages: Victor Serge and the Persistance of the Socialist Ideal," *Massachusetts Review* 22, no. 3 (Autumn 1981): 553–68.
2. See the following reviews: Walter Goodman, "The Conquered City," *New York Times Book Review* (28 December 1975): 14; James Walt, "The Life and Death of Leon Trotsky," *New Republic* (10 April 1976): 25–26; Neal Acherson, "Communist Dropouts," *New York Review of Books* 15 (13 August 1970): 11; and John Leonard, "*Midnight in the Century*," *New York Times* (4 December 1982): C19. Also see J. Hoberman, "Who Is Victor Serge and Why Do We Have to Ask?" *Village Voice Literary Supplement*, no. 30 (November 1984): 1, 12–17.
3. Daniel Singer, *The Road to Gdansk: Poland and the U.S.S.R.* (New York: Monthly Review, 1981), 18.
4. For a comprehensive study of this phenomenon, see Alan Wald, *The New York Intellectuals: The Rise and Decline of the Anti-Stalinist Left from the 1930s to the 1980s* (Chapel Hill, N.C.: University of North Carolina Press, 1987).
5. The announcement of the meeting appears in the *Socialist Call* 14, no. 46 (28 November 1947): 2.
6. The letters from the July 1938 and February 1939 *New International* are reprinted in V. I. Lenin and Leon Trotsky, *Kronstadt* (New York: Monad, 1979), 124–27, 135–39. See also Victor Serge, review of *Escape from Freedom*, by Erich Fromm, *New Essays* 6, no. 3 (Spring 1943): 74–75.
7. See the following issues of *New International*: 14, no. 3 (March 1948): 83–90; 14, no. 4 (April 1948): 123–26; 14, no. 5 (July 1948): 155–58; 14, no. 6 (August 1948): 187–90; 14, no. 7 (September 1948): 220–21; 14, no. 8 (October 1948): 252–55; 14, no. 9 (November 1948): 282–86; 15, no. 1 (January 1949): 30–33; 15,

no. 2 (February 1949): 60–62.

8. See the following issues of *New International*: 15, no. 10 (September 1949): 214–18; 16, nos. 1–2 (January–February 1950): 51–57; 16, nos. 3–4 (March–April 1950): 115–21; 16, nos. 5–6 (May–June 1950): 177–79; 16, nos. 7–8 (July–August 1950): 249–51; 16, nos. 9–10 (September–October 1950): 309–13; 16, nos. 11–12 (November–December 1950): 368–71.

9. "In Memorium: Victor Serge," *Modern Review* 2, no. 1 (January 1948): 7.

10. "Appendix: Victor Serge and Gaullism," in *Memoirs of a Revolutionary* (New York: Oxford University Press, 1975), 383–86.

11. I am grateful to Richard Greeman for an English-language version of "Victor Serge and Leon Trotsky: Relations 1936–40," which appeared in *Vuelta* (Mexico City) 6, no. 63 (February 1982).

12. Peter Sedgwick, "The Unhappy Elitist: Victor Serge's Early Bolshevism," *History Workshop*, no. 17 (Spring 1984): 150–56.

13. Although today avowedly non-Marxist and non-Leninist, Irving Howe in *Leon Trotsky* (New York: Viking Press, 1978) reveals an open attitude toward Bolshevism similar to that of Serge in many respects.

14. Ralph Miliband and Marcel Liebman, "Reflections on Anti-Communism," in *Socialist Register 1984: The Uses of Anti-Communism* (New York: Monthly Review, 1984), 1–22.

15. Letter from Dwight Macdonald to Victor Serge, 27 February 1945, Yale University Library.

16. James T. Farrell, "Generals Die at Dawn," *Beacon* 1 (July 1937): 19–21.

17. *New International* 4, no. 1 (January 1938): 29–30.

18. *Nation* 145, no. 534 (13 November 1937): 531–35.

19. *Saturday Review* 17, no. 10 (30 October 1937): 1.

20. *New Republic* 95, no. 105 (1 December 1937): 105–8.

21. The letter is reprinted in V. I. Lenin and Leon Trotsky, *Kronstadt* (New York: Monad, 1979), 124–27.

22. Ibid., 135–39.

23. Trotsky's piece has been reprinted in Leon Trotsky, John Dewey, and Gorge Novack, *Their Morals and Ours* (New York: Pathfinder, 1973), 55–66.

24. Macdonald's letter is reprinted in *Kronstadt*, 127–31.

25. Letter from Nancy Macdonald to Victor Serge, 1 September 1940, Yale University Library. Also see the references to Serge in Varian Fry, *Surrender on Demand* (New York: Random House, 1945).

26. Letter from Victor Serge to Dwight Macdonald, 1 March 1939 and 29 October 1939, Yale University Library; and Alan Wald, *The Revolutionary Imagination: The Poetry and Politics of John Wheelwright and Sherry Mangan* (Chapel Hill, N.C.: University of North Carolina Press, 1983), 184.

27. Letter from Nancy Macdonald to Victor Serge, 8 October 1940, Yale University Library.

28. Letter from Nancy Macdonald to Victor Serge, 19 October 1940, Yale University Library.

29. Letter from Nancy Macdonald to Victor Serge, 1 September 1940, Yale University Library.

30. Letter from Dwight Macdonald to Victor Serge, 6 July 1942, Yale University Library.

31. "Marxism in Our Time," *Partisan Review* 5, no. 3 (August–September 1938): 26–32.

32. "Conquered City," *Partisan Review* 8, no. 1 (January 1940): 3–17.
33. "What Is Fascism? The Discussion Continued," *Partisan Review* 8, no. 5 (September–October 1941): 418–30.
34. "French Writers, Summer 1941," *Partisan Review* 8, no. 5 (September–October 1941): 387–88; "On the Eve," *Partisan Review* 9, no. 1 (January–February 1942): 23–33; "In Memory: L. D. Trotsky," *Partisan Review* 9, no. 4 (July–August 1942): 388–91.
35. "French Expectations," *Partisan Review* 12, no. 2 (Spring 1945): 232–39.
36. "The Socialist Imperative," *Partisan Review* 14, no. 5 (September–October 1947): 511–17.
37. Letter from Dwight Macdonald to Victor Serge, 22 February 1943, Yale University Library.
38. "The War and the Resurgence of Socialism—An Optimistic Approach," *Socialist Call* (7 May 1943): 2.
39. See the following from *Socialist Call*: "Trust Anti-Fascists in Europe's Prisons," (12 May 1944): 8; "The 'Mystery' Behind Russian Policy," (1 September 1944): 8; "The 'Mystery' Behind Russian Policy," Part 2, (8 September 1944): 8; "Will Stalinism Last?," (14 May 1945): 6; "The Russian People Have Earned the Right to Full Democracy," (20 May 1946): 5.
40. Louis Clair [Lewis Coser], "His Life Was a Living Memorial to Integrity and Socialist Truth," *Socialist Call* (28 November 1947): 2.
41. "Gorkin Stabbed as Mexican C. P. Wrecks Ehrlich, Tresca Meeting," *New Leader* 26, no. 16, pp. 1, 7; and "Jacson: Privileged Assassin," *New Leader* 30, no. 14 (5 April 1947): 5.
42. "Death of Victor Serge," *New Leader* 30, no. 47 (22 November 1947): p. 12.
43. Letter from Victor Serge to Dwight Macdonald, 4 October 1943, Yale University Library.
44. "Stalinism and the Resistance," *Politics* 2, no. 2 (January 1945): 61–62; and "The Responsibilities of Peoples—A Letter from Victor Serge," *Politics* 2, no. 8 (August 1945): 252.
45. "The Communists and Vietnam," ibid. 4, no. 2 (March–April 1947): 78.
46. Victor Serge to Dwight Macdonald, 18 September 1941, Yale University Library.
47. Victor Serge to Dwight Macdonald, 28 October 1942, Yale University Library.
48. Victor Serge to Dwight Macdonald, 18 September 1941, Yale University Library.
49. Victor Serge to Dwight Macdonald, 19 March 1945, Yale University Library.
50. See the following letters from Victor Serge to Dwight Macdonald at Yale University Library: 14 September 1941 and 25 November 1941.
51. Victor Serge to Dwight Macdonald, 13 February 1941, Yale University Library.
52. Victor Serge to Max Eastman, 6 August 1943, Vladimir Serge papers, Mexico City.
53. Victor Serge to Sidney Hook, 10 July 1943, Vladimir Serge papers, Mexico City.
54. Henry Judd [Stanley Plastrik], "Serge's Memoirs," *New International* 17, no. 5 (September–October 1951): 309–10; Irving Howe, "The European as Revolutionary," *Steady Work* (New York: Harcourt, Brace and World, 1966), pp. 258–262.
55. The Fourth International literature on this subject is immense, but the most

comprehensive analysis is contained in "Socialist Democracy and Dictatorship of the Proletariat," *1979 World Congress of the Fourth International: Major Resolutions and Reports* (New York: Special Supplement to *Intercontinental Press Combined with Inprecor*, 1980), pp. 210–225.

3

The New York Literary Left

Terry A. Cooney. *The Rise of the New York Intellectuals: "Partisan Review" and Its Circle, 1934–45* (Madison: University of Wisconsin Press, 1986). 350 pp.

Eric Homberger. *American Writers and Radical Politics, 1900–39: Equivocal Commitments* (New York: St. Martin's Press, 1986). 286 pp.

Mark Shechner. *After the Revolution: Studies in the Contemporary Jewish-American Imagination* (Bloomington: Indiana University Press, 1987). 261 pp.

In the last few years it has become obligatory to commence a review that includes books about the political literati known as the "New York Intellectuals" with the observation that the subject has snowballed into a major sub-field in U.S. cultural studies. The expression "New York Intellectuals" does not refer to all intellectuals making their careers in New York City; only to a particular network coalescing around *Partisan Review* magazine in the mid-1930s.

Inspired by Philip Rahv, Lionel Trilling, Sidney Hook, Mary McCarthy, and others, this informal coterie initially blended anti-Stalinist Marxism (of the Trotsky variety) with a selective High Modernism (represented by Joyce and Eliot). After the Great Depression the group progressively renounced far left politics as it attained an intellectual pre-eminence in the post-war years that has lasted to the present.

The past decade of scholarship about this politico-cultural network has provoked jaded book reviewers into remarking that the road from Trotsky-ism to neo-conservatism is now sufficiently well-trod by authors of Ph.D. theses. There is even a growing sentiment that the reputation of this group of writers will soon become over-inflated, if it has not become so already.

My own view is that the subject is far from exhausted. The scholarship to date remains dwarfed by the significance of the experience embodied in this migration of a talented group of one-time aspiring revolutionaries through central political and cultural dilemmas of our epoch. Many of the issues that perplexed and disoriented the New York intellectuals haunt us yet; some demand resolution with a greater urgency than ever before. That is why the significance of this group derives as much from its intellectual failures as accomplishments.

More precisely, an important source of the enduring fascination of the New York intellectuals is to be located in several unanswered—or inadequately answered—questions that the group posed and tried to resolve. These questions include propositions about the role of the "committed" intellectual in the contemporary world; the liberatory and repressive functions of culture; the antinomies of universalism and ethnic (usually Jewish) identity; and the political character of post-revolutionary societies in the economically underdeveloped world.

To provide a brief summary: Most of the New York intellectuals began as partisans of the industrial and agricultural working class in the U.S. and abroad, but ended by opting for a questionable, self-proclaimed "independence" that some critics (including a few from within the group) feel is a mask for accommodation to a structure of domination within which they have privileges. They initiated their distinctive literary trajectory by decrying the Stalinist manipulation of culture, but, with the exception of Leslie Fiedler, ultimately embraced the elite, Eurocentric patriarchal tradition as a universal standard. They first subscribed to an internationalist identity, but in varying degrees lapsed into either Jewish particularism or Israeli exceptionalism. Finally, they launched their critique of Soviet Communism by rigorously distinguishing between progressive and reactionary features of a complex social formation, all within the context of an over-riding anti-capitalist and anti-imperialist world view, only to succumb in the 1950s to the vulgarities of the U.S. state ideologies of "anti-Totalitarianism" and "liberal anticommunism."

The intellectual achievements of the group vary considerably. But no individual's contribution to date has the soundness and completeness that I find, for example, in the life and work of British contemporaries such as Raymond Williams and E. P. Thompson. The cultural legacy of the group's pre-eminent critic, Lionel Trilling, pales in power and substance next to that of W. E. B. Du Bois. The Marxist literary theorizing of Phillip Rahv, for all the rhetorical brilliance of certain passages and paragraphs, is risible compared to that of Georg Lukács.

The group's most celebrated novelist, Saul Bellow, is prolific and obviously admired by a good section of the reading public and those who award the Nobel prize; yet his "symptomatic" fictional characters such as Henderson and Sammler lack the depth and energy of Toni Morrison's Milkman, Pilate, and Sula. Hannah Arendt, Edmund Wilson, and Leslie Fiedler are all brilliant voices; but they are also quirky and eccentric, each with a distressing "crackpot" feature or two. Irving Howe and Alfred Kazin are humane, rational, and craft-conscious critics; but, whatever their influence through the *New York Times Book Review* and *New York Review of Books*, they are of little importance in the cultural rethinking under way among the new generation of U.S. literary scholars.

It is not that the accomplishments of the New York intellectuals are negligible; rather, my point is that an on-going concern with the lives and work of the New York intellectuals does not betoken adulation. From my own perspective, the story of the New York intellectuals is rich primarily for what it tells us about the perennial issue of the social and political responsibilities of the cultural critic in the late capitalist epoch.

Of course, the problematic of "commitment" (that is, a conscious choice in one's allegiance as opposed to *de facto* alignment with the social forces to which all human actors have a relation) has appeared and has been subjected to study in many forms. What is distinct about its particular incarnation through the experience of the New York intellectuals is the way in which the group's effort to scrupulously choose the form of commitment telescopes many contemporary issues, launching the inquiry on a higher plane of complexity.

For example, what marked this group at its outset in the mid-1930s was its far-sighted break with faith in the Soviet form of "communism" or in any other state ideology, and its refusal to subordinate judgments about the difficult literature of "reactionary" authors to knee-jerk political criteria. Thus, from the initiation of their mature careers, these intellectuals were located in a place at which many of their equally talented contemporaries had yet to arrive.

Second, the New York intellectuals became a group that experienced in a particularly acute form the fate awaiting most radical intellectuals in advanced industrial societies in a period of political stability and economic consolidation. Despite protests to the contrary, most were incorporated in varying degrees into what Louis Althusser provocatively calls the "ideological state apparatus."

That is, the individuals who in the 1950s became the New York intellectuals (during the 1930s, and in some cases the 1940s, the bulk of these considered themselves to be simply anti-Stalin communists) were at first distinguished for their origins as cultural, political, and in some cases ethnic (Jewish) outsiders. Nevertheless, in the post-war era they experienced, and for the most part succumbed to, every temptation to join the system they had once determined to transform. Of course, individual patterns vary considerably, but mostly what we see in the collective history of the New York intellectuals is an astonishing range of rationales for abandoning a youthful pledge to interpret the world from the viewpoint of the exploited and oppressed—the "have-nots" instead of the "haves."

At the same time, one claim persists through most of the rationales: each insists that he or she has remained faithful to original values. With only a few exceptions, the apostate revolutionists argue that their changes in behavior and objective political positions are not the consequence of a need to justify the social system that unexpectedly came to afford them so many privileges (whatever the cost to others). Rather, such changes are said to be warranted by mutations in world politics that fortuitously coincided with the group's own growing power and influence in the cultural establishment. Therefore, the system from which they now personally benefit must be treated with delicacy, if not outright gratitude. The change on the part of the New York intellectuals from revolutionism to reconciliation is thus justified because Communism has turned out to be barbarism; capitalism has proved capable of internal reform; the working class has showed itself incapable of progressive action; Modernism can induce nihilism; etc.

Many of us would agree that the new realities of the post–World War II world necessitated a radical readjustment of all earlier left-wing critiques. But the reversion of the bulk of the New York intellectuals to a political practice that, in spite of some new labels, supported the very social structures and policies that drove them to the Left in the first place, is another matter entirely. The hypocrisy of this position was dramatized when, in the 1980s, Sidney Hook still insisted that he was being faithful to his "socialist" ideals as he endorsed Nixon and then Reagan for president!

Three rich and distinctive new scholarly books reveal both the latest advances and distressing conceptual failures among academics seeking to grapple with this complex phenomenon. Terry Cooney's *The Rise of the New York Intellectuals* is the most intensive scrutiny we have to date of a precise phase (1934–45) of the group's development. Mark Shechner's *After the Revolution* is a brilliant if highly speculative exploration of the psycho-analytical interests and links to Jewish intellectual traditions of several members of the group, who are centered in a study that also treats parallel figures such as Allen Ginsberg and Philip Roth. Eric Homberger's *American Writers and Radical Politics* enhances our understanding of the politico-cultural tradition of which the New York intellectuals are a component, through the presentation of some original research about the broader literary Left during the first four decades of this century.

What is admirable and impressive about Terry Cooney's scrutiny of eleven years in the evolution of the New York intellectuals is the clear and systematic analysis he devotes to a well-chosen group of texts. Cooney treats not just the familiar major essays from leading magazines, but columns, letters, and some unpublished material. Moreover, although he gives sensitive attention to the Jewish backgrounds of many key figures, he does not succumb to the fallacy—as does Alexander Bloom in *Prodigal Sons: The New York Intellectuals and Their World* (1986)—of reducing the whole phenomenon of the New York intellectuals to an expression of Jewish-American upward mobility. Cooney's remarks in this regard are instructive: "The argument presented here will hold that Jewishness was neither the central determinative factor for members of the *Partisan Review* circle nor something irrelevant to them. The attitude of those who were Jews toward their Jewishness can best be understood as an expression of the cosmopolitan outlook they had embraced" (6).

In stating the case for "cosmopolitanism," however, Cooney is also making a bid for a primary category through which to understand and evaluate the New York intellectuals. Here he is successful in demonstrating that the concept of "cosmopolitanism" can afford a lucid narrative framework enabling the re-examination of revealing episodes in the history of the magazine. Still, there is little in the book conceptually new in comparison to the first, and still quite sound, history of *Partisan Review*, James B. Gilbert's *Writers and Partisans* (1968).

At the outset of *The Rise of the New York Intellectuals*, Cooney briefly refers to Gilbert, characterizing the predecessor book as a "survey" and stating that "The present account will depart from [it], and other partial or unpublished studies, through its emphasis on some of the interpretative themes discussed below" (4). I can not agree, however, that Gilbert's book is a mere "survey"; I have always regarded it as providing a striking analysis, and one not fundamentally different from that proferred by Cooney twenty years later. Both depict *Partisan Review* as an internationalist center of intellectual life in the late 1930s that lost the vitality of its vision by the mid-1940s. Neither, however, is willing to embrace any version of *Partisan*'s revolutionary socialism—the source of this salutary internationalism—as a viable perspective for the Cold War years and after. And neither scholar offers even the barest outline of an alternative strategy for successful politico-cultural intervention during that difficult era.

In fact, Cooney's book is valuable largely because it generally adheres to the accurate chronology and thematic perspective of Gilbert's book. While Cooney makes no attempt to correct Gilbert's primary defect—in fact, Gilbert frankly admits that he has no answers for the 1950s, whereas Cooney sidesteps the whole matter by ending his narrative seven years earlier—he does supplement *Writers and Partisans* significantly by offering new details about interpersonal relations and some useful interpretations of literary essays that Gilbert did not treat.

Nevertheless, the book is weakened by Cooney's failure to carefully interrogate his own rather abstract category of "cosmopolitanism." This term is celebrated by Cooney as the pluralistic goal toward which the *Partisan* editors strove, only to grasp it briefly and then lose it. But this brand of "cosmopolitanism" ought to strike contemporary scholars as at least partly a code term for an elite, Eurocentric patriarchal culture. True, there is a beneficial legacy we all have received from the *Partisan* editors' counterposition of this "cosmopolitanism" to narrow U.S. provincialism, the vulgar political criteria of the "proletarian literature movement" of the early 1930s, and the banal sentimentalism of the post-1935 Popular Front. But "cosmopolitanism" of this type must also be understood as an ideological bridge back to the society that the *Partisan* editors claimed to oppose.

Beyond an intelligent examination of literary essays from the vantage point of "cosmopolitanism," Cooney fails to develop the many other elements that went into the distinctive ethos of the *Partisan* circle. For him, their politics is reductively an "anti-Stalinism" that was, first, "radical," and, later, of the Cold War variety. He is either incapable of or uninterested in developing the specifically Marxist, Leninist, Trotskyist, and even pragmatist components of their evolving politico-cultural critique, and he reduces and sometimes botches the story of some of the political episodes playing an influential background role in the history of the magazine.

Mark Shechner's *After the Revolution*, while less incisively organized, is far more original. But it is also much farther removed from rather crucial primary sources, in the use of which Cooney sets a high standard. If we had reason to be confident about many of his crucial judgments, Shechner's book might possibly be an important breakthrough—a *locus classicus* not only in the study of the New York intellectuals, but for our understanding of the "Jewish-American imagination" as a whole. The problem is determining the degree to which one can trust the accuracy of Shechner's speculations and judgments about the motivations and activities of specific writers.

Here we are not at all concerned with the "integrity" of the author, but with a method that has few controls and a narrow context. (However, there may be a problem with integrity of the publisher. The majority of this book has previously appeared in essays and book reviews in journals familiar to those sharing Shechner's interests, such as *Salmagundi*, the *Nation*, and *Partisan Review*. Yet not a single acknowledgement or permission is listed anywhere in this edition.)

At the outset, Shechner forthrightly explains that his book is not a history but "a sequence of discrete windows on a history" (vii), not a "survey" but "the arc of an emotion, a long slow ellipse of thought that brought me from unformed intuitions through a tangled history to idiosyncratic conclusions" (vii). These sentences demonstrate not only the compelling personal voice that wends its way through the study, but also the rich style of Shechner's prose—a style recalling many diverse qualities of his subjects.

Like Cooney, Shechner chooses to work with an entirely plausible, but rather abstract, general thesis. Who can disagree that, after the thirties, many Jewish-American writers turned inward, to personal schemes of regeneration that had ambiguous consequences?

More dubious is Shechner's description of the distinctive Jewish literary tradition: "What Jewish book of importance, from the Bible to *The Interpretation of Dreams*, has not been a quarrel between memory and desire, between melancholy recollection and prophetic longing . . .?" Strangely, I find that this description does not apply to many Jewish-American books of importance, such as Tess Slesinger's *The Unpossessed* and Lionel Trilling's *The Middle of the Journey*. In contrast, the description seems very apt for a good deal of important literature by non-Jewish-Americans—T. S. Eliot's *The Waste Land*, Ernest Hemingway's *The Sun Also Rises*, James T. Farrell's *A World I Never Made*, and Ralph Ellison's *Invisible Man*, to name a few.

It is certainly reasonable to argue for distinctive Jewish or Jewish-American literary traits, but these traits must be demonstrated in some sort of comparative context with controls—not merely asserted by rhetorical force. Since the publication of Stephen Steinberg's *The Ethnic Myth* (1978), all scholars dealing with ethnicity ought to be alert to the Judeocentric dangers of attributing distinctive features to the Jewish-American experience that are actually shared by others and may even have their origins elsewhere.

Shechner's magic sentences are so wonderfully provocative that it is hard to resist falling under their spell. Of Trilling he writes: "[His] brand of anglophilia, one suspects, was a back door Judaism after all, with the novel its Torah and criticism its commentary" (57). Of Kazin: "an accomplished funambulist . . . making an original synthesis out of Winesburg and Williamsburg by draping his American dreams in folds of Baltic melancholy." Of Howe: "[a] self-conscious rebel . . . taking flight from his father's world in youth only to bow to its authority—now become its charm—in middle age."

Yet on reflection it seems to me that none of these striking and memorable characterizations ring true in the context of the full texture and complexity of the lives and works of these accomplished intellectuals; in fact, each characterization is at least partly misleading. Trilling certainly has a strong anglophilic streak, but his attractions to Freud, Hegel, and Marx are equally in evidence, and his writings on poetry, mass culture, and his own fiction should not be occluded by a fixation on his explorations of the novel. Kazin may have blended Winesburg and Williamsburg for a powerful moment in *A Walker in the City*, but this mixture is diminished in the other two volumes of his autobiography and is dwarfed overall by the more significant point that his scholarship as a whole is distinguished by an identification with classic American literature. Howe, of course, wrote with nostalgia and affection of the New York Jewish-American experience in

World of Our Fathers, but he has hardly returned to the family faith; he remains an unrepentant atheist and socialist, and is likely to stay so to the end.

The problem here is too much psychologizing without evidence, and the willingness to sacrifice subtlety when there is a chance to stick in the knife. Kazin, Fiedler, and Howe, we are told early on, wrote *On Native Grounds, Love and Death in the American Novel*, and *Sherwood Anderson*, "from the desire to paste a Yankee stamp of approval on their Jewish mutinies" (6). It is even suggested that Isaac Rosenfeld's early demise was more an act of will than biological bad luck: "Rosenfeld's premature death of a heart attack was the fulfillment of the impossible logic of these crisis years, a death, one might think, of a broken heart" (11).

In short, Shechner's propositions and criteria do not seem to me to grow out of a detailed familiarity with and "feel" for his subjects, especially any empathy for the seriousness of their political commitments. This enables a rhetorical soaring unthinkable to those more grounded in "fact." The problems caused by such license are clearly seen in his detailed portrait of Rosenfeld, probably the central figure in the study and the only one to receive primary research. Among Shechner's claims are that Rosenfeld "was a fierce moralist of pleasure, eager to explore the avenues of sensation, even in the face of the guilt, the shame, the conviction of failure that attended each breakthrough." Moreover, Shechner claims that, unlike the *Commentary* crew of Nathan Glazer, Irving Kristol, and Robert Warshow, Rosenfeld "never made his peace with the American dream" (102).

Unfortunately, it is impossible to grasp precisely what Shechner means by these two assertions. What were the sensual experiments and "breakthroughs" to which Rosenfeld devoted himself? Sexual encounters with many women? With prostitutes? With men? Children? Animals? Did he use drugs? It is not at all clear whether Shechner simply lacks information or for some reason deigns to keep the crucial details secret.

Likewise, the general assertion of uncompromising integrity is not very helpful to those seeking moral guidance in an ambiguous world. After all, Rosenfeld died rather young (age 38), and it is hardly self-evident that he was not idiosyncratically and belatedly en route to the same born-again accommodationism as some of his contemporaries. Moreover, Shechner gives us no standards by which to determine whether or not one has "made peace" with the "American Dream."

Since Rosenfeld moved decisively away from the socialist-internationalist perspective of his youth, his final stance could be the familiar *angst*-ridden posturing of the self-absorbed intellectual. This is, in fact, what is suggested by Shechner's summary description: "Rosenfeld fashioned himself into the last ghetto Jew and pledged solidarity with the ranks of his own dead, who in an age of enormity, bore silent witness to the delinquencies of the living" (120).

There are enough troublesome features of Eric Homberger's *American Writers and Radical Politics* to make one wish the book might have been substantially recast and repackaged to enable its stronger parts to receive more attention than they probably will in the book's present peculiar form. First, the time frame of the book, 1900–39, is unfortunate. We are once taken to a screeching halt at that familiar year when there arrived the disillusioning news of the Hitler-Stalin Pact. It seems to me to be clear by now that the full significance of the radical achievements and foibles of the first four decades of the twentieth century can only be understood in light of the aftermath of World War II.

A second problem surrounds some pretentious claims on the book jacket and in the Preface. According to these, we are supposed to believe that, for the past twenty-five years (presumably since the publication of Daniel Aaron's *Writers on the Left*), the scholarly world has operated under the mistaken impression that all left-wing writers were ideological fanatics, drenched in the sectarianism of Marxist doctrine. Homberger has now come along to set us straight: "They were not the dupes or victims of an alien ideology: even in their socialism or communism American writers were still Americans, imbued with populist, individualist and democratic assumptions. They seldom found political involvement a simple matter. If there is one distinctive note this study brings out, it is that the writers discussed were often equivocal, and not dogmatic, about their radicalism."

It is simply inaccurate and unfair to attribute such ideas to Aaron and subsequent scholars, or, for that matter, to his predecessor, Walter Rideout in *The Radical Novel in the U.S.* (1956). Moreover, there have been any number of studies in the 1970s which emphasized precisely the themes that Homberger claims as his own; most famously, Warren Susman's essay, "The 1930s," and Richard Pells' *Radical Visions and American Dreams* (1973). The result of Homberger's constructing this myth is that the scholarly debate is retarded, returning to ideas quite familiar and by now rather conventional to those working in the field, rather than advancing to new conceptual terrain.

The third and most serious defect of the book is structural. The Preface presents a plausible explanation for the organization of the study: Homberger intends to cover three generations of radical writers, each generation of which receives two chapters and the whole of which is followed by three appendices. Unfortunately, continuity is nowhere carried out internally and there is no conclusion drawing the discrete studies together to offer some lessons or perspectives. The book reads as if it were comprised of six independent essays with only the vaguest thematic relationships to each other, and it's hard for me to understand why internal development, cross-references within the essays, and a conclusion were not requested by the publishers.

But awareness of such lapses should not obscure the book's important contributions. First, while the perspective is not so original as is boasted, it is appropriate and allows for the presentation of the human and distinct features of the writers and their work. This aspect is especially evident in the vivid portrait of Edmund Wilson's patrician radicalism. Moreover, Homberger has a greater understanding of and interest in the Marxist political ideas of his subjects than either Cooney or Shechner, and at least three of the essays are striking for the original research that is competently presented.

The first of these concentrates on the response of Greenwich Village intellectuals to the 1914 massacre of coal miners in Ludlow, Colorado. Homberger demonstrates how and why this event played a powerfully transformative role in the thinking of Max Eastman and John Reed. The impact is compared by Homberger to that of 1937 Barcelona on George Orwell's vision of socialism.

"Proletarian Literature on the John Reed Clubs," a journal version of which has something of a "classic" status among many of us working in the field, provides a background for understanding the stages by which the proletarian literature debate unfolded, bringing some of its subtleties to life in a way that refutes dismissive caricatures. Nevertheless, seeing the essay in book form makes one regret that it wasn't expanded considerably over the past ten years. The body of the essay still remains essentially quotation from secondary sources (such as *New Masses* and *International Literature*), and the descriptions of John Reed Club activities are mostly taken from reports published in journals. Except for the familiar big names—Michael Gold, Max Eastman, and Joseph Freeman—the scores of activists remain unidentified. Who they were, what they individually believed, what they accomplished, and what finally happened to them, remain a mystery that someone else will have to solve.

"Communists and Objectivists" also seems to be salvaged from an aborted project of greater scope. This essay is a crucial contribution as one of the few seriously documented examinations of 1930s left-wing poetry, and perhaps the only study of the relation of this particular group to Communism. But Homberger's conclusion, that the Party bears responsibility for the destruction of the Objectivist movement, is far too one-sided and never adequately proven.

Homberger's book culminates with the publication of a letter from Philip Rahv to Trotsky on behalf of the *Partisan Review* editors, Trotsky's answer, and an answer to the answer. All of these are from 1938 and, considering the date and the discussants, the exchange cries out for a careful analysis— especially in light of all that has been written about *Partisan Review* and Trotskyism. But here, as in several other crucial places in the book, Homberger remains inexplicably silent.

What might we expect from further research into this enticing but elusive topic? First, although these three books will be quite useful to scholars and play a role in the formulation of future agendas and perspectives, I am doubtful that any of the authors will pursue their subjects in any substantial way. The conceptual weaknesses that I have noted in each book are indicative to me of a kind of exhaustion—a failure to sustain a vision of the subject beyond the narrow perimeters of each particular work. Shechner and Homberger, in fact, seem already to have abandoned larger projects in order to concentrate on binding together under a general rubric several earlier, fragmented studies. Cooney is more systematic and persistent but I doubt that his one unifying idea—cosmopolitanism—will sustain him much beyond the stage he has already achieved.

A more telling point is that none of the authors engage contemporary cultural theory. In this sense, the scholarly methodology of all three books is a throwback to the late 1960s and early 1970s. Considering their subjects, it is surprising that the authors never discuss ideology, hegemony, the social functions of intellectuals, or even "culture" in contemporary ways. Even more startling for books appearing at the end of the 1980s, the authors operate exclusively in a white, male, Eurocentric world. To Cooney, the New York Intellectual tradition is a masculine domain, outside of a few passing references to Mary McCarthy. To Shechner, the "Jewish-American imagination" is exclusively male. To Homberger, the radical tradition is not only male but lily white.

One might safely predict that the next few years will witness a new phase of scholarship about the intellectual Left in general and the New York intellectuals in particular. This will be partly due to the enduring and unresolved nature of the concerns with which these types of writers were preoccupied. But I also hold that this next stage will be initiated by scholars more responsive to contemporary cultural theory as well as to issues of class, gender, and race.

Moreover, one other element may need to be present if the new efforts are to surpass the old in order to confront in a sustained and relevant manner the problematic of commitment in all its complexity. Writings of such meticulous intensity are likely to be the products of young women and men who are not only committed—as are Cooney, Shechner, and Homberger—to a frank and unvarnished understanding of the political illusions of the Left in the pre– and post–World War II war eras. Such scholarship can only be animated by a vision seeking to connect lessons of these past experiences to our present politico-cultural situation if it is produced by scholars less conventionally skeptical than these three about the necessity of socialist commitment itself.

4

From Margin to Center: C. L. R. James

Paul Buhle. *C. L. R. James: The Artist as Revolutionary* (London: Verso, 1988). 197 pp. $13.95.

The exponential growth in renown of the Black Revolutionary writer and activist C. L. R. James (1901–1989) may be among the few biographical parallels to Leon Trotsky's famous social law, the "Theory of Permanent Revolution." Trotsky's argument was that, given effective leadership, insurgent movements in semi-feudal societies might strategically combine features of bourgeois and socialist revolutions to politically outstrip the more "advanced" industrialized nations.

Cyril Lionel Robert James (known by his initials "C. L. R.," the Trotskyist pseudonym "J. R. Johnson," "Jimmy," or else the nickname "Nello," which is short for Lionel) emerged from the margins of world industrial development, the African diaspora of the West Indies. He also emerged from the margins of the radical political movement, Leon Trotsky's International Left Opposition.

For more than thirty years, James waged unceasing ideological guerrilla warfare from obscure Marxist groupuscles, or sometimes by himself, on behalf of a remarkably contemporary brand of politico-cultural ideas based on the interests of the subaltern classes. Although he had been known almost exclusively among dissident communists and Pan-Africanists, James in his last decade burst through the dominant culture of Great Britain and the United States to become a recognized figure of international significance not only in the colonies but in the heartlands of imperialism.

The *New York Times* virtually ignored James throughout most of his life, but on his death it published a major, friendly obituary, complete with photograph, respectfully declaring him a "leader of the pan-African movement" and a "prodigious and eclectic intellectual."

While posthumous assessments by leftists are still wending their way into print, there is little doubt that, in the end, his stature will surpass that of most Marxist theorists of his generation. Among New World Africans, for example, James alone is comparable to W. E. B. Du Bois in breadth of accomplishment and general influence.

With the devotion only imaginable of a loyal but independent-minded disciple, Paul Buhle, founding editor of *Radical America* and himself a *sui generis* figure in the U.S. New Left, has written a book that carries out the almost-impossible task of reconstructing the contours of a career defying any conventional notion of shape or form.

First and foremost, in Buhle's portrait, James was an artist who wrote with painful lyricism of the marginalized position of the Black middle-class intelligentsia; this led him, in the opinion of the Guyanese novelist Wilson Harris, to the "exploration of the building blocks of his age seen through various windows and from different perspectives" (quoted in Buhle, p. 3).

Second, James was a cultural critic who, on the one hand, mastered and appropriated the "high culture" of Shakespeare and Melville for his own emancipatory ends; but he also treated the popular culture of sports and film as serious moments of human expression and struggle.

Third, James was a pioneer of a revolutionary nationalist politics who in his historical and theoretical works depicted the emancipation of people of color as the work of the emancipators themselves; yet he also regarded the nationalist stage as one transitional to a truly human internationalist culture.

Finally, James was a prophet of post-Leninist revolutionary movements of non-party workers' councils and a brand of spontaneism that will be central to the coming transformations of capitalist as well as bureaucratized post-capitalist (in Jamesian terminology, "state capitalist") societies.

Buhle's book is replete with examples of the "renaissance" nature of the Jamesian *oeuvre*. In a sometimes awkward sequence of chapters that creatively attempts to combine chronology with a particular theme, Buhle traces James' peregrination from a Trinidadian birth, college education,* and early career as a school teacher and fiction writer (1901–1931), to his sojourn as a cricket columnist, Marxist historian of slave rebellions, and publicist on behalf of Trotskyism (1932–1938).

Among the many fresh and still striking achievements of these years are *The Life of Captain Cipriana: An Account of British Government in the West Indies* (1932), *Toussaint L'Ouverture* (1936, a play performed in London that starred Paul Robeson), *Minty Ally* (1936, still an impressive novel of cultural alienation), *World Revolution: The Rise and Fall of the Communist International* (1937), and *The Black Jacobins: Toussaint L'Ouverture and the San*

---

* At the time I wrote this I was unaware that the Queen's Royal College James attended in Port of Spain was, in fact, not a college but an elite secondary school.

Domingo Revolution (1938), not to mention his editorship of both the International African Service Bureau's *International African Opinion* and the British Trotskyist newspaper *Fight*.

From his arrival in the United States in 1938 until his deportation to England in 1953 during the McCarthyite witch-hunt, James was a charismatic and influential figure in a variety of Trotskyist organizations. Unfortunately, each of these groups suffered from progressively debilitating splits which reduced their efficacy. In this process James's small faction (called the "Johnson-Forrest Tendency" after James's pseudonym and that of his closest and most erudite collaborator, Raya Dunayevskaya) usually played a destabilizing role.

The "Johnsonites" first passed through the Socialist Workers Party (SWP), from which James split in the spring of 1940 along with the followers of Max Shachtman. The immediate issues in dispute were Soviet policies in the wake of the Hitler-Stalin Pact, but the underlying concern was whether the USSR still retained progressive features. Shachtman and James, while holding different theories of the Soviet economy, sought to promote a "Third camp" independent of the capitalist nations and the USSR through a new organization called the Workers Party. Trotsky's followers, remaining in the SWP, held that the USSR still retained social conquests worth supporting in spite of Stalin's political terror.

The Johnsonites left the Workers Party after six years, charging that it was insufficiently proletarian, to rejoin the SWP in 1947, only to split from the SWP a second time in 1950 for reasons that still remain in dispute. In the early 1950s, James's seventy U.S. disciples began publishing *Correspondence*, but, two years after the leader's deportation to England, Dunayevskaya broke off to publish *News and Letters*. In 1961 James Boggs and Grace Lee also struck out on their own, eventually to establish the National Organization for an American Revolution. This left Martin Glaberman, who published *Facing Reality* into the 1970s, as James's primary U.S. disciple.

In these years, James wandered through England, where he resumed his post as cricket journalist for the *Manchester Guardian*; Trinidad, where he edited *The Nation*, organ of Eric Williams' People's National Movement (although James ruptured relations with Williams in 1960 and launched his own unsuccessful Workers and Farmers Party in 1965); and East and West Africa. He returned to the United States in 1968, teaching until 1980 at the University of the District of Columbia and other institutions. After a brief return to Trinidad, he spent the last eight years of his life in London where he witnessed the publication of three volumes of his *Selected Writings* (1977–1984) and a valuable *festschrift* edited by Buhle, *C. L. R. James: His Life and Work* (1986).

While I am persuaded for the most part by Buhle's points of emphasis, and much admire his commentary on James's extraordinarily diverse cultural criticism, I draw back from parts of his method. In my view, Buhle mistakenly assesses and valorizes James in opposition to much of the broader left movement from which he emerged and of which he remained part, even if in an adversarial stance on many issues. In contrast, I find that the contribution and legacy of James is only really fertile in the context of an integrated view of a left movement comprised of many countervailing tendencies and perspectives—each in possession of an element of truth, none the sole bearer of any overall "key" to the strategy of social emancipation.

As a theorist James produced many provocative but mostly partial insights. His numerous essays and lectures on world politics, sports, philosophy, literature, and socialist historiography are markedly uneven. Historical schemas and correlations seem in some places mechanical and thin; his philosophical disquisitions are (to me, at least) often tedious and incomprehensible; and his literary judgments can be off-the-cuff and superficial.

Then there are bizarre elements in James' outlook that appear, for example, in what might be regarded as the "suppressed" chapter of James's book on Melville, *Mariners, Renegades and Castaways* (1953). When the work was reprinted in 1978, the original plates were used or copied, but the highly personal last chapter, "A Natural But Necessary Conclusion," fifty-four pages long, was silently replaced by a two-page "Afterword."*

The most serious deficiency in Buhle's work is that James's major theoretical efforts, his theory of state capitalism and his eccentric interpretation of dialectics, are not seriously summarized and critiqued. These writings will require a more sustained exegesis and interpretation before their full value can be assessed.

Moreover, Buhle, who has made a singular contribution to left historiography through his campaign to view its ethnic and popular culture aspects, turns out to be a supercilious commentator on political organizations with which James came to disagree. In a familiar pattern, those closest to James come in for the hardest knocks.

The Trotskyists are described as "united only in their hatred of Stalinism and in their utter faith in the concept of a vanguard" (p. 68). Buhle claims that, compared to the Dunayevskaya-James "state capitalist" analysis, "all other Trotskyist critiques amounted to a waiting game, waiting for Stalin and his bureaucracy to fall out or be thrust out by some loyal descendant of the old Bolshevik Party" (p. 74). The Black Panther Party is reduced to a

---

* This is not quite accurate; a publisher's note on the copyright page states that "The last chapter of the first edition, which dealt with the author's deportation, is not included in this edition." Martin Glaberman, who was responsible for the new edition, has since informed me that James agreed to the deletion, which saved a fair amount of money on printing and made the publication possible.

"lumpen" organization with "pick up the gun" politics, while the League of Revolutionary Black Workers is praised mainly because of some Jamesian influence (p. 155).

Also, some of the insights that Buhle attributes to James are hardly unique. For example, Buhle cites the following statement made by James for a 1980 symposium as a fresh contribution: "[The] workers and peasants must realize that their emancipation lies in their own hands and in the hands of nobody else" (p. 170). This is not only the foundation of Trotsky's "permanent revolution"—that the workers and peasants must never subordinate their interests to the national bourgeoisie—but also the battle cry of Sandino ("Only the workers and peasants can go all the way") and appears in Marx as well.

Buhle also says of James that "amid the Hungarian revolution [of 1956], he would find his vindication in the substitution of the mass for the party of any kind" (p. 96). However, the revolt of the Hungarian workers and students might well have gone further with an organized instrument of leadership. Does Buhle think that the Nicaraguan revolution could have seized power against Somoza more effectively, or defended itself against the U.S.-backed Contra War more successfully, without the Sandinista National Liberation Front (FSLN)?

One-party states, substitutionism, vanguardism, and bureaucratic-centralist parties obviously cripple the expression and creativity of a diverse and variegated working class. But so far all the evidence suggests that serious political organizations will still be required to transform productive relations and reorganize economies, especially in a world of advanced technology, unevenly distributed resources, and national antagonisms.

Although Buhle also cites Poland in the 1980s to vindicate James's anti-party politics, the Solidarity opposition was forced by the logic of events to increasingly move from a union basis to a political organization. The problem in Poland now is not to abolish extant political organization, which I believe would result in the same process all over again, but to create a new party with democratic controls and a political strategy that will genuinely bring about the rule of the producers themselves.

In my view, it was precisely as a political strategist that James was at his weakest, sometimes inspiring splinter groups that operated as cults. Yet, clearly, there was also an element in Jamesian theory that was sufficiently profound to rebound among larger circles of left activists and that will live on as a constructive and ineradicable component of the revolutionary left tradition.

Some of this influence can be seen in Buhle's own work in creating *Radical America,* and *Cultural Correspondence.* It is also evident in many contributions to his 1986 *festschrift,* and in the work of leading Black radicals in Cedric J. Robinson's *Black Marxism* (1983) and Manning Marable's *African and Caribbean Politics* (1978). To my knowledge, there is no one who used the Marxist sensibility and imagination more variously and creatively than James, which is among the reasons that Buhle's subtitle, *The Artist as Revolutionary*, is most appropriate.

5

Trotskyism in the Sixties: Afterword to Michael Smith's *Notebook of a Sixties Lawyer*

Michael Smith's memoir and selection of his writings from the late 1960s through the late 1980s provide a rare but significant perspective on the major political upheavals and radical movements of that time. Millions of U.S. citizens were galvanized into militant action in ways that changed the political and cultural landscape of the nation. We still live with the consequences of that transformation, and historians are only just beginning to debate the meaning of those events.

What is immediately striking about the material Smith has assembled is that it defies many of the stereotyped conceptions of that radicalization. His writings raise the question of how that history is to be "officially" recorded and who will be the recorder. We are often told, for example, that the 1960s was a "youth" or "student" rebellion of an anarcho-hedonistic character, and that it was only in its later, degenerating phase that participants abandoned their "innocent" New Leftism for the hoary "ideologies" of Marx and Lenin. Smith, however, became radicalized during the 1960s just as he was inaugurating his legal career, and he had already encountered left-wing political ideas albeit at arm's length.

Moreover, the conventional perception of leftists in the legal profession is that they have tended to be either sympathetic to the Communist Party or susceptible to desperate acts of ultraleftism. Smith, however, was drawn to the Socialist Workers Party (SWP) and the variety of Trotskyism that it represented. To me, the SWP's general significance as a political option in the 1960s is that it unambiguously opposed both the politics of Stalinist Communism and the destructive ultraleftism that plagued movements of the 1960s. In Smith's recollection, he was most attracted by the leadership role the SWP was playing in the anti-war movement, its promotion of revolutionary Black nationalism, and its defense of the Cuban revolution. Philosophically, he says that he was impressed by the SWP's roots in IWW and Debsian radicalism, personified by James P. Cannon, who had been an organizer for the Industrial Workers of the World (IWW), a founder of the U.S. Communist movement, and an early Trotskyist. In any event, Smith subsequently abandoned the legal profession for several years in order to aid in the functioning and expansion of Pathfinder Press, the major publisher of the writings of Leon Trotsky and of other books promoted by the SWP.

Although Smith came from a non-conformist Jewish family, he was not, as were so many other recruits to the early New Left, a "Red Diaper Baby" (viz., from a Communist Party milieu). Moreover, despite his strong attachment to jazz and his identification with the struggles of African Americans, his memoir and writing show little attraction to the "cultural revolution" ("sex, drugs, and rock 'n roll") which occupies center stage in conventional depictions of the 1960s.

The point here is not to question the "representativeness" of Smith's book; rather, it is to emphasize that mass-marketed perceptions-from-a-distance rarely catch more than some of the surface features of a complex social movement. Moreover, these surface impressions can often be entirely misleading when it comes to probing the particulars of an individual's political experience. One suspects that, when the history of the 1960s radicalization becomes more fully analyzed, a process that will only come about through the probing of a large number of individual experiences of a cross-section of activists, the nature of the phenomenon might seem very different than the popular images depicted today. In fact, what are currently regarded as the conventional—one might even say, "canonical"—features of the 1960s radicalization and its activists, may prove to be atypical and peripheral. More than a few such perceptions may well be the result of who had access to the press and media at that time and later, or what the media chose to present, rather than experiences of large numbers or even "typical" participants.

In my view, the particular aspect of Smith's book that will most likely make it noteworthy for those studying the 1960s is the new information and insight that it offers on Trotskyism in the United States at that time, or, at least, the SWP and its youth organization, the Young Socialist Alliance (YSA). Smith's memoirs begin with his childhood and adolescence in the 1940s and 1950s, and offer a background for his political and cultural writings of the late 1980s. But the core experience reflected in his book is connected with the fifteen years Smith spent as a militant in the SWP. These were years of great intensity and cohesion in terms of political education and activity. In fact, except for his organizational affiliation, which was severed for reasons beyond Smith's control, the political perspective he holds today, and which he brings to bear in his memoirs and his post-SWP political writings, is still largely informed by that experience.

What, then, was the meaning of Trotskyism in the 1960s? Was its growth and the influence it exerted far beyond its numbers in certain sectors of the radical movement merely a fluke? Was it the result of brilliant strategizing? Was this influence beneficial or harmful to the growth of a viable left alternative in the United States? What can Trotskyism's rank-and-file activists of that era, such as Michael Smith, contribute to the next generation of rebels?

Such questions, of course, are far too large to be answered by Smith's book alone, or by the relatively small amount of material that has appeared on the subject to date.[1] But at least we can contribute to the discussion with a series of observations and hypotheses stimulated by Smith's collection.

First, there is the matter of the organizational and political character of the SWP during the 1960s. Smith was first attracted to the SWP because of its practice and political orientation in opposition to the U.S. war in Vietnam, which was carried out by individuals he came to know and like. The SWP had existed in various forms since its founders were expelled from the Communist Party in 1928. Among the more noteworthy achievements in the SWP's history were the leadership its cadres provided in the 1934 Minneapolis Teamster strikes; its campaign against the 1936–38 Moscow Trials frame-ups; and its opposition to the imperialist war aims of the U.S. government in World War II, for which many of the Party's leaders were imprisoned under the Smith Act.

The SWP and its organizational predecessors left a distinct mark on U.S. cultural life as well. A generation of New York–based aspiring writers and intellectuals were propelled leftward by the national and international crises of the Depression, and began to look to radical political parties for ideas and inspiration. While the Communist Party was the most successful in creating publications, institutions, and organizations for Marxist cultural activity, the Trotskyist movement nevertheless drew to its ranks and periphery a surprising number of literary people who were establishing national reputations or who would become influential in later decades. The most significant in the 1930s were Max Eastman, Sidney Hook, James Burnham, and James T. Farrell. Among those who would later rise to fame, often after abandoning their left-wing politics, were *Partisan Review* editors Philip Rahv, William Phillips, and Dwight Macdonald; the novelists Mary McCarthy, Eleanor Clark, Bernard Wolfe, Saul Bellow, Isaac Rosenfeld, and Harvey Swados; the critics Lionel Trilling, Irving Howe, and Leslie Fiedler; the political journalists Elliot Cohen, Melvin J. Lasky, and Irving Kristol; and many others.

Trotskyism survived into the 1960s, after its high point in the Depression and some brief immediate post-war growth, partly because it was based on an important "truth." That truth was its view of the contradictory results of the Russian Revolution, an event that constituted a kind of "test" for all those calling themselves socialists. The SWP's stance was that the mass upheaval of October 1917 was a model that exemplified revolutionary-democratic action. On the other hand, the course of the Revolution also demonstrated how such an experience could degenerate almost into its opposite. In practice, the SWP's perspective meant championing all the ideals of Bolshevism, including what Marcel Liebman later called the "libertarianism" of Lenin's *State and Revolution*,[2] while repudiating the horrors that emerged full-blown under Stalin as the revolution deteriorated.

The SWP's explanation of the contradictory results of the Russian Revolution was attractive to many newly radicalizing young people in the 1960s who were beginning to expand their political horizons beyond such issues as civil rights or the war in Vietnam. Not only were we trying to come to grips with the complex social transformations under way in Vietnam and Cuba, but we also sought to understand the USSR, China, Yugoslavia, and other post-capitalist societies. Of course, there were many other New Leftists who embraced Mao's China, North Vietnam, Cuba, and even Albania, a phenomenon that needs to be explained if the history of the era is to be complete.

Nevertheless, I, for one, felt that there was simply no credible alternative to Trotskyist conceptions such as the one that argued that, no matter how strongly one supported putative social gains in Third World or any other revolutions, the defense of such achievements could *not* be used to justify abuses of democratic and human rights. The political method of Trotskyism, starting from the perspective of the needs of workers and exploited sectors of the population (and not on support of any particular governments or ruling groups, no matter what their official rhetoric proclaimed), seemed to me a sufficient basis for meaningful political praxis in spite of the small number of the conscious adherents of such a perspective.

Of course, there were many others on the Left who saw and characterized Trotskyism in quite different terms. In particular, both the Communists and Maoists devoted many pages in *Political Affairs* and the *Guardian* to denouncing all forms of Trotskyism as racist, as counter-revolution in disguise, and as middle-class adventurism. At its mildest, this posture led to dehumanizing Trotskyists as "Trots" and making jokes about "icepicks" (a slightly inaccurate reference to the mountaineer's ice axe with which Trotsky was assassinated by a Stalinist agent in 1940); at worst there were violent physical attacks against Trotskyists. On the other hand, social democrats and liberals maintained that Trotskyism was Stalinism out of power; that it was objectively apologetic for Third World revolutionary authoritarianism, and even "anti-Semitic" for its anti-Zionism and its solidarity with the Palestinian cause. While Trotskyism had its flaws and problematic aspects, these kinds of simplifications from both the left and right unfortunately caused great damage to political culture in the United States in the sixties and seventies.

Even more confusing for many was the existence of a variety of other political groups that not only claimed to be Trotskyist, but also insisted that *they* were the true heirs of the SWP tradition. While Smith makes no references to these groups (the number of which ranged from a minimum of three or four at any given moment to as many as twenty when larger groups fragmented), I was acutely aware of their presence and the problem they created for the construction of a genuine left alternative in the United States.

The crimes of "betrayal" of which they accused the SWP consisted usually of various "impurities," such as Popular Frontism, and were never convincingly made. Rather, what distressed me was that, while organized under the same general rubric of "Trotskyism," these groups promulgated an arrogance, sectarianism, ultraleftism, and vulgarity that I saw as the very opposite of those qualities necessary to construct a socialist movement and society. While I knew that many members and supporters of the SWP were able to dismiss these groups with entirely justifiable terms such as "cults" and "sects," I myself could not help but wonder if there were, in fact, connecting links between the SWP's version of Trotskyism and these other versions that my own partisanship rendered me unable to see.

Nevertheless, I am convinced that, whatever potential the SWP had for its own progressive evolution into such a sectarian cult, the organization as it existed in the 1960s was moving in a very different direction; it bore the possibilities of a potentially new kind of development. For one thing, the SWP was an organization that contained many cadres with substantial trade union experience, and leaders who had witnessed the folly of sectarian posturing in earlier decades. All but a handful of these had to be ousted when the SWP completed the process of political transmogrification formalized decades later by its political dissociation from the Fourth International.[3]

In the course of the 1960s, the SWP's vitality was revealed through a surprising initial responsiveness to feminism, gay rights, and even some aspects of the counter-culture. Moreover, the SWP had undertaken a complex evaluation of the Cuban Revolution. At that time it rejected the notion that only an organization modeled after the Bolshevik Party, and by extension itself, could lead a social transformation. But the SWP also reaffirmed its view that the social gains of a revolutionary overturn might be defended even as its absence of political democracy is criticized. This made it possible for people such as myself to accept SWP-type Trotskyism as a political movement with something very valuable to contribute to the left, while rejecting the notion that such a tiny and undeveloped organization was destined to be the political or organizational epicenter of the U.S. or international socialist movement.

In many ways, I see Michael Smith's perceptions of the Trotskyist movement as less "problematic" than my own. In part, this may be due to many specifics of his activist trajectory. He first joined the YSA out of experiences with the YSA's dynamic Madison local. He then moved to Detroit where he was able to develop a remarkably satisfying relationship between his SWP membership and his left-wing law firm that specialized in draft law and defending anti-war GI's. In the Detroit branch he found a political atmosphere that had been largely shaped by George Breitman, certainly one of the most extraordinary individuals I have ever known. After that, Smith moved to New York City, which was the national center of the SWP. There he came to know many of the younger Party leaders first-hand and developed close personal relations with Breitman, who had moved to New York from Detroit years earlier, and with two other long-term SWP intellectuals, George Weissman and George Novack.

In contrast, I became radicalized at an experimental college, Antioch, and was perhaps more immersed in New Left culture, not to mention my own life-long attraction to poetry and fiction. From there I entered graduate school at Berkeley, where several of the local Trotskyist leaders immediately struck me as narrow and bureaucratic. While I, too, eventually developed rather warm relations with the men Smith calls "The Three Georges," the associations were conducted mostly by short visits and correspondence, and occurred mainly during the 1970s when I became decisively alienated from the new generation of SWP and YSA leaders who looked to a Carleton College graduate, Jack Barnes, as their leader.

The result was that I made most of my political contributions through cultural work. I drew sustenance from Trotskyist theory that appeared in articles in *New Left Review*, and in the writings of Ernest Mandel and Michael Löwy. Meanwhile, I also conducted independent research on the cultural left in the United States and studied cultural theoreticians unconnected with the Trotskyist movement (Marxists such as Georg Lukács and Raymond Williams, African revolutionaries such as Frantz Fanon and Amilcar Cabral, and socialist-feminists from the United States and Western Europe).

Thus I am not surprised that Smith seems more sanguine than myself as he surveys SWP policy and practice of the late 1960s and the 1970s. I think we both agree that the SWP's orientation toward the anti-war movement remains a model, recuperable in many aspects, for building a mass opposition to future imperialist slaughters. Then, as now, the strategy of uniting as many forces as possible to force the government to bring U.S. troops back alive seemed to be the soundest way to reach out to the general population. Short of restructuring the economy in a way that was not possible in light of the general level of U.S. political consciousness, this strategy set an empowering precedent (later called "The Vietnam Syndrome") and allowed increased space for struggles for self-determination in the Third World such as those in Nicaragua and El Salvador. Within that context, the crucial work in the G.I. anti-war movement, for which Smith provides valuable documentation, also remains a model to be emulated and advanced.

At the same time, I can't help but wonder whether the relentlessness with which we fought for the single-issue "Out Now" line, despite having an impact that I assess as overwhelmingly positive, didn't have a negative side as well. Smith might disagree, but it seems to me that the kind of "discipline" with which SWP cadres organized and mobilized, with such palpable results, became perhaps the most crucial factor in the rising credibility of the small circle of SWP leaders round Jack Barnes who relied upon a similar kind of self-imposed "discipline" to eventually crush oppositions in the organization.

In this process, in which unity around a general line is only possible by putting aside "secondary" considerations, one comes to feel a contradiction between indulging in individualistic responses and the power to act effectively. Hesitation, listening with a genuinely open mind, and rethinking old positions, become dispensable habits when the clock is ticking, Vietnamese people and U.S. G.I.'s are dying, and rival radical groups are mobilizing for alternative orientations that might set back the struggle for peace. What happens if this mode of behavior is then generalized onto the life of the organization as a whole, rather than episodically countered in some fashion? The history of many left parties from the early Bolsheviks to the Sandinistas shows that, contrary to the SWP, there were times when discipline was balanced against free-wheeling public debates and the infusion of a wide range of perspectives. A sealed-off cadre organization such as the SWP can develop its own internal "dominant culture" to which its members must gradually adapt, if they want to remain members in good standing. This may well occur through an informal process that members may not even be able to recognize for what it is.

This experience of witnessing a political organization progressively transformed by its internal cultural life of "norms" of behavior and interaction is one of the reasons why I, personally, have come to be skeptical about the traditional "Leninist" fixation on evaluation of formal programmatic "positions" in judging the nature of a political organization and therefore of the political effects of an organization's adherents. Those of us on the Left have long recognized that ideologists on behalf of the rich and powerful usually present themselves to be public as the greatest champions of "democracy," "freedom" and "peace." Unfortunately, a wide range of diverse politics can also be mobilized under the broad rubric of "class struggle," "anti-racism," and Trotsky's "Transitional Program for Socialist Revolution."

While the development of theory that can explain world events and guide political action still remains the objective of socialist activists, we must learn more about the ways in which the "subjective factor"—the qualities of talented and often charismatic individuals who lead left-wing organizations—shape the perceptions and interpretations of what appear on the surface to be admirable policies as they are appropriated and carried out by various political groups. Somehow the SWP, although basing itself organizationally as well as politically on a harsh critique of undemocratic features of the Communist Party, and also on critiques of rival organizations frequently characterized as "cults" and ridiculed for their political flip-flops, turned out to be not so very different from them in the end. Yet a substantial number of the SWP's members succumbed to modes of interpretation that allowed a pragmatic rationalization of flip-flops into "steps forward," and of bureaucratic purges into some sort of "defense of the Party" against "disloyal" bad guys.

It is important to recognize that, while forging an organizational culture that would eventually facilitate the SWP's despicable purges of two of the "Three Georges," Smith, and many others, the SWP was able to boast a "formal" constitution and a decision-making process that may have been the most democratic on paper of any group on the U.S. political spectrum! After all, during the period allowed for preconvention discussion (minimally once every two years), all points of view were printed in an attractive and readable format, and many hours of debate were organized in branches across the country. In addition, all sorts of other written and oral discussions were organized.

Moreover, there was the SWP's extraordinary series of educational activities—from internal branch classes on *Das Kapital* to socialist summer schools, weekly forums, presentations on specific topics before branch meetings, and national conferences. In the late 1960s I found myself in the enviable position of having ready access not only to a classical Marxist education (very often prepared by worker-intellectuals, the quality of whose lectures and discussions was enhanced by the absence of academic pretense and by their close association to praxis), but also to serious study groups in African-American and Chicano history, and to the ideas of the burgeoning women's liberation movement.

While it is true that a kind of official SWP orthodoxy prevailed over matters such as economic theory and philosophy (members who challenged the labor theory of value or the dialectics of nature would quickly be taken to task by authoritative party figures), the Trotskyist movement had a general "hands-off" policy on cultural matters. Both Mike and I took full advantage of this, finding the SWP's *International Socialist Review* (*ISR*) a satisfying place to try to make contributions to socialist theory and history. Smith's decision to reprint his own writings on jazz and the history of law from the pages of the *ISR* may help recapture an aspect of Party life that has been generally neglected.

Still, the overall issue remains of how one might assess the political value of these and many other aspects of Trotskyism in the 1960s, of which a brief introduction and preliminary assessment can hardly do justice. My own inclination would be to divide the areas of inquiry into several levels of analysis. One would obviously be an institutional history of the Trotskyist movement. This means a study of its ideas, organizational structure, and practice, not only from the top-down perspective of its leading theoreticians and major documents, but also from the perspective of rank-and-file activists and local experiences. It is here that Smith's book could play a most significant role.

The second level would be a comparative study. What were the most distinguishing features of the Trotskyist movement, in the radicalization that began in the 1960s as well as earlier, in comparison to other left-wing organizations? In this area, the problem will center around gaining a synthetic analysis, somewhat "above" the factional claims and the counterclaims of various political tendencies, although without any illusion of having total "objectivity" or of achieving a "value free" perspective.

A third level will involve an examination of the establishment of criteria for political efficacy. What, exactly, are the means by which one determines positive and negative contributions to the development of a socialist left? At this level, of course, one enters into momentous debates about overall trends in U.S. and world history—ones that may never be fully resolved prior to historical experience itself.

Seen from the latter two larger perspectives, the contributions of Smith may seem relatively small. Readers cannot approach his or any other retrospective on the 1960s radicalization with the expectation of easily learning the answers to such large questions. At best, such writings must be treated as source materials for activists who are trying to discern what connections might exist between earlier radical activities and the needs of the present moment.

I also think that it is particularly noteworthy that Smith's memoir shows that his is the story not merely of a person radicalized by an organization, but of a person radicalized by the injustices of a society. His subsequent decision to join a socialist organization was seen as a means of acting upon and enriching existing values and commitments. This is yet another indication that the phenomenon of "Trotskyism in the Sixties," among other things, was a historical product of diverse individuals working out the problematics of their historical conditions. Whether one chooses today to idealize or vilify Trotskyism, there is no possibility of simply reproducing the SWP's most attractive features nor of fully avoiding the reccurrence of its most repulsive. The moment of Trotskyism's greatest influence in the 1960s has now entered history as part of the larger legacy of the Left out of which new generations of socialist activists, along with surviving veterans of the past, will have to create new instruments for social transformation under continually changing conditions.

Notes

1. Other than materials published to promote the perspectives of various political groups, assessments of Trotskyism in the 1960s remain sparse. The views of a veteran of Trotskyism of an earlier generation who saw the 1960s from the SWP's perspective can be found in Ben Stone's *Memoirs of a Radical Rank and Filer* (New York: Prometheus Press, 1986), and a scholarly study that treats U.S. and French Trotskyism comparatively with Maoism is A. Belden Field's *Trotskyism and Maoism: Theory and Practice in France and the United States* (New York: Praeger, 1988).
2. See Liebman's *Leninism Under Lenin* (London: Marlin, 1975).
3. While the break wasn't announced until the middle of 1990, the process was initiated in the early 1980s. Of course, the SWP for legal reasons had not held membership in the Fourth International, but it had politically defined itself for many decades as the most orthodox Trotskyist and "proletarian" current of that world political organization.

PART II
Communism and Culture

6

Remembering the Answers

As a Marxist historian and teacher of left-wing political culture, I followed the radical press's coverage of the 9–12 October 1981 American Writers Congress in New York City with considerable interest. I was searching for signs that the left was overcoming its perennial difficulty in explaining the connections between politics and culture. What I found instead was a strong and understandable desire to forge links with past traditions of politico-cultural commitment, but this good will toward radical ancestors was mixed with an all-too-familiar reluctance to acknowledge the ambiguities present in those very traditions.

My concern is not with the Congress itself but with the linking of the Congress through its name and historical reference to an earlier organization, the League of American Writers, initiated by the Communist Party. The League was founded in 1935 and collapsed in 1941—collapsed, not because of any pressure from the right but in disgrace because of the mass defection of both radical and liberal writers who felt that it had too often subordinated culture to political expediency. While cultural historians of the right seem capable of responding to this legacy only by Red-baiting, much of the left seems to exhibit the equally superficial responses of evasion, amnesia and the creation of sentimental myths.

For example, Margot Cohen and Dave Lindorf [see "Writers' Unions: Solidarity—Ever?," *The Nation*, 3 October 1981] made reference to the manipulative presence of the Communist Party at earlier Congresses but failed to explain the precise political purpose of this manipulation (was it simply a power play by the party or were more serious issues at stake?) or even to mention that these Congresses created and enforced a certain type of cultural style on the left. On the other hand, *The Guardian* ("Writers Congress Calls for Cultural Unity," 21 October 1981) simply quoted Meridel Le Sueur's idealized recollection that the Congresses of the 1930s "struggled against war, against fascism, and for civil liberties."

I was particularly frustrated by Josh Kornbluth's report in *In These Times* ("Scenes from a Congress," 21–27 October 1981), which offered the following reminiscence of one-time American Newspaper Guild organizer Paul Romaine: "Romaine chaired the plenary session of the Second Writers Congress in '37, at which a small group of writers led by James T. Farrell made a motion to raise the proletarian banner by singing the 'Internationale.' Romaine, himself a Communist but dedicated to a 'united front,' was thrilled when like-minded participants rejected the notion on the grounds that it would alienate non-leftists. 'That showed the consciousness of the writers present—how united they were against war and fascism. It was a very good sign.'" Thus the myth that the American Writers Congresses of the past wedded politics to culture in a salutary unity—a unity that we might well emulate today—is perpetuated by a newspaper that, ironically, hopes to initiate a new socialist movement in this country that won't repeat the mistakes of its predecessors.

Kornbluth and Romaine's "history lesson" demonstrates on a small scale the familiar deficiency of intellectual curiosity I have noted in discussions about the politics of culture on the left. Romaine's anecdote was told to suggest that radical critics of this remarkable instance of anti-fascist unity in the 1930s must have been like Farrell, perverse left sectarians. But anyone who reads histories of the Congresses will discover that Farrell's proposal to sing the "Internationale" was made not at the 1937 Congress but at the 1935 Congress—which was held just before the Popular Front was announced— and that it was not rejected by the delegates but approved. Farrell, a pro-Communist sponsor and speaker at the first Congress in 1935, was motivated by cultural as well as political concerns. Much admired by the younger people at the gathering, Farrell was angered by the Congress's decision to exclude from membership the unknown and working-class writers (many of whom were from ethnic minorities) who had been organized into the John Reed Clubs to pioneer a new radical culture. This decision stemmed from the party's desire to make the League into a showcase for the big-name writers whose cultural achievements many non-Communist radicals regarded as debauched by commercialism.*

As for the 1937 Popular Front Congress, Farrell was simply not present, and this time the explanation is primarily political: while the Congress allowed dissent within certain perimeters, neither Farrell nor any other radical American writer who had dared to criticize the Moscow Purge Trials was invited. As the *Socialist Call* (5 June 1937) pointed out, "The primary test by which writers were chosen to take part in this Writers Congress was not their moral and intellectual and literary standing, but

---

* "Richard Wright wrote bitterly about this policy switch in *American Hunger* (1977) and elsewhere. Kornbluth is also incorrect in referring to the Communist policy as "United Front" instead of "Popular Front," but that's the subject of a different essay.

their attitude toward the Moscow Trials." Instead of independent Marxists and left-liberals such as Farrell, John Dewey and Edmund Wilson, figures such as Romaine—who publicly lauded the trials' verdict that resulted in the executions of thousands of Soviet dissidents (*Daily Worker*, 28 August 1938)—were given positions of authority.

My concern here is not to rehash the history of the 1930s, and it is certainly not to suggest that the excoriation of earlier writers' movements should have been a purpose of the latest Writers Congress, which had its own, more pressing, priorities. But I want to draw attention to the failure of many radicals and others to come to grips in a thoughtful way with the inherent political dimensions of all cultural phenomena. It is precisely this connection between politics and culture that the recent mythologizing of the earlier American Writers Congresses seeks to oversimplify or ignore. The 1935 shift away from a cultural orientation that claimed to support needy and unknown writers was intrinsically linked to the Communist leaders' political desire to engineer a pseudo-unity with liberals based on the lionization of figures like Ernest Hemingway and Archibald MacLeish as antifascist heroes of the people. It was fear of disturbing what appeared to be a successful alliance, and scaring off the superstars as well as the liberals they attracted, that caused many sincere leftists to rationalize the fact that thousands of unnamed "Trotskyites," "Zinovievites," "Bukharinites," anarchists, POUMists and innocent bystanders were being executed by the same Stalinist political movement in the Soviet Union and Spain.

Many radicals of the 1930s may be excused for not having recognized the political implications of this aspect of the radical cultural movement at the time. But left-wing cultural historians of the present will lose their credibility and moral authority if they continue to gloss over the politics of the Communist-initiated cultural activities in their attempt to make the traditions of American radicalism into a usable past. There is sufficient scholarly material to clarify the record on these matters, but perhaps the ascendancy of the right has made many radicals unwilling to ask basic questions.

Three biographies of cultural figures associated with the Communist Party that were published this year confirm that radical cultural history has simply reached an impasse in this respect. David E. Shi's *Matthew Josephson* (Yale University Press); William Alexander's *Film on the Left* (Princeton University Press), which is in part a collective biography of the radical film makers Sam Brody, Leo Hurwitz, Ben Maddow, Ralph Steiner and Paul Strand; and David King Dunaway's *How Can I Keep From Singing: Pete Seeger* (McGraw-Hill) all exhibit the liberal or radical historian's characteristic uneasiness about the relationships among politics, culture and American Communism. Shi and Alexander, both of whom are competent scholars and present important information about their subjects, depart from their usual high standards when discussing the politics of culture on the left. Shi adds little to David Caute's *The Fellow-Travellers: A Postscript to the Enlightenment*, which describes radical intellectuals as heirs of the eighteenth-century humanist and rationalist traditions. Alexander rallies sympathy for ambiguous "progressive" causes while expressing weak reservations about the Soviet Union's "repressive measures"—a euphemism for mass murder, frame-up trials and torture.

Dunaway's book, the most drastic example of this phenomenon, deserves attention because Seeger is still alive and personifies for many of us the committed cultural figure of the left. Dunaway does provide a good deal of information about the evolution of contemporary folk music in association with left-wing politics since the 1930s, but his scholarship is virtually useless as an account of Stalinist Communism and the cultural style of the Popular Front—two related factors that were crucial to his protagonist's development. Even worse, Dunaway is hopelessly confused, and confusing, in his attempt to explain Seeger's peculiar relation to the Communist Party. And this is so in spite of the book jacket's boast: "Here, for the first time, [is] an inside history of . . . Seeger's involvement with the Communist Party."

Dunaway's problem is not his political bias but his inability to confront the political nature of certain cultural phenomena. He depicts the pioneer of the contemporary folk-song movement as a man refreshingly simple in his moral values but outrageously simple-minded in the translation of those values into political loyalties. He admires Seeger for his empathy with rural and urban working people, his courageous stand against the 1950s blacklist, his popularization of the "citybilly" music that was forged through his collaboration with Woody Guthrie, and his front-line participation in the civil rights and anti-Vietnam War movements.

At the same time Dunaway's version of Seeger's association with the Communist Party repeatedly hints at some profound defect in Seeger's integrity or intelligence without providing a forthright explanation or analysis. After joining the Communist movement while a student at Harvard in the late 1930s, Seeger wrote lyrics that coincided with the "radical patriotism" of Franklin Roosevelt's New Deal. But when the Hitler-Stalin Pact was announced in 1939, Seeger and his first singing group, the Almanacs, accommodated themselves to the new party line by performing songs *against* Roosevelt and his war preparations. In the third stage of this tortured progression, after Hitler invaded the Soviet Union in 1941, the Almanacs followed party dictates once more, producing chauvinistic pro-war songs and putting "Talking Union" on the back burner so as not to contradict the party's vigorous support of the no-strike pledge. Seeger was apparently shaken by the rapid transmogrifications but, unlike some of the others of his generation, failed to conclude that the party's policies might be retarding more than advancing the struggle for socialism. Dunaway states, "Opposing the pact would have cut him off from friends and jobs in New York. The Soviet Union's *Realpolitik* was hard to overlook, but Seeger had forced himself."

According to the narrative we are given, Seeger never really "broke" with the party. Dunaway claims that he dropped his membership at the beginning of the witch-hunt era "more from an instinct of self-preservation than any political difference." As the biography explains, Seeger abstained from public criticism of the party and therefore had the privilege of not being denounced as a "renegade." Thus he remained silent about the Soviet Union's massacre of Hungarian dissidents in 1956 and its invasion of Czechoslovakia in 1968. But Dunaway does not tell us whether or not Seeger was suppressing substantive criticisms. After examining voluminous notebooks and journals and conducting 110 interviews, Dunaway tells us that Seeger never said anything harsher of the whole Stalin era than that it involved "an awful lot of rough stuff." His only recorded objection to Soviet society (which he witnessed on several tours) concerns "a few polluted lakes and the Siberian weather." Dunaway is disturbed by this feature in a man he otherwise admires, but not sufficiently so as to present us with anything more than an ingenuous conclusion: "Pete always had a blind spot to the excesses of socialism-in-the-making."

This statement, appearing at the end of *How Can I Keep From Singing*, might have been a satisfactory conclusion for a newspaper journalist who had undertaken a one-shot interview for a Sunday magazine supplement. A cultural historian should have acknowledged that it is the familiar cliché about Communists and their fellow-travelers, one that begs to be analyzed. Shi uses a similar formulation in describing Josephson: "Josephson was . . . the victim of moral blind splits." Although this way of putting it places Josephson himself, rather than the dead and imprisoned, in the role of "victim" of his moral blind spots, Shi at least tries to account for this behavior. Dunaway's study never even gets around to asking the most fundamental question about Seeger's relation to the Communist Party since his membership lapsed: has Seeger remained a convinced Stalinist or does he have important differences with the party which he refrains from expressing for fear of giving ammunition to the right? Or is Seeger just a naive do-gooder, someone who took the Popular Front view that "Communism is Twentieth-Century Americanism" too literally?

It is clear from Dunaway's book, and from other reports, that Seeger is an enigmatic figure who closely guards his personal life; he is a man who appears anti-intellectual and warm-hearted in public life, but who is said to be quite otherwise in private. Many biographers have had to distinguish their subject from his or her mask, and the enigma of Seeger and his mask is an especially crucial one for radical cultural historians to explore. Not only does he share a history with as many as a million other Americans who were at one time either supporters or members of the party but he is a living link between the experience of Great Depression leftism and the political radicalism of our own time.

Furthermore, the search for facts about the nature of Seeger's Communism should not be regarded as a destructive endeavor, an attempt to undermine or discredit. There are many things to admire in Seeger and we need to understand him. Wherever there has been a struggle for social justice in the United States since the 1950s, Seeger has been there. His refusal to attack the Communist Party has been coupled with a very un-Communist refusal to attack other groups on the American left.

I suspect that liberal and radical biographers such as Shi, Alexander and Dunaway are evasive in their assessments of American Communism and the politics of culture because they cannot imagine an analysis that is neither Red-baiting nor pro-Communist; in all instances they fail to understand, or to believe, that Stalinism can be condemned from a militantly anticapitalist or revolutionary Marxist perspective.

The recurring pattern in these three books, as well as in other recent works about politics, culture and American Communism—for example, Bruce Cook's *Dalton Trumbo* and Malcolm Cowley's *The Dream of the Golden Mountains: Remembering the 1930s*—is the failure to provide a clear view of either the nature of American Communism or the Popular Front culture celebrated and codified at the Writers Congresses of the 1930s and 1940s. The fact is that Popular Front culture meant the abandonment by radical intellectuals of their traditional association with vanguard ideas for the sake of creating a popular art that would reach a mass audience on much the same terms as the commercial mass culture created by capitalism already did. As Robert Warshow pointed out in 1947 in his essay "The Legacy of the Thirties," this sort of cultural practice embodies a major ambiguity. On the one hand, it can raise the level of popular art; on the other hand—and Warshow believed that this came to be the predominant feature—it can "distort and eventually destroy the emotional and moral content of experience, putting in its place a system of conventionalized 'responses.' In fact, the chief function of mass culture is to relieve one of the necessity of experiencing one's life directly." The ambiguities involved in the creation of simplified and conventionalized responses are central to an understanding of the political nature of Popular Front culture; they are crucial to our assessment of Josephson's popular histories, and several of the late-1930s films discussed by Alexander, and Seeger's songs.

In 1970 Nathan Glazer published a collection of essays called *Remembering the Answers*. Its title comes from an anecdote reported in Norman Podhoretz's autobiographical memoir *Making It*: "William Phillips [editor of *Partisan Review*] once told the New Left minded English critic Kenneth Tynan that he could not argue with him about politics, because Tynan's arguments were so old that he, Phillips, could no longer remember the answers." Glazer's book is important mainly for its documentation of the author's transformation from a "1950s radical" into a neoconservative, but the concern with the historical record reflected in his title should be ours as well. A body of knowledge has accumulated about the experience of American radicals in cultural matters. Radical cultural historians of the present can choose whether they want to extend that legacy or reassess it, but in both cases the first step is to ask the critical questions and remember the answers that have already been attempted.

7

The Legacy of Howard Fast

For nearly fifty years Howard Fast has produced novels that have entertained millions of people while introducing them to radical politics. Many of today's liberal and socialist activists grew up in households that had copies of *Citizen Tom Paine* and *Freedom Road* on the bookshelf. A new generation is encountering Fast's books in the high schools, where several of them are standard reading. Now sixty-eight years old, Fast recently completed a series of four best-selling novels: *The Immigrants* (1977), which also became a two-part television film, *Second Generation* (1978), *The Establishment*, and *The Legacy* (1981). Dramatized in these works are racism, class prejudice, war profiteering, labor struggles in the Great Depression, the Spanish Civil War, the McCarthyite witch-hunt, and the rise of the new radicalism in the 1960s.

Such a career might be cause for celebration among those who would like to see fiction with a radical perspective reach a broader audience. What is discomforting is that none of Fast's books has earned a reputation as a truly distinguished work of art. One can recall some stirring episodes and vivid portraits, but, when compared to outstanding political novels such as Dostoyevski's *The Possessed*, Silone's *Bread and Wine*, and Gordimer's *Burger's Daughter*, much of his writing appears two-dimensional and lacking in subtlety. The sometimes crude political messages embedded in many of Fast's novels may elicit discomfort as well. While the notion of a direct correlation between political line and literary quality has long been discredited among serious Marxists, Fast's career suggests to me the importance of recognizing that an author's relation to particular kinds of ideology may in certain instances enhance or narrow the scope and complexity of artistic vision.

Fast's literary career began to take shape mainly while he was a supporter of the liberal-Communist Popular Front in the latter half of the 1930s; he joined the Party during World War II, when the Popular Front was once more in full swing. The cultural orientation of the Popular Front was distinct from the Proletarian literary line that prevailed during Communism's "Third Period" before 1935; it celebrated "little people" instead of workers and waved the flag of idealized patriotism instead of socialist internationalism. In technique, radicalism's traditional ties with the avant-garde were definitively broken during the Popular Front. What we now call Modernism (typified by Eliot and Joyce) was condemned as antipeople and protofascist, and replaced by Hollywood and Broadway. At one time, endorsement lists for Communist-initiated cultural activities were headed by John Dos Passos and Edmund Wilson; in the Popular Front days they were replaced by Rex Stout, Donald Ogden Stewart, Dashiell Hammett, and eventually Howard Fast, whom Leslie Fiedler characterized as the Communist movement's "most faithful middlebrow servant in the arts."

However, the young Fast made an individual contribution to this development. While he tended to choose famous subjects and historical events as the topics for his novels, he frequently focused on lesser-known episodes, taking an unusual angle of presentation or even telling the story from the reverse of the conventional point of view. He also refused to idealize many of his historical portraits—frankly depicting George Washington as troubled, Tom Paine as a drunk and a braggart, and John Peter Altgeld as having ascended to power through corrupt means. Furthermore, the books frequently had a clear thesis that had more to do with his own political philosophy than with the fashions of the moment. Most often Fast wanted to make some point about the universal nature of the struggle for freedom. As a literary technician, he was frequently praised for his narrative skill and flair for characterization—important qualities in any writer.

Nevertheless, from the start of his career there were some commentators who noted an affinity between Fast's technique and the conventions of mass culture. For example, *Conceived in Liberty* (1939) was said to be "like all other great war stories that people have been reading for twenty years; only the setting is different." In the 1940s several critics noted that Fast gave his short stories happy endings that were a "concession" to the magazines where they first appeared. In the following decades his work was observed to have the "flavor of a movie spectacular," with much of the dialogue "escaped from the women's magazines or daytime television." The novelist Harvey Swados argued that "Mr. Fast's conception of history is really not that much different from that of Cecil B. De Mille."

To these negative observations we can add that there are facets of his career that have elicited the charge of opportunism. While in the Party his books were sold widely in Soviet-bloc countries were he was vastly overpraised, which may have been a factor in the longevity of his membership. In fact, the USSR, where he was regarded as a world-class novelist, awarded him the Stalin Peace Prize in 1954. Immediately following his sensational break with and public excoriation of the Party in *The Naked God: The Writer and the Communist Party*, he dashed off to Hollywood to become a scenarist for Universal, Paramount, Pennybaker, and Hitchcock studios. Finally, even though historical novels have been the center of his work, he gives an appearance of having swamped his major efforts in a deluge of stories for children and adolescents, simple history books with photographs and drawings, science fiction stories, mysteries, Zen stories, and a score of books that he himself calls "entertainments."

Yet the view of Fast as an opportunist money-maker hardly explains why he produced explicitly Communist books such as *Silas Timberman*, *The Story of Lola Gregg*, and *The Passion of Sacco and Vanzetti*, published by his own press and paid for by his own resources, during the height of the Cold War when no commercial publisher would touch him. In 1950 the House Committee on Un-American Activities ordered him to provide the names of all those who had contributed to the support of a hospital for Spanish Republicans in Toulouse, France, with which he had been associated during the Spanish Civil War. When he refused, he was thrown in jail for three months, during which he wrote most of the novel *Spartacus*. Blacklisted upon his release, he initiated his own Blue Herron Press and turned the novel into the only self-published best-seller in recent history.

The point is that during the Cold War, Fast was not writing on fashionable topics but produced according to the social and political convictions that were both the inspiration for and objective of his creative drive. Had American mass culture in subsequent decades become dominated by right-wing sentiments, he might well have drifted into obscurity. Instead, the shift in our culture to the more democratic, antiracist, and antiwar moods of the 1960s and 1970s made possible his return to the best-seller charts on a more regular basis. Even the series of books about "wise, brave and gallant women" he has issued under the pseudonym "E. V. Cunningham"—such as *Phyllis*, *Alice*, *Shirley*, *Lydia*, *Penelope*, *Helen*, *Sally*, *Samantha*, *Cynthia*, and *Millie*—and his detective novels about a Nisei cop, Massao Masuto, working out of the Beverly Hills Police Department, contain social criticism that would be unacceptable in a less liberal cultural environment. So the reason for Fast's new success is not simply that he accommodated his art; American culture changed as well.

The manner in which Fast dramatizes his political ideas in fiction is clearly demonstrated in the plot of his newest series of best sellers that traces the rise to fortune and power of the fictional character Daniel Lavette. Lavette is the son of Franco-Italian immigrants who settle in San Francisco in the late nineteenth century. Orphaned by the 1906 San Francisco earthquake, he uses his fishing boat to create a financial empire during World War I. His personal life is torn between his wife, a Nob Hill socialite, and his mistress, the librarian daughter of his Chinese bookkeeper. The mistress finally becomes his second wife at the end of the first volume, *The Immigrants*, allowing Fast to sustain throughout the rest of the novels a contrast between Lavette's two sets of relatives—the snobbish and bigoted WASPS and the decent and hardworking Chinese.

Although Lavette loses his fortune at the start of the Great Depression, he returns in the second volume, *Second Generation*, to his millionaire status through another windfall of war profits, made this time through World War II. However, May Ling, his second wife, is killed by stray bullets while visiting Hawaii during the Japanese attack on Pearl Harbor. Lavette then remarries his WASP wife and the focus thereafter shifts to their daughter, Barbara, a novelist and journalist.

Barbara never subscribes to any radical ideology, but she breaks from her mother's elitist bigotry and her father's cynicism about social reform by aiding longshoremen in the period just before and during the 1934 San Francisco General Strike. Harry Bridges appears in the novel as a minor character. Then she moves to Paris, where she falls in love with a French journalist who dies of wounds incurred in the Spanish Civil War. At the end of *Second Generation* she marries Bernie Cohen, a Jew who resembles her father in every way except that Cohen's passions are abetting Zionism and killing Nazis instead of aggrandizing wealth.

At the start of the third volume, *The Establishment*, Cohen becomes a gun-runner in Palestine at the time of Israel's formation and is killed in combat with Arab troops. Meanwhile, Barbara is framed before HUAC [House Un-American Activities Committee] and eventually serves a prison sentence for refusing to divulge the names of people who gave donations to the Toulouse hospital where her French lover died.

The final volume, *The Legacy*, takes us into the 1960s where, after a brief marriage to a Los Angeles publisher rendered sexually impotent by his inability to break free of his conservative family, Barbara overcomes a writer's block by researching an historical novel about the wife of an American president. She watches her son, Sammy, and his cousins and friends, become active in the new political movements against racism and the Vietnam War. Barbara herself becomes a feminist and the founder of Mothers for Peace.

The Lavette novels have a number of features that render them hard to take very seriously. Their structure—the large cast of characters with interconnecting lives and the large number of short scenes—is reminiscent of a television soap opera; indeed, one reviewer referred to *The Immigrants* as "soap history." While the didactic quality of the books is nothing new in Fast, the lessons here seem unusually trite and aimed at an audience that watches soaps. In the concluding volume, Barbara learns the social lesson that "there was no happiness in the legacy of the rich," and the personal lesson that the abused notion of love must be replaced by "trust," which is the knowledge that someone will "be there when you need him."

However, it would be simplistic to conclude that Fast has merely tried to dope out what a mass audience is willing to buy and then churned out the requisite product. Fast is trying to reach a large number of people with his values, and there is nothing reprehensible in that. But the very way he conceives of his medium restricts the possibilities of his craft. From the time of the Popular Front to the present, Fast has retained a notion that in order to reach a large audience one's novels must resemble a Hollywood spectacular, and that the typical reader has the sensibilities of a rather unreflective movie fan; this most recent effort amounts to sugarcoating his messages in a big, splashy, sentimental story. We like to think that authentic artists simply write their best in the hope that readers will eventually respond to such an effort on its own terms. Of course, the truth is that most artists probably have to struggle somewhat before making a few necessary compromises with publishers and the expected audience; but Fast gives the impression that such struggles are far in his past, and that his medium now controls him as much as he controls it.

The result is not only that his art can hardly be assessed outside of the terms one would use in treating mass media, but also that his unique contribution—the left-liberal doctrine with which he infuses his books—is not just simplified but fatally trivialized. He consistently refuses to complicate any matter that he thinks might confuse the reader or distract from the action. For example, Fast is eager to extract just one simple meaning from the witch-hunt years: that the McCarthyites framed people as Communist dupes in order to manufacture headlines. And so he fails to address the civil rights of those who were real "subversives" in the eyes of the witch-hunters. Thereby he makes it possible for readers to conclude that it is only the excesses and abuses of the HUAC hearings that should be condemned, rather than the entire process. Since Fast's nonfiction writings show that it was the process itself that he abhorred, his attempt to write down to the imagined level of his readers has betrayed his own values.

Further, the social and political essences of the antiwar and women's movements of the 1960s are embarrassingly trivialized when Barbara becomes a pacifist and feminist leader. Her naive view, as revealed in a major political speech at a women's rally, is that war would cease if women played a more prominent role in society—because women are mothers and wouldn't allow their children to be killed. Barbara's political opposition never transcends this pseudo-analysis. She thinks that the Vietnam War has nothing to do with the right of colonial people to self-determination. Similarly, in her capacity as a feminist leader she denies that feminism involves a basic critique of the family as a social institution in class society. The problem here is not that Barbara's ideas are politically "incorrect"; it is that Fast's attempt to simplify them for consumption by a mass audience renders them banal to the point of falsifying the historical movements which she leads.

The result, ironically, is that Fast, who has been influenced by Marxism and no doubt seeks to disclose the "real" meaning of history in his novels, writes books that bear a striking resemblance to the kind of literature that the Marxist critic Georg Lukács stigmatized as "naturalist," as a means of distinguishing it from authentic "realist" literature. By naturalist, Lukács meant a work that, regardless of the subjective intentions of the author, only captures the superficial features of reality, as in a photograph or mirror, missing the true complexities of humanity in its dynamic interaction with class and social institutions. Lukács was not opposed to experimental techniques, difficulty, or ambiguity, as long as artistic goals didn't obfuscate the depiction of social truth in all its complexity.

As an example of naturalist simplicity, Lukács pointed to Zola, a socialist who produced his books according to a theory of scientific determinism; as a realist counterpart, he cited Balzac, a reactionary monarchist whose artistic grasp of character and social reality brought truths to the pages of his books that his own philosophy would deny. If the character of Barbara Lavette, who was born in the same year as Fast (1914) and who shares so many of his experiences, was intended to reveal the political dimensions of his life with more candor and subtlety that can be found in his non-fiction writing, the results are disappointingly "naturalist." The multi-layered human drama of being a member of a corrupt Communist Party in a corrupt capitalist society is evaded by depicting Barbara as an innocent non-Party member victimized by unscrupulous right-wing politicians. The social truth of the McCarthy era is only superficially captured.

Part of the explanation for Fast's inability to develop more fully as a "realist" in Lukács' sense may be that, despite several phases in his political and philosophical evolution, he has never outgrown a constricting style of thought and some erroneous assumptions about the functions of art that he acquired from the ideology in which he was immersed during his formative period. Even today, with his Communist Party membership twenty-five years behind him, this latest quartet of books, especially *The Legacy*, still exudes the Popular Front sensibility of the late 1930s and World War II years. It does so first of all in its promulgation of a simple "progressive" program of peace and liberal reform that will appeal to "the masses," but also in its promotion of relationships among good people of all classes and races and in its absence of precise ideas and emotional candor. It is intriguing that Fast has changed so little, and also that the public is so responsive. That this orientation, first championed by the Left five decades ago, could be reborn in a national best-selling series of novels in the 1970s and 1980s, impressively testifies to the real power of Popular Front ideology; it also seems to confirm Harold Rosenberg's observation that "collapsed ideologies are not blown away by the winds. On the contrary, they spread throughout our society and take the form of popular culture."

This shrewd observation, about the ideological origins of ostensibly unsystematized popular thought, was part of a polemic against the "middlebrow"—a type of writer with which Fast is sometimes identified. The middlebrow is usually depicted as one who is posing as a mediator between the complexities of high culture and a mass audience intellectually unprepared for those complexities—although in truth the middlebrow is operating on the principle that culture is a commodity to be sold for profit. The argument that Fast is a middlebrow in spite of his radical politics is largely based on the interpretation of Popular Front culture itself as a middlebrow phenomenon.

It is true that after World War II the Popular Front collapsed and Party chairman Earl Browder was expelled. But Fast never felt very comfortable with the subsequent shift in cultural policy from celebrating an idealized American democratic tradition to excoriating the defects of the same tradition. In fact, when he eventually broke with the Party he was in sympathy with John Gates and other "neo-Browderites" who sought in large measure to return the Party's politics to the old Popular Front days. In 1957, shortly after Fast made public his resignation, Irving Howe predicted that, since middlebrow values are "pervasive to our time . . . the middlebrow in Fast may yet survive the old Stalinist, bringing him success of a kind parallel to that which he has enjoyed during the past two decades."

This astute prediction, striking as it is, stems from a rather simple notion that the middlebrow writer fabricates his or her books to respond to whatever standard is set by public demand—which is the only standard that interests one who sees all literary subjects as commodities to be exchanged for money. But this formulation and its assumptions do not embody an adequate appreciation of the nature of the creative process (how easy is it for a writer to consciously and successfully write beneath his or her genuine talents?) and of the legitimate desire of some artists to exploit conventional forms and themes in order to influence a wider milieu. Furthermore, Howe's prediction does not anticipate that the ideas promoted by the Popular Front of the 1930s and 1940s might percolate down into popular culture at a future time, as they apparently have.

The point is that the dismissal of Fast by Howe and other critics as merely a middlebrow—that is, as one who pretends to respect the standards of serious art but who actually waters them down, vulgarizing them for profit—is too constricting and unfair to be the last word about his achievement, even though it does disclose some important features of his technique. His early works in particular display strengths of craft and creativity that, under other circumstances, might have enabled him to develop into a novelist of greater distinction. In the 1940s he made a unique mark on our literary history that ought not to be undervalued. Furthermore, there is nothing in money-making activities, extreme productivity, or widespread popularity that inherently discredits Fast as an artist. Edgar Allen Poe was an unabashed money-maker, Balzac was incredibly prolific, and *The Education of Henry Adams* was a leading best-seller in 1919.

Of course, no one has yet suggested that Fast is an author of the same importance as Poe, Balzac, or Adams. In his case one can legitimately question whether something has been sacrificed because of his emphasis on quantity and by his total devotion to the exploitation of almost every opportunity that arises in the commercial arena. No doubt Fast received a good deal of monetary and psychological benefit from his U.S. and Soviet fame, but it also seems likely that he paid a heavy price for his machine-like production of books and screenplays. In a 1945 critical essay Granville Hicks showed distress that Fast was writing so fervently that he was unable to reflect sufficiently to recognize that some qualities of his work were declining after the high point of *Conceived in Liberty*, *The Last Frontier*, and *The Unvanquished*. He warned Fast that "the creative imagination refuses to be hurried" and pointed out ways in which Fast's haste was already bringing about carelessness and lack of attentiveness. The problem has only grown worse since then.

Exacerbating this weakness is the shallow eclecticism and lack of clarity reflected in his political thought. He shares this trait with other writers, many of them artistically successful, but it is a special handicap in an author like Fast who puts so much emphasis on the rather simple lessons he programs into his books. Hicks' 1945 essay correctly noted that Fast's "naiveté on the intellectual level" rendered him especially inept in treating ideas, pointing out that Fast "only half understands" his revolutionary formulas. Since the 1940s his formulas have become less revolutionary, but he still proceeds at times as if he were sketching in scenes somewhat mechanically on the basis of a simplistic broad thesis. A truly first-rate political novelist ought to give the sense that an active imagination is operating throughout his or her works, which is not incompatible with the transmission of a precise political vision.

In the United States at present, we don't have to look back to the classical novelists such as Balzac to demonstrate the kinds of qualities that seem absent from so much of Fast's work and that Lukács honorifically calls realism. The books of writers such as Maxine Hong Kingston, Toni Morrison, and Leslie Silko aim to recreate historical consciousness through the perception of history as a concrete totality and complex process—not, like Fast, by simply depicting the immediacy of historical experience from one person's liberal or radical perspective. While Fast's admirable concern with racial oppression led him to oversimplification and abstraction (his black characters in *Freedom Road*, for example, have been criticized as being virtuous beyond believability), Kingston, Morrison, and Silko dramatize in Asian-American, Afro-American, and Native American Indian settings what Raymond Williams has described as the dialectic between the domination of cultural hegemony and the resistance of residual and emergent cultures. Their protagonists are neither idealized not artificially "balanced"; they are fully human in Lukács's realistic sense of being typical yet individualized. Furthermore, these three authors have achieved some degree of popularity through their integration of "difficult" ideas—the kind usually identified with "serious" art or high culture—with quite accessible narrative and vivid characterization. This suggests that the old theory of a schism among mass culture, middlebrow culture, and high culture is no longer so relevant today. It may even raise the question of whether it ever *was* a sound and comprehensive approach to understanding cultural phenomena, rather than a mechanism for legitimizing the elitism generated by the prejudices of a society divided by class, gender, and race.

Based on what we know about Fast, it would be an overreaction to conclude that politically committed writers should turn their backs on the possibility of reaching a mass audience for fear that their ideas will become trivialized. Such a strategy would run the risk of returning to a form of elitism like High Modernism that no longer has the revolutionary impact on our culture that it had in the 1920s and 1930s. Furthermore, one might question whether it is useful to judge Fast's books according to the same standard one would use in discussing a novel by Balzac, Silko, or Morrison, especially when their artistic strategies and objectives seem so markedly different. Isn't there room in our society for a frankly popular kind of writing—a genre of lightweight page turners that provides entertainment and escape along with mild doses of history and politics? If so, shouldn't we be grateful simply for the existence of a writer like Fast who brings relatively enlightened values to a mass-market audience that might otherwise be reading Harold Robbins and Rosemary Rogers?

There are significant problems with this line of argument, but I think it is the most effective way we have at present of responding to the elitism of a single standard for evaluating diverse cultural phenomena. Where I feel it may not do justice to Fast is in regard to the ambiguous promise of his early work. If he had been formed in a different period of American culture or been subject to different influences after achieving his initial success in the 1940s, he might have made a contribution to our literature that commanded more respect even if it had resulted in fewer sales. Simply put, the ideology of the Popular Front inculcated Fast with the notion that radical politics could be transmitted to a large audience in the garb of liberal sentiments and idealized patriotism, all aimed at a reader imagined to represent the "common man." That Fast achieved considerable success in this genre constitutes an important chapter in radical cultural history; that he was unable to develop as an artist or even to sustain the quality of his work is testimony to the inadequacies of this approach.

As it stands now, the legacy of Howard Fast is an ambiguous one. But so are the legacies of many of his predecessors in the history of American literary radicalism, such as Jack London and John Dos Passos. The dilemma of the radical artist's relationship to mass culture in fiction, as well as in film, music, and the other arts, is not one that can be resolved through blueprints, formulas, or precise models. More effective might be an uninhibited and wide-ranging dialogue between young artists and politically active workers and intellectuals about the cultural problems of late capitalism. In isolation, artists seeking a mass audience may well revert to worn-out conventions that may subvert their radical intentions; in the ferment produced by the creative exchange of ideas, at least there is the hope of assimilating the best from the past and forging new pathways to the future.

8

Aspects of the
Communist Experience

Tethered to the Past

Norman Macleod. *The Distance: New and Selected Poems* (1928–1977), ed. Liam Hunt (Pembroke, N.C.: A Pembroke Paperback, 1977). 120 pp. $3.00.

In *The Little Magazine: A History and Bibliography* (1946), Frederick J. Hoffmann and his coauthors present a composite portrait of the avant-garde literary personality. They describe the little magazine editor and contributor as animated by a rebellious discontent with the unjust, boring, or ridiculous features of the publishing institutions perpetuating the status quo: "He views the world of publishers and popularizers with disdain, sometimes with despair." Hoffmann *et al.* identify Eugene Jolas, Norman Macleod, Ezra Pound, Ernest J. Walsh, and William Carlos Williams as the models from which the portrait is drawn.

Norman Macleod is the sole surviving member of this group, and, at seventy-two years of age, a rebellious discontent remains a distinguishing trait of his poetry and literary activities. From beginning to end, his writings retain a characteristic dysphoria concerning the human condition. This volume of new and selected verse demonstrates the refractory poet's relentless struggle over five decades to extract his personal satisfactory meanings from the elementary experiences of life and death.

Continuity in Macleod's literary activities is also shown through his editorship of *Pembroke Magazine*, in which some of the more recent poems first appeared. When he received a grant from the North Carolina Arts Council to initiate the journal in 1968, Macleod put an end to the twenty-year hiatus from the public view during which he worked in total obscurity. A successor to his earlier experimental publications—*The Morada* (1929–30), *Front* (1930–31), and *Briarcliff Quarterly* (1944–47)—this international journal of the fine arts features tributes to aging and deceased poets of our time, as well as to behind-the-scenes figures such as scholars and printers.

Macleod's editorial orientation reflects his concerns as a creative writer. In his own poetry, his rebel temperament is inextricably linked to ponderings about his past. *The Distance* emphasizes his fixation, constant throughout all phases of his work, on lost cultures, disintegrated families, and dead friends and relatives. These common features of the poems transcend the diverse elements in his writing derived from Macleod's having been a poet who has lived through several generations of literary development, and who has traveled widely, using many geographical locations as settings for his writings. The editor has grouped the poems into three sections corresponding to chronological periods, but an equally useful tripartite division for these mournful ruminations might be to consider them as regional, political, and philosophical in subject matter.

The bulk of the regional work derives from two locations—the Northwest (primarily Oregon and Montana) and the Southwest (primarily New Mexico and Arizona)—although the selection also contains several later poems drawing on Macleod's personal and ancestral ties to Scotland. In his youthful work we are presented with the recurring images of the poet as a boy in his stag shirt or mackinaw; we are shown glimpses of his family life; and we are introduced to the Western spirit of community, reflected in the frequent use of the pronoun "we" and in the descriptions of collective activities. Western shrubbery (the syringas), geographical locations (the Bitterroots), and wildlife (the ptarmigans) are the center of the imagery.

But these poems are regional only in the sense that they constitute an imaginative response to the landscape, history, folklore, and language of these areas. The poems are in no way localized or restricted, either in form or content. Indeed, it is important to remember that Macleod was one of the first Modernist poets from the West.

Like many of the Imagists, and the experimentalist contributors to *The Dial* in the 1920s, Macleod, in some of these poems, is less concerned with communicating his ideas about culture than using art as a vehicle for the vivid organization of physical, mental, and imaginative experiences. Macleod sought to bring into interaction the new literary experimentalism and the regional materials at hand.

Macleod is most successful in this project when carrying out Ezra Pound's injunction to recharge the poet's vocabulary by striving for the immediacy of effect that arises from the close association of word and object. The short poem "Inquest" exemplifies this in its description of villages of penitentes (the secret lay order of the Southwest noted for its flagellating rites during Holy Week). Sunset over the adobe huts is depicted in the vivid imagery of Christian ceremony ("cup of earth," "wine of life") intermixed with that of the flagellating rites ("welt upon the body," "redder than any lash").

At other times Macleod employs impressionistic techniques reminiscent of Stephen Crane and John Dos Passos. In "Shadowbox: In a Milltown," he describes a sunset as "when color ran riot into the evergreen," and in "The Little People of Twilight," he depicts bluebirds shot down by children's air rifles as "Red Grief/On a grey shed."

But other regional poems depart from the aesthetic purity of the Imagist perspective, and are fused with the social and political consciousness typical of left-wing writers of the late 1920s and early 1930s. The subject of a number of lyrics and elegies is the lives of the common people (miners and loggers) and the fading of native cultures (that of the Pueblos, the Nez Perces, and the Navajos).

Many of Macleod's poems of the West appeared in specifically regional publications such as *Jackass* (which Macleod edited in 1928–29) and *Troubadour* (which tried to establish a fraternity of poets of the Pacific Coast during the same time), as Macleod attempted to fuse Imagism, regionalism, and political consciousness. The founding of *The Morada* (the name refers to the chapel of the penitentes) constituted Macleod's last major effort in this area; following its demise he entered a period in which revolutionary politics played a dominant role in shaping his writing.

Unfortunately, the poetry of Macleod's revolutionary period is rather poorly represented in this selection. In the early 1930s he served as a contributing editor of the Communist-sponsored *New Masses*, but his most important magazine venture may well have been *Front*. This was a trilingual publication produced in Holland which, for a year, managed to sustain an alliance of first-rate experimental literature and left-wing politics. However, poetry from *Front* is not included in *The Distance* and the writings reflecting Macleod's encounter with radicalism are limited to a few stating his empathy with the poor and oppressed; several which express his doubts about and, later, his opposition to the course of the Stalinist leadership of the USSR after the 1930s; and a paean to the triumph of the once-illegal movement of industrial unionism.

Yet, there is evidence that Macleod's political radicalism continued to persist in later years—perhaps in a form akin to the anti-authoritarianism that Edmund Wilson maintained until his death. A poem probably written in the late 1940s or early 1950s ("The Pigeons in the Park") describes a presidential election as a nation's vote for "its own death":

> Big lie's harlot flags
> Announce the approaching Siberia
> Whose Army will police the mind. . . .

In a poem dated as recently as 30 June 1975 ("The Seagulls Are Crying For You, Jock"), Macleod fears that

> The West approaches the twilight
> An auguring Spanish Inquisition. . . .

Many of Macleod's regionalist and politically-conscious poems in this volume are drawn from a similar perception in that they look backward, judging the present negatively in relation to a more satisfying past. (In some cases this past is a time of romanticized youthful innocence; in other cases it is a period when the Russian Revolution seemed healthful and progressive.) But in the poem "Bellvue Hospital: 1934," which appears a third of the way through the volume, Macleod's obsession with his relation to his past assumes a pivotal role. As his eyes survey New York harbor from the window of a mental institution, the voice of the poet struggles to speak. But, his body confined to a straight jacket (". . . his hands beside him"), he is overtaken and paralyzed by a bleak vision of his own psychic state:

> . . . the huge hulk of an ocean liner docked
> As I am, tethered to the wharf of my past.
> The contemplation of no new journeys
> Hoists the anchor.

This paradox of moving forward only by ceaseless lucubrations of the past is decreed to be Macleod's fate. But it is an unacceptable fate, leading logically to death, as he later expresses in "My Jack on the Beanstalk":

> I must come to some loving embrace with the past
> Or it will destroy me.

In another poem, "Way," Macleod describes the process by which the past, to which he clings, controls and torments him—the more so because it is eroded by new events:

> Fire flows through the forest
> Like war, disaster consumes our past
> And bone, trunk, brittle with envy,
> Hoists their last flag.

These sentiments are the underpinning of the pessimistic and skeptical philosophy which—while present in embryonic form in earlier work— comes to the foreground and overshadows most of the poems of his later phase. The poems of his middle and old age are more personal: Whereas a few of the earlier poems occasionally refer to quarrels in Macleod's family, the later ones indulge in endless meditation over divorces, separations, infidelities, strained relations with children, and, most importantly, a profound estrangement from his son, whose picture in a cowboy outfit haunts the poet in several pieces:

> a windswept length
> With leg holster strapping; therefore
> With a sombrero singing through afternoon
> Blithe blessed and whistles of living
> Even the sun's circling crescendo that
> Will take him from me soon.

The philosophy suggested by this focus on himself as an individual cast adrift in a sea of uncertainty is very much akin to the ideas of some of the Existentialist thinkers. Man is shown as a frail and isolated creature. (In "A Nightscape With Figures," Macleod likens himself to a private creature quivering with the "stretched ears of my mustache.") We are trapped in an irrational universe, the superficial order of which could explode at any moment:

> For the individual is held in place
> By the concrete objects which have
> Him as their focus—break these
> And man is utterly destroyed
> and distributed as god.

In particular, Macleod's outlook suggests parts of the philosophy of Martin Heidegger. The poet probes the past, after all, in a desperate search for the meaning and structure of Being. But there is an important difference: whereas Heidegger's *Daseinanalytik* (analysis of human being) is disciplined and proceeds according to a phenomenological method, Macleod's analysis is fragmented, chaotic, and ultimately psychological.

The psychology, however, is not exactly Freudian: references in the poem "Shadowbox: In a Milltown" suggest that it might more accurately be associated with the ideas of Arthur Schnitzler, the Austrian playwright and fiction writer of the *fin-de-siecle* period: Schnitzler viewed man as essentially an animal who is subjected to various emotional sicknesses (such as sexual passion); his literary talents inclined toward creating atmospheres of decadence and melancholy. Macleod approximates Schnitzler's mood in poems such as "An Apple For My sweet":

> What beauty lives
> Is a busted apple crate;
> Have an apple, lady?
> Here is one the worms left.

What is the basis of Macleod's recreation, through poetry, of a philosophical disposition similar in so many respects to the skepticism of Schnitzler and the bleak vision of the Existentialists? The roots of Macleod's alienation and angst lie in the experiences and values of the avant-garde writers of the 1920s, to which Macleod has always remained faithful. Poets of that generation felt that there was no place for them in the post-World War I world, and literature became a tool for forging new terms for existence.

The precise reasons why Macleod remained in the Waste Land of despair while others, such as T. S. Eliot, moved on to find religion or achieve some other *modus vivendi*, probably can't be disclosed short of a full-length biography. But, as these poems make clear, a decisive factor was Macleod's early attempt to assimilate and preserve the Western experiences of his youth through his experiments as a regional poet. His natural resistance to the urbanized landscape of industrial capitalism is communicated quite early in the poem "Subway," in which Macleod describes himself as a moose, hamstrung and bloodied by the alien environment of New York City.

In his later, more philosophical verse, the Western theme becomes transformed from mere nostalgia to a mood of lonely grandeur, as in "Chief Joseph the Nez Perce," one of the most moving poems in the entire collection. Macleod compares his role—as a poet, true to the original values of his generation—with that of the famed chief of a group of Nez Perce Indians. Chief Joseph resisted orders to leave land that had been ceded to the United States government by a fraudulently-obtained treaty. He has gone down into the history books as a triumphant figure, primarily because of the role attributed (somewhat inaccurately) as the mastermind of the heroic fighting retreat of the Nez Perces as they sought to evade confinement in a reservation by escaping to Canada. But Macleod's ending for the story is different:

> tomorrow the son I then will be
> will renounce not only the men
> who were his anchor in the past
> but also his race, name, those
> poems he will never know, there
> fore he will die as I will die
> grey as the ultimatum motorized
> transport move upon, atomizing
> our tablet in this world's mind.

In characteristic fashion Macleod cannot accept the historical triumph of Chief Joseph in 1877 as anything but a mark to be corroded away. Like the experiences of the poet's own life—the dissolution of his four marriages, the estrangement from his beloved son, the eclipse of his literary reputation after the 1930s and 1940s—the victory of the moment begins to be undermined by the disintegrating process of time at the very instant of triumph.

Reading, Writing, and Red-baiting

Ellen Schrecker. *No Ivory Tower: McCarthyism and the Universities* (NY: Oxford University Press, 1986). $19.95 (cloth).

"Present-mindedness," the interpretation of the past according to the political climate of the present, is an old problem in the historiography of the United States. Most historians now agree that the early 1950s was a time of considerable antiradical repression, reaching its apogee in the sensational charges of Joseph McCarthy, the Republican Senator from Wisconsin, that various U.S. government agencies were infiltrated by Communists. Yet the causes, scope, significance, and effects of that repression are still under dispute in ways that are a commentary on our own times as much as on the events of three decades ago.

Among scholars, shifting attitudes toward the meaning of McCarthyism have produced a considerable body of controversy—for instance, the famous debate between Richard Hofstadter and Michael Rogin as to whether McCarthyism was a populist phenomenon. In the mid-1970s, an array of films and books—Woody Allen's *The Front* and Lillian Hellman's *Scoundrel Time* are the best known—registered the view that the witch hunt was brutal and unconscionable, and its victims—especially those who resisted—admirable defenders of democracy.

Ironically, just as many of these films and books were being released, the mood of the country was moving toward the right. This shift was reflected in Hilton Kramer's 1976 *New York Times* essay, "The Black List and the Cold War," which argued that, despite regrettable excesses, the Communist threat to U.S. security had been a real one, and the victims were by and large authentic Communists who lied about their beliefs and associations. Moreover, these Communists had persecuted others wherever they had power, not only in the Soviet Union, but also in cultural circles in the United States: "Unmentioned [in these books and films] . . . are the vicious attacks that anti-Communist liberals and radicals were obliged to endure whenever they attempted to reveal the bloody truth about what Miss Hellman delicately describes now as the 'sins' of the Stalinist regime."

When David Caute's encyclopedic *The Great Fear: The Anti-Communist Purge Under Truman and Eisenhower* appeared in 1978, Sidney Hook, a leading philosopher with firsthand experiences in the political controversies of the 1950s, wrote a sharp rebuttal in *Encounter* which challenged every aspect of Caute's highly critical view of American society during the witch hunt. "Even at the height of Senator McCarthy's power," wrote Hook, "the leading newspapers were criticizing, indeed denouncing, him. His methods, tactics, and words were under impassioned attack in almost every large educational center of the nation."

Ellen Schrecker's new book provides strong evidence that Caute was justified in calling the witch-hunt phenomenon "The Great Fear." It demonstrates that there was a blacklist in academia as comprehensive as the more famous one in the entertainment industry. And it strengthens Caute's charge that there was complicity on the part of Cold War liberals with the witch hunt—the one assertion most angering Kramer and Hook, who defend and wish to revive that Cold War liberal tradition.

For it was possible to enforce the antiradical campaign even if one dissociated oneself from the more discreditable statements and actions of McCarthy himself. Indeed, using American colleges and universities as a case study, Schrecker convincingly shows that anything short of militant rejection of the witch hunt only served as grist for the rationalization-producing mills that enabled administrators to persecute faculty for their views in the name of "academic freedom." At each step most universities slavishly followed the national trends, quickly and shamelessly abandoning any legitimate claim to being havens for dissent.

Central to her argument is the claim that the ideology and even certain features of the apparatus of the future witch hunt in academia were already in place long before McCarthy launched his campaign, and before university trustees and administrators felt forced to capitulate to outside pressure. The most significant academic precursor was the 1940 investigation of Communist college teachers in New York City by the Rapp-Coudert Committee, a special state legislative body which "pioneered the techniques that later state and congressional investigating committees would employ. It developed evidence, elaborated arguments, and even trained personnel that its successor committees would appropriate, unchanged." Some of the accused New York teachers were not Party members, but most were and lied in a futile effort to save their jobs. The one teacher who pled the Fifth Amendment was fired instantly.

In the Board of Higher Education hearings that followed, the precedent was established that the actual classroom conduct and scholarly activities of the faculty were irrelevant to the judgment passed. Conduct "unbecoming" a professor was defined simply as membership in the Communist Party. As Schrecker demonstrates, by the 1950s unbecoming conduct was expanded to include any refusal to cooperate in the witch hunt by informing on suspected Communists.

Despite her recording of such events, Schrecker's study is by no means a sensational revelation of witch-hunt scandals. Indeed, many of the episodes she recounts will be familiar to those acquainted with the literature on the subject. The strength of the book lies, rather, in her careful dissection of the stages of the witch hunt, and in her sensitive portrayal of the victims' initial engagement with Communism, their response to the trauma of the academic purge, and their efforts to survive in subsequent years.

The witch hunt evolved through two stages. First the state, acting through the agency of investigating committees and the FBI, identified "political undesirables" on campus. Then the universities themselves took over, finding ways to "get rid of the targeted individuals." Again and again, Schrecker shows, persistence on the part of trustees and administrators broke the will of even those university faculties in which sentiment against the purges was strong at the outset. In the University of California system, for example, fifty per cent of the faculty refused to sign the loyalty oath when it was adopted in 1949, even though noncompliance meant not receiving a letter of formal appointment for 1949–50. Leading scholars on the campus rallied to the principle that the state Regents did not have the right to interfere with tenure and faculty self-determination. Yet, at the end of a long series of compromises, hearings, and modifications in the oath, divisions had developed among the nonsigners to the extent that those resisting were reduced to a helpless handful.

As in the case of the Hollywood purges, the object was not to gain information—the FBI already knew more than the subpoenaed faculty could remember—but to break the will of faculty rebels by forcing them to name names. Thus, when three faculty members were dismissed from Jefferson Medical College in 1953, they were told by the dean and a trustee that admitting their own past membership in the Party was insufficient: "We would like to have evidence that you have broken, other than to say that you have, and the best evidence you can possibly give is to become an informer."

Often, the victims themselves inadvertently assisted in their own victimization. Some resigned quietly when they came under attack, in the hope that a lack of publicity would enable them to find future employment. Others, recognizing that open acknowledgement of a Party association would result in a loss of their jobs, lied or at least were evasive about their political associations—and were later dismissed for perjury or noncooperation (grounds the administration preferred to dismissal for the holding of political views alone). To be sure, the blacklist that followed the purges was an informal procedure. But, operating as it did through letters of recommendation (to which the job-seeker did not have access), it worked so successfully that "almost every academic who lost a job as a result of a congressional investigation had trouble finding a new one."

Through an extraordinary number of personal interviews and a thorough examination of papers in scores of archives and personal collections, Schrecker has broken through the barriers of silence imposed by McCarthyism as has no previous historian. She can talk confidently about who was and wasn't an authentic Party member, and about the motives for resistance or cooperation in each case. Moreover, she takes her story back to the 1930s to show the conversion experience of an important part of a generation of young scholars to communism, and re-creates in some detail their political lives on campuses and in Party units.

What emerges is not a portrait of foreign agents or aliens—although, as she frankly acknowledges, a disproportionate number of Communist intellectuals were of Jewish background—but of radical scholars all too human. They were naive about the Soviet Union and the nature of the Communist Party in the United States, and they committed a number of blunders that may have helped in their own undoing. Most of all, they were preoccupied by fear of losing their jobs—not only because of income, but also because they dreaded having to work in a field where they could not pursue their scholarly and scientific interests. In the 1930s, this insecurity urged them to maintain secrecy, to disobey Party norms of behavior, and to refrain from classroom propaganda or even from close association with students—even though, ironically, they would later be purged in part because of their alleged devotion to subverting the young.

How well does Schrecker respond to those who now defend the behavior of the 1950s Cold War liberals? In my judgment, she is devastating in her claim that one could participate in the witch hunt—as did the liberal Cold Warriors of the Sidney Hook variety—even as one insisted that one was "standing up to McCarthyism and defending free speech and academic freedom"; the real test was in actions, not words.

She also demonstrates convincingly that the purpose of the witch hunt was not to ferret out unknown Communist agents who were abusing their academic positions, but to induce universities to enforce the general political climate needed to assure acquiescence in the Cold War. Her empirical data confirms the argument of Ralph Miliband and Marcel Liebman in *The Uses of Anti-Communism* that anticommunist ideology functions in the West as a means of discrediting all movements for social change by tainting them with the crimes of Stalinism.

Finally, she renders entirely explicable the deceitful behavior of the Communists and former Communists when they were under attack (even though another approach might arguably have worked, such as the forthright affirmation of the right to Marxist beliefs made by the Trotskyist James Kutcher). Based on what they had seen before, it seemed reasonable to them that, if they wanted to keep their jobs but not name names, they had no choice but to plead the Fifth Amendment or in some other way evade specific statements about their views and affiliations. Without the widespread prejudice against Communist political affiliation (a prejudice based as much on ignorance as on an authentic understanding of Stalinism), most professors would probably have acknowledged their past and present affiliations quite openly.

Where Schrecker is a bit weaker in answering the new defenders of the witch hunt is in regard to its ultimate justification; that is, if the Soviet Union had been, as the Cold War liberals saw it, a form of "Red Fascism" expanding throughout the world, and members or affiliates nothing less than brownshirts in academic garb, would an investigation and purge of academia still have been justified? Does "academic freedom" mean freedom to work to destroy the freedom of the majority?

Schrecker is unambiguous about her lack of sympathy for either the Communist Party or the Soviet Union, although the reasons are not entirely clear. Stalinism to her is objectionable as sectarian, authoritarian, and subservient to Moscow. Yet her book shows no real evidence of disgust at the real horror of the Stalin era—the millions imprisoned and murdered during the Purge Trials; the anti-Semitic persecutions; the repeated sacrifice of the lives of even the most loyal Communists for opportunistic reasons; the betrayal of revolutionary movements in Greece and elsewhere.

Of course, a study such as this one does not need to pillory the Soviet Union. But it does seem important to offer a perspective on the social, political, and moral nature of the regime that so deceived the Communists and fellow travelers. One might then argue that what befuddled many U.S. Communist professors was, in Miliband and Liebman's words, the "two-sided nature of Soviet-type regimes," in which advance and progress are accompanied by dictatorship and repression. They were thus blinded to the Soviet Union's totalitarian political order by their passionate support for what they believed to be its social and economic achievements.

C. P. Ups and Downs

Maurice Isserman. *Which Side Were You On? The American Communist Party During the Second World War* (Middletown, CT: Wesleyan University Press, 1982). 305 pp. $17.95.

Maurice Isserman's *Which Side Were You On?* is a careful reconsideration of the American Communist Party from its successful use of the Popular Front strategy in the mid- 1930s to its decline following Khruschev's revelations of the crimes of Stalin in 1956. Hardly an academic exercise, the book's clear and unpretentious style ought to appeal to a broad readership of radicals intent on the lessons to be learned from the generation of American Communists he examines.

The main facts about the party's changes during World War II are familiar. In 1939 the Hitler-Stalin pact exploded the American Communists' Popular Front alliance with liberals. For the next two years, until Hitler's invasion of the Soviet Union in June 1941, the party downplayed antifascism and demanded that the United States not intervene in the European war. Then, in a characteristic *volte-face*, it embarked on a patriotic campaign supporting U.S. intervention which involved endorsing the no-strike pledge and the internment of Japanese-Americans.

Finally, in an effort to assure America's rulers that Communists were completely loyal, party chairman Earl Browder announced in 1944 the abolition of the party itself; it was replaced by the Communist Political Association, an organization predicated on the idea of postwar harmony between classes. But only one year later, in April 1945, Moscow denounced Browder; following his subsequent expulsion, the party was reorganized under the leadership of William Z. Foster and adopted policies that eventually led to its isolation and disintegration.

The originality of Isserman's study is supported by new archival material and by interviews that provided him with details about changes and developments within the party and its affiliates. His work should be seen as part of an effort by younger historians—such as Paul Buhle, Roger Keeran, Mark Naison and Kenneth Waltzer—to challenge traditional histories of American Communism. Like Isserman, these historians are critical of the Fund for the Republic's project on "Communism and American Life," by Theodore Draper, David Shannon, Nathan Glazer, Clinton Rossiter and others, and of Irving Howe and Lewis Coser's *The American Communist Party: A Critical History*. Isserman is particularly distressed by the way these writers have depicted Communist Party members as "malleable objects" in the service of Soviet Foreign policy. In response, he and his contemporaries want to show that there were times when the party was "flexible, imaginative, principled, rooted in neighborhoods and workplaces, and enjoy[ed] popular support."

Isserman also disagrees with New Left historians such as James Green, Nelson Lichtenstein, Staughton Lynd and James Weinstein who have criticized the party for its role in housebreaking the American labor movement during World War II. As a consequence, a good part of his book is devoted to defending Browder's wartime policies. He argues that "'Browderism' held the potential for leading to something other than itself—sheltering and lending legitimacy to the efforts of those American Communists who had the capacity for and commitment to finding what would later be described as the 'American Road to Socialism'—even if in 1944 and 1945 taking any road to socialism was the last thing on Browder's mind."

A central achievement of *Which Side Were You On?* is that it manages to humanize the Communist movement and at the same time to be objective about the most controversial personalities and events of the period. Isserman is able to demonstrate that important differences of opinion existed within the party, and he shows how some members used the party for their own ends instead of being completely shaped by it. But nowhere does he offer evidence to challenge the basic analyses of those who emphasize the party's political dependence on Moscow. For example, he shows that in the late 1930s, Foster and Alexander Bittleman thought that a Hitler-Stalin pact was inevitable, while Browder believed it was impossible; that many party members were disconcerted by the pact and were relieved when it was ruptured; that the 1941 convention of the American Youth Congress refused to go along with the latest turn in Communist Policy; and that in 1942, Elizabeth Gurley Flynn objected to the Communists' attitude toward women workers. But none of these episodes alter the fact that, in the end, party members either followed the political line that was handed down from Moscow or, like Browder, suffered expulsion.

Since he is in a unique position to do so, it is a shame that Isserman does not do more to help us understand how and why so many fine people— people characterized even by Howe and Coser as some of "the best of their generation . . . the most intelligent, selfless and idealistic"—could have behaved in this manner. He does offer a partial explanation when he suggests that there were "social bonds" that kept party members in check. In describing how the party membership voted unanimously to support the Hitler-Stalin pact, he notes that "Communists were a . . . highly concentrated minority. They tended to live in the same neighborhoods, they spent most of their social life with other Communists, and their children played together. Breaking with the party over the pact would have meant accepting a status as a social pariah."

The notion of the party as a community or even an extended family provides us with a far more plausible explanation of the membership's repeated acquiescence to the Moscow line than does the conventional metaphor of Communist politics as religion. Had Isserman pursued this idea further, he would have made a much broader contribution to our understanding of the American Left, since the double-edged concept of "party loyalty," which can induce both self-sacrifice and servility, is a feature of so many left-wing organizations.

Instead, Isserman devotes the heart of his book to a defense of Browder's policies during the war. He calls the party's support of the no-strike pledge "a difficult but principled political stand," although he thinks Browder went too far in proposing that pay increases be dependent on productivity. And he tries to refute the criticism that Communists "abandoned" or "suspended entirely" the struggle for black equality during World War II, claiming that all the party did was limit "its struggle for black rights to those areas that it believed benefitted the war effort." But here, as in his response to the scholars who have stressed the party's subservience to Moscow, Isserman's arguments are too weak to be convincing.

To justify the Communist Party's labor policy he must accept the party's post-1941 depiction of World War II as a straightforward conflict between democracy and fascism. He ridicules the party's earlier position (1939–41) that it made no difference whether the fascist or democratic capitalist nations were victorious, but in doing so he avoids the more difficult questions raised by revisionist historians such as Gabriel Kolko, who maintains in *The Politics of War* that "the American economic war aim was to save capitalism at home and abroad," and Howard Zinn, who argues in *A People's History of the United States* that World War II was, after all, an imperialist war.

As for Isserman's defense of the party's policy on the struggle for black rights, he may be correct that the party never "abandoned" the struggle; however, he has ignored a number of instances where the party acted against the interests of blacks and Third World peoples. These included not only the party's opposition to the black community's "Double V" campaign ("Victory over discrimination at home" coupled with "Victory over the Axis abroad") and its denunciation of the 1943 Detroit race rebellion as Nazi inspired but also its support for slashing the budget of the Fair Employment Practices Commission and its refusal to campaign in defense of the black sharecropper Odell Waller, who was electrocuted for shooting his white landlord in self-defense. He has also forgotten the party's demand that colonies of the Allies cease their struggles for national independence so as not to disrupt the war efforts of their imperialist masters. In his discussion of Communist policy toward segregation in the armed forces, it is unfortunate that Isserman chooses to quote James Ford's ambiguous statement in the October 1941 *Communist* that the "main task" must be "the destruction of Hitler," rather than Browder's unequivocal dictum in the 4 March 1945, *Sunday Worker* that the party's "studied policy" had been (and would remain) "to refrain from public discussion" of the issue of Jim Crowism in the army.

Throughout *Which Side Were You On?* Isserman refuses to use a theory of Stalinism as a way of explaining the contradictions within the American Communist Party as it carried out the policies of its mentors in the Kremlin. To the contrary, the political conclusion of his book seems to be that if one excludes the Fosterites—whose heirs are said to control the party today—

one would find within the party's pre-1956 ranks democratic individuals with "a deep feeling of patriotism," who under Browder almost transformed the party into a truly "democratic socialist" movement. But such a view is at best problematic, especially since the Communist Party today is, in many instances, still carrying out the same Popular Front policies embraced by Browder and the generation that left in 1956. Furthermore, Isserman never explains what he means by the ambiguous term "democratic socialist."

What exactly are the political lessons that Isserman wants us to learn from his book? He holds that the generation that left the party in 1956 bequeathed to us the lessons that "the American left could not be built on foreign models; that civil liberties and democratic institutions should be at the center of any vision of the American socialist future; and that Marxists had as much to learn from other political traditions as they had to teach about American political realities." But how much new and useful wisdom is contained in these general statements? A wide range of people—from revolutionary Marxists who follow *New Left Review* to conservatives who read the *New Leader*—could agree with these sentiments, depending on how they are interpreted; and, of course, these same opinions were articulated by liberals and socialists long before the "generation of 1956" came of political age.

Regrettably, Isserman is presenting a set of old political propositions as if they were a new beginning for healing the current fragmentation of the American Left. One can only applaud his desire to find some basis for unity on the Left, but one wonders what sort of unity he actually advocates.

The impressive achievement of this book is qualified in many respects because Isserman's political horizons are circumscribed by the very limitations that hindered the party members he admires. In short, he identifies too closely with the political trajectory of the 1956 generation. Their understanding of Marxism was so affected by their bitter experiences with Stalinism that many of them did little more than return to the same social democratic ideas they had once rejected. It is to Isserman's credit that he is able to draw our attention to their story; it is testimony to the political confusion of the present day that he fails adequately to assess this political odyssey for what it really was.

A Radical Writer Rediscovered

Elinor Langer. *Josephine Herbst: The Story She Could Never Tell* (Boston: Little, Brown and Company, 1984). 374pp. $19.95.

Josephine Herbst (1892–1969), along with her friends John Dos Passos and Ernest Hemingway, was regarded in the 1930s as one of the outstanding novelists of the Depression era. By the beginning of the next decade she was already slipping into obscurity. When she died fifteen years ago at age seventy-seven, only those members of the younger generation who had read Walter Rideout's *The Radical Novel in the United States* (1956) and Daniel Aaron's *Writers on the Left* (1961) were able to recognize her name in the obituary columns.

Elinor Langer's biography, the first major attempt to rescue Herbst's reputation, also aspires to demonstrate the relevance of her tumultuous life to the experience of radical activists in the 1960s. The result is a pathbreaking study in which the author has consulted many original sources: manuscripts, correspondence (including an explosive body of material that Herbst marked "destroy" but nevertheless preserved), files obtained under the Freedom of Information Act, journalism and fiction, and extensive interviews with friends and acquaintances.

This makes it all the more regrettable that so much of the attention the book has received has been devoted to a nine-page chapter in which Langer conjectures about a distant connection between Herbst and the famous case in which the former State Department official Alger Hiss was accused of espionage by Whittaker Chambers.

During an interview with Ruth Herrmann (the second wife of Communist Party member John Herrmann, who had previously been married to Herbst), Langer was told that John Herrmann claimed to have introduced Chambers to Hiss in a Washington restaurant in 1934. Even though there is no substantiation of the recollection, several articles in the *New York Times*, as well as a number of early book reviews, have treated this alleged episode as if it provided significant evidence against Hiss's claims that he was the victim of a frame-up.

Such political exploitation of this book is even more disgraceful since Langer admits at one point the irrelevancy of this information to the actual case and even quotes Herbst as saying that Hiss was "innocent." Nevertheless, Langer bears some responsibility for this abuse of the book. Early in Chapter 26, she writes, "Reader: If your peace of mind is still dependent on a sacrosanct version of the Hiss case, this is not the chapter for you." When asked by the *New York Times* why she never bothered to check with Hiss the accuracy of Ruth Herrmann's account, Langer responded: "I'm not in the Hiss business . . . and it is a business, a veritable industry. I've seen many people disappear into it and never come out."

This lapse, however, should not blind one to the merits of *Josephine Herbst*. Langer directly confronts the more problematic aspects of Herbst's life. With a high degree of intimacy, yet in a frank and unembarrassing way, she discusses Herbst's sexual activity. From an unidealized but sympathetic perspective, she considers the personal and less glamorous side of

Communist political and literary activity in the thirties. With disappoint-
ment, but never censure, she probes Herbst's pathetic dependency on her
lovers, especially one man and two women, all much younger than herself.

Langer is enthusiastic about Herbst's now-forgotten literary achievement, although she provides insufficient analysis of the novels to permit a
firm judgment. However, readers will soon be able to sample Herbst's
fiction for themselves; this year, the Feminist Press is reissuing *Rope of
Gold*(1939), the final volume of her important trilogy about the decay of
capitalist society. (The other volumes of the trilogy are *Pity Is Not
Enough*[1933] and *The Executioner Waits*[1934]. In addition, Herbst's first
novel, *Nothing Is Sacred*[1928] has already been reprinted by Arno Press in a
series called "Rediscovered Fiction By American Women.")

Herbst's journalistic achievements are presented as almost equivalent to
her career as a novelist. As a correspondent for publications ranging from
the *New York Evening Post* to the *Nation* and *New Masses*, she was in Iowa
during the farm strike of 1932; Cuba for the 1934–35 general strike and
Batista's counterrevolution; Germany in 1935 to observe anti-Nazi resistance; Flint, Michigan, for the 1937 sit-down strike; and Spain later that
year where she witnessed the bombardment of Madrid.

Those who saw the film "Reds" may think of Herbst as a Louise Bryant
who actually "made it" as a writer, as well as a woman and a radical could at
that time. Like Bryant, she had her literary beginnings in the West and came
East in search of opportunities in Greenwich Village Bohemia. Born in
Sioux City, Iowa, in 1892, she immersed herself in literature at a young age
and attended four colleges, finally graduating from the University of
California at Berkeley at twenty-six. By then she had a small reputation in
San Francisco literary circles, but in 1919 she moved to New York City
where she associated with the *Masses* and *Liberator* writers such as Max
Eastman, Floyd Dell, and Michael Gold. Subsequently she joined the
expatriates in Western Europe and at age thirty-two married twenty-three-
year-old novelist Herrmann.

Like many other writers of their generation, Herbst and Herrmann were
radicalized by the onset of the Depression and made the transit from
Bohemianism to Communism. Rather unsuccessful in literature, Herrmann, a minor figure in the *transition* group, now found his true calling as a
Communist speaker, organizer, and underground agent working with New
Dealers in Washington, D.C. Langer is insistent that Herbst was never
more than a fellow-traveler, carefully guarding her independence from the
party. However, even after her marriage dissolved in 1935 and the 1939
Hitler-Stalin Pact, which caused her considerable distress, she only grew
disaffected from but never totally disloyal to the Communist movement.
Her radicalism stayed with her into old age when she was an enthusiastic

supporter of civil rights protests and student demonstrations in the 1960s.

As for her literary career, a combination of emotional turmoil and political harassment seems to have been responsible for its decline. Here Langer deftly uses the concept of the "graylist," a status in which opportunities for publication never completely dry up but become mysteriously meager.

Herbst's radical past came to national attention in 1942 when she was suddenly fired without explanation from the German desk of the Donovan committee (associated with the Office of War Information) in Washington, D.C. Langer's examination of government files on Herbst indicate the discharge was due to malicious lies by an old friend, novelist Katherine Anne Porter, who told FBI agents Herbst was a Communist spy.

The unique qualities of this biography are perhaps best expressed in a segment where Langer presents, side by side and on the same page, excerpts from Herbst's notes on the Cuban revolutionary struggle in the 1930s and passages from letters recording her sexual frustration and loneliness in her effort to be an independent woman. Through this kind of synthesis of the personal and political, Langer has written a book unlike any other about a radical writer of the 1930s.

To Live without Hypocrisy

Dorothy Doyle. *Journey through Jess: A Novel* (Inglewood, Calif.: Ten Star Press, 1989). 349 pp. $10(paperback). Order from P.O. Box 2325, Inglewood, Calif. 90305-0325.

During the past decade radical scholars have given increasing attention to a number of writers within the U.S. Communist literary tradition who might be called "The Premature Socialist-Feminists." This group includes women such as Tillie Olsen, Meridel Le Sueur, and Josephine Herbst. Others can be found in the 1987 Feminist Press anthology *Writing Red*, edited by Charlotte Nekola and Paula Rabinowitz.

What is distinctive about their fiction and poetry is that these Communist women writers promoted women's liberation from class-conscious and anti-racist perspectives in advance of official Communist Party theory and practice.

Dorothy Doyle's *Journey through Jess*, published thirty years after her Communist Party experiences, extends that tradition in remarkable new ways. Her novel dramatizes the transformation of a Party militant into a socialist-feminist against the background of the McCarthyite witch-hunt.

The central female character is Ada, married to a liberal Hollywood screenwriter gradually caving into the pressure to give anti-Communist testimony before a Congressional Committee. Against her initial impulses, and to some extent out of racial guilt, she is drawn into an affair with Jess, a new Black Party member with whom she is working in a civil rights coalition.

A monumentally defiant man, Jess is committed to working with the Party because it does fight racism, but he also insists on maintaining his own autonomy and Black identity. Hardly idealized, he personifies the contradictions of his situation.

On the one hand, his personal anger and his corrosive skepticism about whites provide powerful insights into the paternalism of certain aspects of Party practice. On the other hand, the depth of these same qualities disable him so that he cannot develop discipline in his political or personal life.

Although Ada gradually sees Jess's weaknesses, she progressively takes inspiration from his sense of self and his relentless exposés of the ways in which men are seeking to dominate and manipulate her, insights often gained through analogies he sees between racism and sexism. Finally, a feeling that one "can't separate . . . love and politics," as well as a desperate desire "to live without hypocrisy," lead her to disclose the affair to her husband and comrades.

To her dismay, the revelation only brings the latent racism and sexism among her white associates to the fore. Her husband strives successfully to receive full custody of the child. A number of her comrades virtually command her to dissolve the relationship, which they see as a "scandal" that will hurt the Party's image.

The book moves toward a climax in numerous interconnected ways. The Rosenbergs are facing execution on the East Coast, but the increasingly perverse Jess refuses to join a protest march on the grounds that Black people have been executed for centuries without comparable attention. At the same time, Ada debates whether or not to abort the child she has conceived with Jess. Finally, in powerfully closing scenes, Ada, whose only personal bonding is with Paul, a gay and religious Party sympathizer, takes dramatic actions in defense of her autonomy.

From one angle the book seems to end somewhat unsatisfactorily— utopian-style, with a pastoral retreat from city to a rural commune. But the steps Ada has taken before her flight guarantee that she will have to continue her battle for autonomy on other fronts. In effect, there is no closure; the struggle must continue.

Among the most striking and original features of this novel is that Doyle builds unabashedly upon first-hand experiences in the Communist movement of the late 1940s and early 1950s, writing in the language of the time. Unlike her predecessors, such as Olsen, Doyle finds Party life experiences themselves to be worthy material for dramatization.

Never before have we been offered such vivid depictions of Party meetings, mass organization meetings, branch discussions, branch trials, day-to-day activism, Party social life, and interpersonal relations among Party members. One feels the sexual dynamics of the interracial dances and hears the familiar tropes of political debate.

Another feature is that Doyle's story of a white middle-class Communist woman's interracial affair searingly centers the complex intersections of class, gender, and race with an explosive tension unmatched in any piece of writing of which I am aware. The naturalistic energy of the descriptive prose recalls Ann Petry's *The Street*. The verbalized domestic quarrels—both in Ada's disintegrating marriage to Dave and her anguished relation to Jess—surpass in pain even those in James T. Farrell's *This Man and This Woman*.

This is a book that is uncompromisingly anti-racist and class conscious in its roots and sensibility; it is a work defiantly posed against the hegemony of capitalism, and capitalism's racist and patriarchal culture. But within that context many voices are heard as Ada battles her society and her own psyche to gain control of her life.

Some of the most powerful of these contradictory voices are from within the Communist movement itself. On the one hand we are shown, from a rank-and-file perspective, the siege mentality of the secondary leaders at the branch level and of the membership as they continue to mobilize against racism and for working-class rights during the domestic Cold War, with its witch-hunt committees and Smith Act imprisonments. The dangers of a "vanguardist" mentality are exposed, but at the same time the roots and to some extent the necessity of that mentality are also presented.

In retrospective debates on Party policy, Doyle's book provides a good case for a left-wing political critique of the Party. This is especially in regard to its subordination of the domestic struggle to a blind loyalty to an idealized Soviet Union.

But characters in the novel also make plausible cases for the Party loyalists who in fact represent a diversity of perspectives. Moreover, their "on-the-line" situation makes more understandable their rationalizations and justifications of the commandism, monolithism, and simplistic analyses promoted by the leadership.

In my view, Doyle's perspective exemplifies the kind of critical consciousness we all need when examining our own political and personal lives so as to make sense of them for the next generation of militants.

In recent years, there has been a spate of scholarly books attempting to analyze the many contradictions of the U.S. Communist experience. However, with the exception of Vivian Gornick's *The Romance of American Communism* and a few autobiographies, none have remotely approached the core of the experience in the way that Doyle does in *Journey through Jess*.

In part, this is due to her passion to remember and learn from events that touched her life, in order to constructively advance the socialist movement from which she first drew inspiration. But it is also because she has developed a craft and artistry enabling her to refract the political through the personal in ways that many of us will long remember.

Marxism in the United States

Paul Buhle. *Marxism in the USA: From 1870 to the Present Day* (London: Verso, 1988). $12.95. 299 pp.

Paul Buhle's new book has several different titles and subtitles on it. If read according to the implications of that on the front cover, *Marxism in the USA: From 1870 to the Present Day*, one is likely to become confused and frustrated. This is by no means a straightforward introduction to the history of the influence of Marxist thought over the past one hundred and ten years. Indeed, most of my undergraduates who read the book for one of my courses could hardly comprehend it.

However, if read from the perspective of the subtitle that appears inside the book, *Remapping the History of the American Left*, one is confronted with a remarkable and provocative challenge to most previous ways of theorizing this experience. In short, the heart of the book is a series of seven essay-interventions into numerous facets of left-wing thought and activity.

The result is a work that stands as the most comprehensive and ambitious work of the school of "New Historians of American Communism," a heterogeneous group mostly influenced by the experience of the New Left of the 1960s. Their complaint is that earlier histories gave too much weight to official pronouncements, the role played by the Communist Party leadership, and Soviet domination of Party policy. Their project is to retell the "story" of U.S. Communism by emphasizing the role played by the rank-and-file who, as active agents, had an impact far richer, more diverse, and more substantial than previously recognized.

Marxism in the USA extends this methodology in many new ways. First, Buhle covers not only the Communist movement in its influential period but numerous left-wing movements before and after. Second, Buhle sets aside the traditional chronology and categories for organizing the study of the U.S. Left, which are usually around key dates (1914, 1919, 1929, 1939, etc.) or decades (the thirties, the fifties), or areas of primary influence (labor, Afro-Americans, intellectuals). Buhle's essays are thematic, shifting focus among alternative primary categories such as immigrants, culture, Leninism, and post-Leninism.

The third area of expansion is the manner in which Buhle tries to de-center the traditional constructs of "Marxists" that we have received. He achieves this not by excluding well-known figures but by reducing the focus on them and giving more attention to matters such as the work of non-English language publications and groups, the religious roots of indigenous radicalism, and issues of popular culture.

The fact that Buhle is a proud and unabashed veteran of the New Left, with its special focus on racism and, later, sexism, assists enormously in his ability to review this terrain with a fresh eye. However, as a heterodox follower of many of the ideas of the brilliant West Indian C. L. R. James (James receives four-and-a-half solid pages of analysis in the book; Earl Browder receives two paragraphs), Buhle tends to emphasize race more than gender, and, in this regard, restricts himself too much to Afro-Americans. In the thirties period, material is absent about the very important involvements of the Left with Chicano strikes on the West Coast and in the South West, and with Japanese-American struggles against deportation and Filipino union organizing on the West Coast. In the sixties period, material on people of color other than Afro-Americans, while present, is still sparse.

The most impressive feature of the book to me is the way in which Buhle tries to tell the story "whole." By putting Marxism and Communism in a larger setting, and by showing the diversity and interconnections of the Left experience, he effectively disintegrates the old mythology that Marxism and Communism were "foreign" parasites on an indigenous radicalism that really wasn't all that radical.

I am especially appreciative of this effort because I write as someone who spent fifteen years researching and publishing about the Left under the belief that, due to the horrors of the Stalin regime, the central tradition of the U.S. Left has to stand apart from the Communist Party. It was only in the early 1980s that I concluded that this couldn't be done because the Communist Party *was* central, and the other traditions too narrow to constitute an independent foundation. Buhle's ability to range back and forth among almost all of the Left currents, praising and criticizing as he sees fit, is a model for the integrated conception of the Left tradition on which we need to build.

Buhle also has a fantastic preface where he acknowledges his own membership in this tradition of diverse left-wing ancestors—even if, like members of a large and quarrelsome family, they have fought with and vilified each other brutally.

Nevertheless, as in the case of any fresh challenge to traditional methods, new answers to old problems bring about new questions. Frankly, while I fully support Buhle's expansion and enrichment of the terrain, I don't find a convincing overall methodology in the book. The weaknesses of the methodology is illustrated by Buhle's maxim that "Marxism is as Marxism does" (19). This is admirably non-sectarian, but who is to determine whether something is "Marxism" so as to decide whether or not to embrace its accomplishments? Sidney Hook claims to be a Marxist, but I fail to see his pro-Reaganism as a Marxist project.

Without straightforward criteria for judgments and evaluation, I frequently feel that Buhle has not employed a well-worked out strategy in the way he divides up his material (such as the decision to halt "Rise of the Culture Critique" in 1940, and to then move to a chapter called "Somewhere Beyond Leninism, 1940–50"), nor in his selection of figures and events on which to focus.

This results in some incoherence, imbalance, infelicitous cramming, and other problems that hurt the book a bit from the point of view of its use as a scholarly reference. Occasionally there are even factual inaccuracies, such as the statement that "left intellectuals Albert Maltz, Lillian Hellman, Clifford Odets, John Howard Lawson and Donald Ogden Stewart . . . could be counted among Popular Front sympathizers" (p. 179). All of these had a period of Party membership, some briefly and Lawson for his entire life; moreover, even when these were "out" or not public members, most remained ideologically Communist for some years. This false impression may not have occurred if the chapter had been organized more conventionally with sub-sections on "Communist Writers" and "Fellow-Traveling Writers."

Although Buhle has tremendous credentials as an "insider" in regard to the Left, he can sometimes be glib and make arcane references. For example, in his Conclusion Buhle refers knowingly to "Socialist Workers Party leaders who declare Trotskyism to be a theory of Latin American revolution (262)." But all documentation points to the opposite: the Socialist Workers Party leadership concluded in 1983 that Castroism, not Trotskyism, was the appropriate theory of Latin American Revolution, and repudiated in print Trotsky's argument for combining bourgeois–democratic and socialist demands.

Two other minor gripes: (1) The index is very superficial. (2) Too often Buhle does not give the name of the source of an opinion or quotation, which limits the reader's ability to evaluate.

Finally, one of the most intriguing aspects of this important book is that, while effectively repudiating mechanical Marxism, Buhle moves in the direction of a spiritualistic personal testament. In fact, at the outset he announces that the book "began as a reassessment of U.S. Marxism from the wealth of new historical evidence available," but ended as "an installment in collective autobiography"(4). This doesn't undermine the book's value, but it should underscore the fact that many of Buhle's choices about which events and individuals on which to focus are determined by very strong personal responses.

Moreover, while the emergence of Liberation Theology requires all of us to rethink our attitudes toward the politics of religion, the consequences for Buhle seem to be an attitude much too uncritical in his new evaluation of religious elements in the U.S. radical tradition. The apparent influence of Liberation Theology also results in a disturbing concluding paragraph where he identifies those of us in the Red Tradition as "God's own fools." By this he means that, while we have been made fools of by the unexpected ironies of history, we have also acquired "glimmers of wisdom" which, "along with an undying revolutionary faith, have allowed all types and generations of radicals to keep a light in the window" (274).

While I am a proponent of the notion that those on the Left must create a culture of humanity that binds us together and that preserves and advances our culture, our story, and our vision, in contrast to the culture, story, and vision of the forces of domination and exploitation, I simply draw back from the word "faith." It seems to me that repudiating "faith" of any kind is what a remapping of the Left is all about. What is required instead is the constant rethinking and reworking of data and ideas so as to approximate as closely as is possible what has happened in the past and what we may expect in the future.

"Faith" in anything—countries, leaders, even the international working class, if one does not have a foundation in scientific inquiry—gets in the way of the critical consciousness required for such an undertaking, just as does a chronic skepticism that will accept no working hypotheses. Of course, what makes left-wing scholarship so exciting today is the presence of diverse voices, such as the unusually impressive and distinctive one of Buhle's. But my own conclusion would be simply that it is in our own best collective self-interest to understand the forces shaping our lives and to continually project new strategies for human self-emancipation.

9

Down the Academic
Memory Hole

Cary Nelson. *Repression and Recovery: Modern American Poetry and the Politics of Cultural Memory, 1910–1945* (Madison: University of Wisconsin Press, 1989). 187 pp. text, 59 pp. illustrations, 90 pp. footnotes and bibliography.

When the history of twentieth-century U.S. poetry is finally written in response to authentic cultural achievement, rather than ideological constraints of institutionalized cultural elites, Cary Nelson's new challenge to the canonized version of Modern poetry is likely to be vindicated as a prophetic work. Indeed, even at present, *Repression and Recovery* ought to be heralded as a major sign-post, a courageous gesture toward the liberation of culture from the academy's class, gender, and race-bound orthodoxies of the past fifty years.

Despite its brevity, *Repression and Recovery* is a major reformulation of the aims and objectives of committed literary scholarship based on impressive new primary research combined with a complex and mostly-persuasive theoretical apparatus. While Nelson's aim is ostensibly to demolish the assumptions underlying the naturalized myth that the course of twentieth-century poetry was qualitatively transformed by a relatively small number of canonical Modernist texts, the implications of his research and theoretical acuity extend to virtually every area of literary-cultural practice. Indeed, the most cogent parts of his argument cohere around the theme that struggles over literary value and history are indissolubly linked to the broader effort to forge an equalitarian, non-racist, and non-sexist social order.

Less satisfying is the highly self-conscious, self-reflexive, post-Modernist literary form in which Nelson has chosen to cast his argument. One can only hope that this experimental approach will facilitate the process of communicating his multi-faceted argument as fully and richly as he would wish. However, such an idiosyncratic text, even if regarded mainly as a

126

compendium of suggestions and provocations, may not reach much beyond the small number of *cognoscenti* already converted to canon revision.

In my own view, the machinations of dominant cultural discourse, interlocked among numerous sites of cultural production—from the "common-sense" hegemony inculcated by family and peers, to the official proclamations and symbols of the state—require systematic, thorough, and rigorously-documented refutation. Moreover, such an effort can only be preparatory to a projection of alternative paradigms and models of cultural analysis to be demonstrated in depth and detail.

In contrast, Nelson, while equally aware of the intricate character of "the enemy," has chosen the long meditative essay as his mode of critique. Moreover, he de-centers particular arguments—of which there are a host of fascinating ones—in order to avoid a "master narrative." Yet this is an objective that he simultaneously acknowledges to be near impossible.

The result is two-hundred pages of eloquent text, without chapters or subheadings of any kind, characterized as a "prolegomenon to what I imagine to be a series of future projects" (xi). So far as I can tell, the argument of the book proceeds more by the logic of association within the author's own head than according to a plan systematically elaborated at the outset. Readers may well be divided as to whether the advantages of subverting a master narrative are as felicitous in practice as they sound in theory.

It is no surprise that *Repression and Recovery* is a work that can not be outlined, apparently by intent. Major and minor arguments are often indistinguishable. New themes, issues, and examples are sometimes introduced at unexpected moments. Well-developed claims are presented on the same level as highly speculative ones. Many of the pithy endnotes might as well appear in the body of the book. Even the center-stage status of Nelson's most frequently-discussed topic, the multifaceted suppression of left-wing poetic practice from cultural memory, is erratically undermined by many examples from and excursions into writings and writers outside the political Left.

Finally, in an unprecedented move with double-edged results, Nelson informs us that he intends to block this study from becoming part of the conventional discourse that regards all challenges to the canon as entries into a hierarchical competition of "great" texts and writers. This is accomplished by severely limiting the examples from and analysis of any particular poet, thereby minimizing our capacity and temptation to make such judgments. Unfortunately, there are ways in which this approach is ironically complicit with the drive of the dominant culture to depict all but the canonical master texts as ephemeral and insubstantial.

Nelson tells us that he designed his book to be read in a single day. The testimony of my personal experience confirms the reasonableness of this expectation; many left-wing cultural workers will fall quickly under the spell of the argument. Indeed, as someone who has been tilling the vine-yards of U.S. left-wing literary theory and practice for over two decades, I found myself thrilled by the "shock of recognition" in Nelson's ability to disentangle central from diversionary issues. I was also full of admiration for the way in which such a relative newcomer to the field gets so many complex things "right," and then extends the terrain of cultural inquiry into new and important areas.

At the same time, I had to continually fight a sense that the method of the book tends to diffuse the issues. I also feared that the non-organization (or *sub rosa* organization) of Nelson's book might allow me to project my own priorities inaccurately onto his work. And I wondered about which aspects of Nelson's rapid-fire sequence of contentions may or may not be "heard" by others not quite so intent upon listening as myself.

Although Nelson might disagree, I find the most compelling part of the book to be his general exposition of the damage wrought by the ideology of "literariness" in academic discourse. Never before have I encountered such powerful and convincing arguments on behalf of the centrality of the multifarious social dimensions of poetry. On the other hand, his theory of the ideological construction of literary Modernism largely on the basis of idealized Romantic assumptions is plausible but inadequately documented.

In trying to situate Nelson's achievement, it is important to remember that, while a considerable body of polemic already exists on the "canon debate," far too little represents theory derived from an extensive encounter with the excluded "others." Yet this is precisely the feature of Nelson's book that gives a power and incisiveness to his claims about what Modernist and New Critical valorizations of a small number of elite poetic texts have caused us to "lose" in U.S. literature. These losses include:

• A more complex view of the possibilities of literary tradition in the first half of the twentieth century. Here the Modernist myth tends to awkwardly bifurcate tradition between code-breaking and conventional forms, allied respectively with content that veers toward the avant-garde in the former case and varieties of gentility in the latter. Nelson demonstrates not only the hybrid character of much Left poetry, but later he observes that several key Modernist texts are themselves subject to "reversible" readings that refuse other variations of such strict dichotomies.

• A grasp of the centrality of the "mode of production" of literary texts, which Nelson demonstrates through a magnificent selection of book and magazine covers, and illustrations to various poems. These are combined with facts about circulation, collaboration, sales, historical context, and alterations in selection of texts for later publication. Many of Nelson's "readings" of visual materials are truly spectacular, changing forever my own appreciation of various poems and cultural projects.

• An understanding of the way in which literary value, and the literary history that collaborates in the production of that value, derive primarily from the psychological and cultural needs of our own time. Nelson bluntly raises fundamental questions that are generally ignored. He suggests, for example, that "English professors should be pressed to explain why . . . the poetry sung by striking coal miners in the 1920s is so much less important than the appearance of *The Waste Land* in *The Dial* in 1922" (p. 68).

Nevertheless there are certain aspects of Nelson's argument that in their present form appear far more tentative and less convincing. These include:

• An uncertainty of meaning in regard to Nelson's own notion of literary value. His stance is that the criteria that render texts "aesthetically compelling" are "always changing and always ideological" (p. 41), and he consecrates this book to recovering the social function of poems that "do vital cultural work" (p. 22) in our time as well as in the past. To me, the former stance is evasive and the latter remains an unexplained formulation that seems reducible mainly to the valorization of radical political content.

• His treatment of "cultural difference" among writers of color and of gender difference in women's and gay literature seems perfunctory. In particular, the discussion of the former lacks a broader view of writers of color—including, at least among the Left, the poetry of Carlos Bulosan and H. T. Tsiang—along with a consideration of the debates over "internal colonialism" and "the national question."

• The methodological foundation of the book, in which post-structuralism and Marxism are said to provide "corrective impulses" (p. xi) to each other, is attractive but potentially the seat of many ambiguities. One wants to know more about the larger context in which the "corrective impulses" are to be realized. After all, "impulses," no matter how "correct," are inadequate for sustained cultural critique. While Nelson's central categories of "discursive formation" and "articulation" are shown to be helpful theorizations of cultural mutations, the book bears an uncertain relation to the dubious "post-Marxism" (arguably a return to a pre-Marxism, based upon a caricature of classical Marxist texts) that has become the latest stage of theorists such as Ernesto Laclau and Chantal Mouffe.

Perhaps the most promising methodological feature of *Repression and Recovery* is Nelson's argument for an antagonistic tension between literary history and canonizing efforts. Nelson insists that an incestuous relation has hitherto existed, "one of unthought dependency, with each providing unreflected support and grounding for the other" (53). In contrast, he proposes that literary history focus upon "poetry of significant historical and cultural interest," regardless of the numerous claims and counter-claims of literary merit (p. 41). From this broad empirical base, it will then be possible to construct self-consciously relative and explicitly problematic models of literary value.

However, this proposition remains difficult to realize in light of the present relations of power among literary resources. Nelson informs us that many of the texts invoked in his essay are not even physically available to more than a handful of scholars, and many publications (not to mention individual poets) to which he refers have been allowed to entirely "disappear" from our cultural landscape.

At the present time, not a single journal, institute, foundation, newsletter, or network exists for perpetuating the memory—let alone exploring the cultural achievements—of the cultural Left of the first half of the 20th century. A movement that was central for decades in ways far greater and more various than can even be encompassed by Nelson's broad scope, this cultural Left was largely destroyed by the ideological and material onslaught of decades of virulent anti-communism—among the ugliest moments in U.S. culture, in which elements of liberalism and even radical anti-Stalinism were significantly complicit. The results have been so devastating that even the efforts of many of the post-1960s generation of scholars to reform the canon have largely ignored the Left tradition that anticipated so many contemporary concerns.

From this point of view, Nelson's agenda for future research might say far more about the need for cultural workers to debate and discuss in rather precise terms the relations between cultural memory and organized movements for social change. After all, a key lesson of Nelson's book is that partisans of cultural, economic, and political equalitarianism cannot count on the internal dynamics and networks of extant institutions to preserve even the most rudimentary material artifacts of oppositional culture. Therefore, Left cultural workers in such institutions fatally err in limiting their associations to "colleagues." Rather, they need to find new ways to forge activist relations with oppositional social forces, many of which have the objective need to produce counter-institutions of cultural memory of their own.

PART III
Race and Culture

10

The Culture of "Internal Colonialism": A Marxist Perspective

After reading the papers and panelists' remarks from the December 1980 Modern Language Association (MLA) program on "Ethnic Literature and Cultural Nationalism," I feel that I should devote my comments to explaining why it is important to sustain continuity in theoretical work between the highly creative era of the 1960s and our own more conservative time. While I am unhappy about criticizing co-workers who are toiling in this beleaguered area of scholarship—a still fragile discipline that deserves support especially because it remains suspect and unorthodox in the eyes of academia—I also believe that it would be a disservice to mute my conclusion that some of the contributions to the MLA panel represent a *de facto* throwback to modes of discourse that are too simple in light of our collective experience over the past twenty years. Frankly, some of the material in the MLA program fails to provide fresh, incisive analysis, and falls short of treating the cultural issues with the subtlety of thought that they deserve. Other contributions are designed to educate us about principles that are correct but already familiar.

However, on the positive side, I am impressed by the degree to which the more provocative and penetrating interpretations—found in parts of the contributions by Alurista, Martin, Ortiz, and Saldivar, but especially in Vivian Davis's "Selected Black American Literature: A Cultural Interpretation"—derive logically from the kinds of radical cultural analysis first worked out in the 1960s and, in some cases, more fully realized in the 1970s. Reading these particular materials reconfirms my sense that the most appropriate framework for analyzing the literary practice of Blacks, Chicanos, Native American Indians, Asian Americans, and Puerto Ricans remains a politico-cultural notion of "internal colonialism." In what follows I

133

will review this notion and explain why it takes my thinking in a different direction from the thinking of literary scholars who conflate the study of all cultural subgroups in the U.S. into the ambiguous category of "ethnic," "multi-ethnic," or "minority" studies. I will also offer examples of creative and critical practice that ought to be among the centerpieces of the counter-hegemonic cultural perspective we need to extend from the 1960s and 1970s into the 1980s.

1. IMMIGRANT AND COLONIZED MINORITIES

Who can deny that the 1960s was a decisive decade for our work? It was a period of tumult in which literature by and about racially-oppressed groups erupted on the scene in a manner somewhat analogous to the way in which literature about working-class, immigrant, and "bottom dog" life burst into the pages of American literature during the Great Depression. The thrust of much of the widespread politico-nationalist thought in the 1960s was to argue for the existence of a unique cultural achievement by Blacks and certain other groups whose incorporation into American society bore a greater resemblance to a colonization process than to an immigration process. Thus, Chicano culture was no longer viewed as an adaptation of Mexican culture to the Euro-American environment, but was said to be a unique blend—Chicano; Black American culture was defined by Black writers as neither African nor a "damaged" variety of Euro-American culture, but as something new and positive—Afro-American; and so on.

Unfortunately, the complexity of this argument is not adequately captured by William J. Harris in his MLA contribution called "*The Yardbird Reader* and the Multi-Ethnic Spirit." He begins his essay by stating that the 1960s and 1970s were dominated by forms of "black nationalism which assumed that race was the most significant factor in a black person's life. . . ." But, to document this claim, he quotes Amiri Baraka that "Black people are a race, a culture, a Nation . . .", a formulation that clearly tells us that discussions of race consciousness took place in a much broader context than is ever disclosed in Harris's critique. Although Harris sees the achievements of the 1960s as preparatory to a new and higher stage that he identifies with the "multi-ethnic spirit" of *Yardbird Reader* in the mid-1970s, I feel that the exigencies of his thesis cause him to caricature black nationalism by reducing a complex politico-cultural development to a sort of mirror image of white nationalism, which he then indicts for extolling one culture at the expense of another.

This approach to nationalism, in which he more or less equates black and white cultural nationalism, is quite the reverse of the Marxist understanding of nationalist movements. Lenin, of course, made the famous differentiation between the nationalism of an oppressed group (one that has been deprived of control of land, language, economy and culture) and the nationalism of an oppressor group (one that rules land, language, economy, and culture through force and hegemony). Most contemporary Marxists use this differentiation as the starting point for the evaluation of precise nationalist movements in terms of existing class forces and relationships in a particular society at a particular time.

In any event, I simply can't agree with Harris that the major thrust of the politico-cultural nationalist movements of the oppressed in the 1960s was one that was opposed to any kind of unity with other oppressed and non-dominant groups; the question was—and remains to this day—*how* and *on what basis* should this unity be achieved? While I'm sure that Harris and I have much in common in our values and objectives—and I feel that he performed a service at the MLA panel by drawing our attention to the noteworthy achievements of *The Yardbird Reader*—I do not feel that he in any way resolves the difficult issue of the relationship between immigrant and colonized minorities by writing as if, prior to the 1970s, the necessity for alliances and cultural diversity was unrecognized or even opposed by the rebellious politico-cultural movements of the day.

In fact, the single most influential theoretical work of the earlier period was Frantz Fanon's *The Wretched of the Earth* (English translation, 1966), which unambiguously argues that the re-establishment and valorization of the culture of the oppressed is only a preliminary step to the achievement of a truly international culture. In his conclusion to "Reciprocal Bases of National Culture and the Fight for Freedom," the most frequently discussed section of the book, Fanon affirms that the correct orientation toward promoting the nationalist consciousness of a colonized group

> is of necessity accompanied by the discovery and encouragement of universalizing values. Far from keeping aloof from other nations, therefore, it is national liberation which leads the nation to play its part on the stage of history. It is at the heart of national consciousness that international consciousness lives and grows. And this two-fold emerging is ultimately the only source of all culture. (*The Wretched of the Earth*, p. 199)

There is no doubt that in the ferment and heat of the 1960s many ambiguous and poorly thought-out—and even foolish—things were said and done. What we really need is a thorough book that scrupulously examines the decade in a way that distinguishes what was central from what was epiphenomenal, and which puts individualized spokespersons such as Karenga in a proper perspective. However, because Harris's contribution—and the passages he quotes from *The Yardbird Reader*—tend to emphasize the most limited aspects of the legacy of the 1960s, I will try to balance this by extracting those elements from the 1960s that I feel to be the most positive.

For example, part of the declaration of cultural independence that occurred in the 1960s on the part of racially-oppressed minorities involved a crucial polemic against liberal notions of assimilation and integration. Harold Cruse and others demonstrated that such notions could simply be euphemisms for advocating that racial minorities should have the "freedom" to acculturate to Euro-American values—a doomed effort that could only bring humiliation and failure for the masses of the oppressed. After all, one of the hallmarks of Euro-American culture is its deep-rooted racism, and a society based on such a culture—and which needs divisions among races for economic reasons—will never grant true equality to the majority of its darker-skinned members.

Another part of the politico-nationalist argument of the 1960s was that blacks and certain other groups had some features of an "internal colony" within the larger context of American capitalist society. There was never any agreement as to whether "internal colonialism" was primarily a metaphor, a description of real economic relations today, or a legacy of past experience that persists in spite of the major economic changes that have occurred in twentieth-century American capitalism. The main point—stated clearly by Robert Blauner in *Racial Oppression in America* (1972), and recently theorized in a more comprehensive fashion by Mario Barrera in *Race and Class in the Southwest* (1979)—is that colonized minorities differ from the European immigrant ethnic minorities in at least three respects: historically, the colonized minorities were incorporated into the nation by force and violence (for example, as slaves kidnapped from Africa or as the population of a territory that was invaded by outsiders); economically, the colonized minorities became special segments of the work force (for example, as chattel or migrant laborers); and culturally, the colonized minorities were subject to repression and misrepresentation on a scale surpassing the experience of any European ethnic immigrant group in the United States (for example, the extirpation of African languages and religions, and the banning of certain Native American Indian religions).

The point of the "internal colonialism" argument was never that colonized minorities suffered cultural discrimination while immigrant European ethnic groups did not. There is abundant evidence that even blond and blue-eyed Scandanavian-Americans have grown up with feelings of self-hatred and a belief that their own culture is inferior. Furthermore, there is substantial documentation showing that the cultural achievements of women and workers within these immigrant groups have also been unfairly disparaged. So the difference between the cultural discrimination suffered by immigrant minorities and colonized minorities must be understood partly in terms of the degree of intensity of the discrimination and partly in terms of the historical context in which the particular discriminatory act occurred. (For example, the denial of the legitimacy of bilingualism to the Chicano population is qualitatively different than it is to the Franco-American population, because the Chicanos are still inhabiting what is historically their own land.)

In reminding the reader of this "internal colonialism" analysis, my purpose is not at all to discourage comparative analyses of, for example, Afro-American and Jewish-American writing; it is to defy any simplistic and sentimental analogies between colonized groups and immigrant groups to the effect that "we are all hyphenated Americans," or "we are all minorities of one kind or another against whom there has been discrimination," etc. This is a pseudo-universalism that can serve to obscure important differences in cultural formation and in degrees of oppression. And here I must criticize the MLA forum for not being forceful enough in confronting and clarifying the differences in the cultural patterns of the immigrant and colonized groups—for one of the crucial tasks of the 1980s will most certainly be the necessity of having a theoretical framework for explaining why racial minorities still confront special forms of oppression in the United States. This point will have to be cogently defended against school administrators who are arguing that students must go "back to basics" (often a code term for the exclusive study of Euro-American culture from the Euro-American perspective) and against politicians who are advocating the old racist doctrine that "anyone who really wants to make it in our egalitarian society can do so," as they eliminate the minimal Federal assistance that has been given to oppressed groups under previous administrations.

Of course, I am completely in sympathy with Black, Chicano, and other scholars from racially-oppressed minorities who resent the depiction of their cultures as exotic or narrow; and I can understand why many artists from these groups feel they ought to be recognized as artists first and not immediately pigeon-holed as a special type of "minority" artist. But it must also be understood that, regardless of our personal yearnings to step beyond the hypocritical terms of Euro-America's prejudice and stereotyping, there can be no genuine cultural equality achieved in this society without a complementary struggle for social equality. The truth of the matter is that the facile conflation of colonized and immigrant groups into the same ambiguous category of "ethnic studies," in addition to being historically inaccurate, plays into the hands of those who, in this more conservative Reagan era, are dedicated to the abolition of affirmative action programs in regard to university hiring, the establishment and maintenance of special institutes, and the inclusion of the culture and history of racially-oppressed groups in the curriculum. We must not forget that the entire basis of the affirmative action argument is that certain groups have historically experienced *special* oppression and currently face *special* obstacles to equal treatment. I believe that in the 1980s, writers, scholars, and students working in the culture of "internal colonialism" will have to play a vanguard role in defending the need for such programs and for increasing available resources.

In order to carry out the counter-hegemonic task described above, it is necessary for us to rely on the best theoretical acquisitions and examples of cultural practice of the 1960s and 1970s. For example, in that time there was a considerable influence wielded by Third World activists in the colonial revolution. Some writers and critics found themselves spontaneously taking up Amilcar Cabral's call to "return to the source"—to revitalize and learn the hidden and distorted and almost erased cultures that the colonizers have tried to wipe out as part of their struggle to dominate colonies in the Third World as well as "internal colonies" in the United States.

What is important in Cabral's work, as well as in the work of Fanon and others, is that he gave expression to the thesis that, for a colonized people, the cultural struggle is inherently political; even an activity as basic as the accurate reconstruction of the history of an oppressed group can threaten the hegemony of the ruling class. Thus, in contrast to the experience of the American left during the 1930s, when politics and literature often existed in awkward and contradictory relationships, the 1960s and 1970s produced works of imaginative literature that are truly remarkable in their harmonious blending of cultural affirmation and undoctrinaire but politically-revolutionary concepts.

2. CREATIVE AND THEORETICAL PRACTICE

An extraordinary example of this phenomenon is Leslie Silko's *Ceremony*, a 1978 novel by a woman who grew up on the Laguna Pueblo Reservation in New Mexico. In my judgment, this book represents not only a genuine advance in the evolution of Native American Indian literature, but it is precisely the kind of work that those of us devoted to studying the culture of "internal colonialism" ought to point to as exemplary of what ought to inspire creative practice in the 1980s. The book has, of course, already been the subject of several essays that have emphasized its remarkable technical innovations and its cultural derivation from Native American oral tradition. Consequently, in the comments that follow, I will augment these earlier discussions by giving special emphasis to some of *Ceremony*'s political dimensions—some of which may be present by design, and others of which may have unconsciously worked their way into the text. My view is that Silko has in this area transcended all hitherto known thematic boundaries in Native American Indian fiction. This is done through the startling perspective she brings to bear on the way in which capitalism objectively unites people of color through its domestic violence and international wars.

Ceremony is the anatomy of the mental breakdown of Tayo, a World War II veteran from the Laguna Pueblo Reservation. Tayo's alleged psychosis is precipitated by a combat incident when he is ordered to execute some Japanese soldiers lined up in front of a cave with their hands over their heads. Tayo finds himself unable to shoot because he believes that he sees his uncle Josiah—the most beloved member of his family, the one who kept closest to the Pueblo traditions—in the middle of the Japanese prisoners. After the executions are carried out, Tayo collapses in uncontrollable crying and his condition is diagnosed as "battle fatigue."

When he returns to the United States, Tayo is treated in a Los Angeles mental hospital, but on the day of his release a second incident occurs. He faints in a train station and awakens to find himself surrounded by a Japanese-American family recently released from a relocation camp. Staring into the face of the youngest boy, Tayo hallucinates that he sees Rocky, his cousin who was killed in action in the Pacific. Tayo is then seized by an attack of nausea and imagines that he is trying to vomit the image of the boy's face out of his mind.

A third traumatic episode occurs when Tayo is back in New Mexico at a bar near the reservation. He is in the company of other Native American Indian veterans who are frustrated because they have lost the temporary sense of equality with whites that they had known in the service. They now pass their time bragging about military and sexual exploits. But when Emo, the most rabidly anti-Japanese of the group, displays a bag of teeth that he knocked out of the head of a dead enemy soldier, Tayo stabs him with a broken beer bottle.

Eventually Tayo learns that his sense of sympathy and identification with the Japanese is not the result of psychotic hallucinations but the consequence of a higher order of perception. He tells Betonie, a heterodox medicine man, about his vision of Uncle Josiah among the Japanese prisoners, and Betonie answers: "It isn't surprising you saw him with them. . . . Thirty thousand years ago they were not strangers" (*Ceremony*, p. 130).

After this reminder that most Native American Indian tribes are descended from Asian clans that crossed the Bering Straits during the Pleistocene Ice Age, Tayo progresses to a deeper understanding of the ways in which American capitalism devalues the lives of people of color in its inherent drive to expand and dominate. In a climactic scene, when Tayo is trying to escape from Emo and other veterans who are threatened by his "crazy" ideas, Tayo hides in a uranium mine. In this setting he recalls the fact that Trinity Site, where the first atom bomb was exploded, is only three hundred miles to the southeast of his reservation, at White Plains.

After a moment of reflection, Tayo comes to the realization that there is a tragic connection between the slaughter of Native American Indians for their land and the holocaust at Hiroshima: "The top-secret laboratories where the bomb had been created were deep in the Jemez Mountains, on land the Government took from the Cochiti Pueblo" (*Ceremony*, p. 257). Tayo concludes that "He was not crazy; he had never been crazy. He had only seen and heard the world as it always was: no boundaries, only transitions through all distances and time" (*Ceremony*, p. 258). He understands that the victims of Hiroshima and his own people are united by the white man's system in a "circle of death" (*Ceremony*, p. 258).

One of the more popular misconceptions about Native American Indian literature is that it is a variant of romanticism, advocating an impossible return to an idealized, pre-technological existence. Although the cultural values underlying Silko's critique of capitalism are complex and perhaps contradictory, one of the most prominent threads of her narrative seems to offer a refutation of this sort of characterization.

This thread can be traced by starting with the title of the book, *Ceremony*, which refers to the curative treatment that Tayo experiences under the tutelage of Betonie. While Betonie is a character partly intended as an answer to the white psychiatrists who had tried to "cure" Tayo by convincing him that he must adjust to the sick society, Betonie is also counterposed to a traditional medicine man, Ku'oosh. This is not only because of Betonie's eccentricities (his medicinal paraphernalia includes telephone books collected from all parts of the country), but also because he is an innovator who teaches that new ceremonies must be developed to respond to the contemporary situation.

Betonie believes that the source of evil in the world is neither white people nor their brutal, inhuman machines. He argues that the whites themselves are victims of a value-system that transforms a vital natural world into "objects" (142). As an antidote to this socially-induced perceptual distortion that recalls Marx's discussion of commodity fetishism in volume one of *Capital*, Betonie advocates ceremonies that will restore a sense of collectivity among all people and a harmonious existence in nature. But such ceremonies cannot be acted out by a medicine man alone, because, as Betonie says, "the people must do it" (*Ceremony*, p. 132).

Throughout *Ceremony* it is the individualism of the whites—especially as expressed in Christian theology with its emphasis on individual suffering and individual salvation—that is the focus of attack. Silko sharply distinguishes between "ritual," in which the false lessons of history are simply re-enacted, and "ceremony," a praxis-like activity in which a consciously controlled creative act restores humanity to its correct relation to the world.

Ceremony is a first novel and not without certain flaws and limitations.

Silko may have to some degree sacrificed the psychological realism of some of her characters to the daring aesthetic achievements of her fresh, dramatic language and her provocative flashbacks, juxtapositions, and transitions. A few of her characters may seem to be contrived to exhibit different modes of assimilation to or resistance against the dominant culture. Sometimes they are one-dimensional—either replete with self-hatred or else mystically sensual and bound to nature.

Nevertheless, I find Silko unequalled in the way she has used craft and imagination to provide a longer range perspective for the kinds of sentiments expressed by rebellious youth of the 1960s and 1970s. I sense that she is trying to transfer the political themes of anti-imperialism and Third World solidarity characteristic of the Vietnam era back to the less-questioned World War II era, in order to suggest that similar mechanisms of racism and economic exploitation are involved in *all* wars waged by the United States. In summary, *Ceremony* is the culmination of what was best in the politico-cultural rebellion of the 1960s and 1970s. On the one hand, it offers profound testimony to the creative resources of the Native American Indian cultural tradition. On the other hand, Silko's political intuition and insight surpass other writers who fail to see that American imperialism's crimes against people of color are not simply aberrations that can be reformed out of existence, but that they inhere in the character of the social structure itself.

If *Ceremony* is the novel that represents the best traditions of creative practice in the last twenty years, Raymond Williams' *Marxism and Literature* (1977) is the theoretical work that I feel can most effectively guide our critical work in the 1980s. This book presents the British Marxist's theoretical conclusions flowing from a half-dozen earlier books of literary and cultural analysis that he has published. It is not intended as an introduction to Marxism or Marxist literary theory, but, rather, as a critique of past critical practice (of both Marxist and non-Marxist critics) and an argument for the development of a new approach that Williams calls "cultural materialism," and which he identifies as "a theory of the specifities of material culture and literary production within historical materialism" (*Marxism and Literature*, p. 5).

To me, the most compelling section of the book is his argument that virtually all of our received Euro-American literary categories—not only literary traditions, genres, and conventions, but also the very notions of "aesthetics" and "imaginative literature"—serve hegemonic functions in the sense of inculcating us with attitudes toward cultural phenomena that serve the interest of the status quo. Like all seminal works of Marxism, Williams' book is primarily a creative synthesis of insights that many others have produced in their studies of class-biased, patriarchal, and chauvinist cultures of advanced industrial societies. As such, *Marxism and Literature* joins *Ceremony* in re-arming the cultural left for the coming decade of struggle against the ideologies of ethnocentrism and racism that continue to deform our national life and the role of the United States in international politics.

11

Hegemony and Literary Tradition in America

INTRODUCTION

The issue of hegemony and literary tradition in the United States is one that urgently requires extensive and highly detailed investigation. In order to provide a precise focus and to allow room for the analysis of several texts, I shall confine myself in this essay to only one aspect of the larger issue: the treatment of racial minorities in college literary anthologies.

My contention is that what we refer to as our "literary tradition" or "canon" of major works, as codified in literary histories of the United States and in classroom texts and anthologies, is neither a scientifically determined nor an arbitrary phenomenon. Regardless of the subjective intentions and rationalizations of the literary historians and anthologists themselves, the dominant tradition objectively serves dominant class interests and thus contributes to the maintenance of a class society.

This means that the United States literary "tradition" is actually a *selective* tradition that ratifies certain works as important and excludes others, not according to any measurable standard of quality but in response to the national self-consciousness as registered among, and interpreted by, privileged social layers, within the limitations of a certain world view at different historical junctures. This analysis of the underlying function of tradition does not mean that theories of aesthetic quality are irrelevant to its making, or that market considerations are beside the point, or that the canonizers and anthologists are without autonomy. But it does suggest that these and many other mediating factors in the process of canon-formation are subordinate to deep-rooted cultural prejudices and prevailing social trends.

Here one might adapt a famous statement by Karl Marx: "Literary scholars and anthologists make their own literary canon, but they do not make it just as they please; they do not make it under circumstances chosen by themselves, but under circumstances directly encountered, given, and transmitted from the past." A cogent elaboration of this theoretical perspective is offered by Raymond Williams in his book *Marxism and Literature*:

> From a whole possible area of past and present, certain meanings and practices are selected for emphasis and certain other meanings and practices are neglected or excluded. Yet, within a particular hegemony, and as one of its decisive processes, this selection is presented and usually passed off as "the tradition," "the significant past." What has then to be said about any tradition is that it is in this sense an aspect of contemporary social and cultural organization, in the interest of the dominance of a specific class. It is a version of the past which is intended to connect with and ratify the present. What it offers in practice is a sense of predisposed continuity.[1]

Thus it seems fair to conclude that literary tradition is largely an ideology; that is, an expression of what Marx called "definite forms of social consciousness," expressing the interests of groups and classes. As an ideology, literary tradition serves, among other things, to organize, monitor, and transform power in society.[2] This is why, according to the accompanying table of United States literature anthologies used in undergraduate and graduate courses during the past decades [Table 1], there were few works by women and Blacks in the standard texts until those particular sectors of the population revolted anew in the 1960s and 1970s. Then, retrospectively, certain writers and books (although far too few) became partially integrated into the canon. The belated inclusion of Kate Chopin and Charles W. Chestnutt in many of these anthologies is an example of the revision of the canon under social pressure.

Moreover, the preface to the 1979 edition of *The Norton Anthology of American Literature* reports that the editors decided to make the changes that appear in the new version, including the addition of more female and Black writers, after polling seventeen hundred teachers.[3] In other words, these seventeen hundred teachers suddenly voted the culture of women and Afro-America into existence, as far as this canon-making textbook is concerned. What will it take before these same teachers or their counterparts decide to vote Chicano, Native American Indian, Puerto Rican, Asian American, gay, working-class, and other nondominant cultures into existence as well?

A further point I wish to argue in this polemic, and to demonstrate by example, is that cultural hegemony—that is, in Antonio Gramsci's conception, rule by consent, with which the ideology of literary tradition is ultimately bound up—operates so subtly that even the *terms* in which we learn to evaluate culture are biased in favor of Euro-American patriarchal culture, in which Shakespeare is the paradigm for great literature while oral and folk cultures are often regarded as inferior.[4]

AMERICAN CULTURE

The mechanism of bourgeois hegemony is very visibly at work is the conventional notions of "American literature" or "American Culture" that most of us in the United States have received. To begin with, it is my view that to talk as if there exists in the United States a single, only moderately differentiated, clearly identifiable literature or culture is a dangerously misleading oversimplification that can disarm us. And the reason it disarms us is that it tends to misrepresent the entire history of the formation of the United States as a modern nation.

This one-sided history is dispensed in the "Introductions" to many of the anthologies listed on the accompanying table, as well as in standard literary histories such as *The Literature of the United States* by Marcus Cunliffe, who writes: "America is, of course, an extension of Europe in Europe's expansionist phase. It has been peopled mainly by Europeans. The 'involuntary immigrants'—Negro slaves—from Africa are an exception, and their presence has modified American society. . . . Culturally speaking, America might be called a European colony."[5] More popularized versions of this history from the point of view of the victors is dispensed in television shows, movies, comic books, and patriotic ceremonies on national holidays, in which there is usually a great deal of talk about "our Pilgrim forefathers," "the winning of the West," and, of course, George Washington as "the father of our country."

Unfortunately, such symbols of national history hardly explain the reality of North American historical and cultural development. It is true, of course, that *one aspect* of the historical formation of our nation involves European expansionism, Puritan pilgrims, settlers moving westward, and the leading role of a wealthy slaveholder named George Washington in fighting the British and serving as president.

But this history has only to do with the trans-Atlantic immigrants to the North American continent; that is, it has only to do with the history of those Europeans who crossed the ocean to improve their life circumstances. Some of these immigrants were explorers serving in the name of their kings and queens; others were mercantile capitalists trying to get rich; others were victims of religious persecution in Europe; and still others were masses of poor people from Italy, Ireland, Jewish shtetls in Eastern Europe, and elsewhere, driven from their homelands by poverty or intolerance and looking for work in the "New World."

Of course, a good deal of the cultural legacy of this last group—the poor immigrant masses—has been neglected, obscured, or distorted. That is, we are much more likely to read and know about the diaries of British explorers such as Captain John Smith or the political documents of a famous

TABLE 1   American Literature Anthologies Currently in Use[a]

TITLE OF TEXT	TOTAL NO. OF CONTRIBUTORS	WHITE FEMALES	BLACK MALES	BLACK FEMALES	AMERICAN INDIANS	CHICANOS	PUERTO RICANS	ASIAN AMERICANS
Major Writers of America (Harcourt, Brace & World, 1962)	28	1	0	0	0	0	0	0
American Literature (Washington Square, 1966), 3 vols., 18th & 19th centuries only	108	7	0	0	0	0	0	0
American Poetry and Prose (Houghton Mifflin, 1970), 5th edition	102	8	9	2	0	0	0	0
Anthology of American Literature (Macmillan, 1974), 2 vols.	124	10	7	2	0	0	0	0
Literature of America (Wiley, 1978)	127	17	23	3	19[b]	0	0	0

The Norton Anthology of American Literature (1979), 2 vols.	131	25	12	2	0	0	0
Major American Short Stories (Oxford, 1980)	34	8	2	0	0	0	0
American Literary Survey (Viking, 1980), 3rd expanded edition	119	15	10	2	0	0	0
Magill Surveys in American Literature (Salem, 1980), 4 vols.	147	28	9	2	0	0	0
The American Tradition in Literature (Random House, 1981)	164	28	8	1	14[c]	0	0

[a] These statistics have not been double-checked and may contain some errors.
[b] All the contributions are anonymous except for one by N. Scott Momaday and four speeches.
[c] All the contributions are anonymous.

slaveholder named Thomas Jefferson than we are to study the letters, memoirs, poems, and songs of the impoverished working people who came here from various parts of Europe, especially in the great waves around the turn of the century. Much of this material has not even been preserved, let alone published in classroom texts.

Nevertheless, keeping these qualifications in mind, I think we can still say that it is mainly the culture of males from European immigrant groups that is taught in United States educational institutions as supposedly representing all of "American Culture." What the cultures of these groups have in common—and what makes them seem to cohere as a unified entity—is that they are all based upon the Judeo-Christian tradition (expressed in the Bible, which contains a group of myths about which just about everyone in the United States is taught) and they are all derived from literature of the European tradition that goes from Homer and the Greek dramatists, through Dante and Shakespeare, and then up to the novel, which became, after the rise of capitalism, *the* generalized literary form throughout all of Europe.

Thus, a selected patriarchal Euro-American literature and culture, based upon and adapted from parts of the immigrant population of Europe, is commonly mistaken for what is known as "American" culture; hence, what is purported to be "our" canon is centered around Cooper, Hawthorne, Melville, James, and so on, with a sequence of literary themes centered around Puritanism, Independence, Westward Expansion, the Gilded Age, Expatriatism, and so on. But this is only part of the story, for there is an entirely different sector of the population living on the section of the North American continent that falls within the borders of the United States, for whom the notion of racist slaveholders, such as Washington and Jefferson, as the founders and fathers of "their" country and "their" culture is not only absurd—it is probably insulting and repugnant.

I am referring here, first of all but not exclusively, to those groups who might be called the "colonized minorities," as a means of contrasting them to the immigrant minorities. These colonized minorities are Blacks, who were kidnapped from various parts of western Africa to be used as slaves throughout our hemisphere; there colonized minorities are members of several hundred very diverse tribes of Native American peoples whose ancestors were here at least thirty thousand years before the Europeans invaded the continent; these colonized minorities are Chicanos, who were literally invaded and conquered by the colonizers in 1848, when the United States expanded its borders to take in the northern part of Mexico, which became Texas, California, Arizona, Colorado, and other Southwestern states. And these colonized minorities might include several other groups, such as Puerto Ricans and Asian Americans, whose incorporation into

American society bears a much greater resemblance to colonialism than it does to immigration.

It is crucial to recognize that for each of the colonized cultures excluded from the Euro-American canon and tradition, there are alternative traditions—traditions that are wholly apart from, or else engaged in a complicated interaction with, the dominant tradition. The point is that the ideology of the Euro-American literary tradition does not operate merely to shut out the specific literary achievements of the colonized minorities and other groups; it is that these groups have diverse and internally complex cultural traditions of their own that are suppressed or not understood. We must recognize that the very terms with which we have been trained to discuss and evaluate Euro-American literature—Romanticism, Frontier Epic, Alienation, National Consciousness—are inadequate or must be radically redefined for the nondominant cultures.

NONDOMINANT CULTURES

This general proposition can be made concrete by contrasting two examples of writing. The first is an excerpt from T. S. Eliot's 1922 *The Waste Land*:

> Unreal City,
> Under the brown fog of a winter dawn,
> A crowd flowed over London Bridge, so many,
> I had not thought death had undone so many.
> Sighs, short and infrequent, were exhaled,
> And each man fixed his eyes before his feet.
> Flowed up the hill and down King William Street,
> To where Saint Mary Woolnoth kept the hours
> With a dead sound on the final stroke of nine.
> There I saw one I knew, and stopped him, crying: "Stetson!
> "You who were with me in the ships at Mylae!
> "That corpse you planted last year in your garden,
> "Has it begun to sprout? Will it bloom this year?
> "Or has the sudden frost disturbed its bed?
> "O keep the Dog far hence, that's friend to men,
> "Or with his nails he'll dig it up again!
> "You! hypocrite lecteur!—mon semblable,—mon frere!"[6]

This is a segment of what is possibly the most important and influential poem in the English language. I am using it to demonstrate, perhaps with an extreme example, just how dependent "American literature" can be on what is really a distinctive Euro-American culture. As we can see, even the location or setting of the poem is Europe—as evidenced by the references to

London Bridge and the Church of St. Mary Woolnoth. Moreover, all the literary allusions in the poem come from European predecessor poets. The phrase "Unreal City" is borrowed from the French poet Charles Baudelaire, while the line "death had undone so many" and the passage about people flowing "with eyes fixed before their feet" are borrowed from Dante's *Inferno*, to suggest that life is comparable to a living hell.

The poem depends also on a knowledge of London geography and the Europeans' Christian Bible when it says that St. Mary Woolnoth "makes a dead sound on the final stroke of nine." St. Mary Woolnoth overlooks the financial district of the city, so it can reasonably be assumed that the crowds depicted in this poem are largely made up of bankers, businessmen, and stockbrokers. Moreover, there is a special significance in the hour that the church clock strikes because, as the Gospel of Matthew records, Christ died on the cross at the ninth hour. So there is an association here between the financial district clock's striking nine to announce the new working day and the murder of Christ and whatever values for which Christ stood. In other words, when the business day starts, authentic Christianity dies.

I won't go on with other examples; the point is that most of the social, historical, and cultural substance of this portion of the poem is *Euro-American*. The difficulty of the poem is caused not only by its being an intellectual poem that requires a wide range of knowledge before the reader can fully appreciate its complexity; the difficulty is also that this intellectual content is almost exclusively European-derived. One has to know something about European haberdashery to see the significance of naming a man "Stetson" (which is a special kind of hat); one has to know something about the Roman naval victory over the Carthaginians at Mylae to understand the reference to the battle in the poem; and one would have to know the work of other European writers—not only Baudelaire and Dante but also the playwright John Webster—to appreciate the other literary allusions at work. Finally, one would have to know French in order to interpret the last line.

Now let's examine a second poem, "Plainview: 2," by N. Scott Momaday:

> I saw an old Indian
> at Saddle Mountain.
> He drank and dreamed of drinking
> and a blue-black horse.
>
> Remember my horse running.
> Remember my horse.
> Remember my horse running.
> Remember my horse.

Remember my horse wheeling.
Remember my horse.
Remember my horse wheeling.
Remember my horse.

Remember my horse blowing.
Remember my horse.
Remember my horse blowing.
Remember my horse.

Remember my horse standing.
Remember my horse.
Remember my horse standing.
Remember my horse.

Remember my horse hurting.
Remember my horse.
Remember my horse hurting.
Remember my horse.

Remember my horse falling.
Remember my horse.
Remember my horse falling.
Remember my horse.

Remember my horse dying.
Remember my horse.
Remember my horse dying.
Remember my horse.

A horse is one thing.
An Indian another.
An old horse is old,
An old Indian is sad.

I saw an old Indian at Saddle Mountain.
He drank and dreamed of drinking
And a blue-black horse.

Remember my horse running.
Remember my horse.
Remember my horse wheeling.
Remember my horse.
Remember my horse blowing.
Remember my horse.
Remember my horse falling.

Remember my horse.
Remember my horse dying.
Remember my horse.

Remember my blue-black horse.
Remember my blue-black horse.
Remember my horse.
Remember my horse.
Remember.
Remember.

"Plainview: 2" by N. Scott Momaday, 1965[7]

The central contrast between the Momaday poem and the Eliot poem ought to be clear at once. It is as if they came from two different cultures, even though both can claim to be poems by Americans. But Momaday's poem has no direct allusions to the Christian Bible, no citations from European history, no references to famous metropolises, no quotations from famous writers—and all of the other stuff out of which the dominant Euro-American element United States culture is comprised. Yet this second poem is in a sense more truly "American" than the first; not only because of the author's Native American Indian ancestry, but also because the setting of and characters in this poem could only be North American. But, ironically, I think that many students and teachers of American literature—trained by our ethnocentric educational system—would have some difficulty coming to grips with Momaday's poem, even though it is written in the English language and even though the events depicted are in certain respects more comprehensible (though not necessarily "simpler") than those in the excerpt from *The Waste Land*.

The problem for such readers would be, I think, that the aesthetic experience is remarkably different. To begin with, Eliot's poem is intellectual and meant to be read carefully and studied for multiple layers of association, denotation, and connotation piled up on each line. But the Momaday poem is really some sort of chant; it is, at least in terms of the tradition from which it derives, some sort of oral poem. A chant, of course, is meant to be sung to a rhythm provided by drums in the background. While Momaday himself is a contemporary writer, a professor of English whose work is not wholly free of Euro-American and possibly other non-Native American Indian influences, we must still recognize the centrality of the chant to this piece.

The primary feature of the chant is, of course, repetition. The whole poem is, in fact, a variation of the first stanza, with the extended and repeated description of the horse's death. In the ninth stanza we do have the hint of some sort of philosophic meaning—"A horse is one thing./ An Indian another; /An old horse is old, /An old Indian is sad." But the meaning here is relatively clear, or at least it is not enigmatic, so that one must recognize that the aesthetic dimensions of the poem will have to come from an appreciation of things other than its potential for generating Eliot-like allusions and literary puzzles.

Probably, if this chant were read effectively or chanted to rhythm or music properly, the repetition would lead to an intensification of the important themes of the poem, which have to do with the role of the horse in Native American Indian culture, the significance of Saddle Mountain, the significance of the aged person as the link to a fading culture, the tragedy of living through memory, and so on.[8]

The point is that this poem grows out of a different life experience than the segment of Eliot's poem. It is not derived from the Western cultural tradition that dominates Euro-American literature, and it therefore represents one of the kinds of literature still largely excluded from the canon. Only on rare occasions have I seen a survey course in "American Literature" that included the literature of the first Americans; most purported "surveys" start in the seventeenth century with the writings of the European invaders.

My interest then is not really in reforming the canon nor even in advocating a mere pluralistic expansion of it; my objective is more akin to an overhaul or abolition. Naturally, after the ground is cleared and the cultural complexity of our continent revealed in all its diversity and complexity, anthologies will have to be assembled and histories written. But this time, among other things, "aesthetic merit"—if such a term survives—will have to be derived, not from any illusory universal qualities (which are often only masks for select themes that ratify the dominant culture), but from the cultural context of each nondominant grouping itself.

However, constructing the theoretical apparatus for such work is still far off. In 1979 Howard Zinn published *A People's History of the United States* describing the formation of our nation "from the bottom up": from the viewpoint and life experience not exclusively of the businessmen, generals, and politicians who reaped the benefits, but also from the perspective of the women and men, immigrant and indentured as well as kidnapped, conquered, and colonized, who forged the history and culture of the continent with their own labor. Our first step is to write something analogous in United States literature.

Notes

1. Raymond Williams, *Marxism and Literature* (Oxford: Oxford University Press, 1977), 115–16.
2. Terry Eagleton, *Marxism and Literary Criticism* (Berkeley: University of California Press, 1975), 6. For a useful study of ideology and hegemony see Göran Therborn, *The Ideology of Power and the Power of Ideology* (London: New Left Books, 1980).
3. Ronald Gottesman et al., *The Norton Anthology of American Literature*, 2 vols. (New York: Norton, 1979), 1: xxiii.
4. The definition of hegemony used in this essay is the basic one, as can be found in Walter L. Adamson's *Hegemony and Revolution* (Berkeley: University of California Press, 1980), 170–71. However, the concept can be developed in more subtle and complex ways than I have had an opportunity to explore in this short piece.
5. Marcus Cunliffe, *The Literature of the United States*, 3d ed. (Great Britain: Penguin, 1968), 14–15.
6. T. S. Eliot, *The Waste Land and Other Poems* (New York: Harvest, 1962), 31–32.
7. N. Scott Momaday, *Angle of Geese and Other Poems* (Boston: Godine, 1974), 6–8.
8. For a number of insights into "Plainview: 2," I am grateful to Roger Dickinson-Brown, "The Art and Importance of N. Scott Momaday," *Southern Review* 14, no. 1 (Winter 1978): 30–45.

12

Racism and Academe: Issues in the University of Michigan Struggle

The following essay is based on a talk given at the April 1988 Socialist Scholars Conference in New York City under the title, "Anti-Racist Movements and the Responsibility of Socialist Scholars"

INTRODUCTION

For the past fourteen months, the University of Michigan, like many other university campuses across the country, has been the scene of militant mass marches, sit-ins, and explosive confrontations ignited by explicit acts of racism. Almost every day, the student-run *Michigan Daily* and the city's *Ann Arbor News* print articles, editorials, letters, and guest viewpoints decrying racism on the campus. On weekends, they sometimes publish entire supplements devoted to the subject.

Every week, the *University Record* appears, funded by a very frightened university administration that knows that it cannot directly oppose an anti-racist movement in a liberal community such as Ann Arbor and in a state with a large Black population such as Michigan. Almost always, the *University Record* will contain sophisticated propaganda pieces about alleged achievements in the recruitment of students and faculty of color.

Moreover, the *University Record* more and more frequently displays photographs of darker-skinned university guests—temporary visitors, of course—who have suddenly been invited to give lectures and to receive awards. It also publishes long apologias by the administration in which various deans and executive officers vie with each other in claiming that *they themselves* are the ones in the vanguard of the movement for what they call campus "diversity"—which is their euphemism for what the students have been calling "anti-racism."

The administration's efforts to neutralize the movement have been to little avail. Every week there continue to be rallies, teach-ins, forums,

155

debates, and leaflets by anti-racist organizations. In these events and publications, the claims of the liberal administrators are disputed and some of the
administrators' statements endorsing "diversity" are themselves characterized as "racist."

Virtually every meeting of the Regents of the university for the past year
has been the scene of a confrontation; several of these have ended with the
president of the university and the other officers grabbing their briefcases to
flee from the room in the face of relentless chanting by their critics—the
composition of which is primarily Black students.

On Martin Luther King Day, 18 February, tension was so great that
adherents and opponents of an anti-racist boycott of classes nearly came to
blows at the main entrances of buildings on central campus.

What, then, is the political responsibility of socialist scholars in light of
this new anti-racist movement on the campuses? This is an issue that needs
to be addressed rather precisely, although it is also one that obviously has
broader implications, and the campus struggle is hardly separable from the
struggles in the larger society.

1. A TWO-FOLD CHALLENGE

In my view, the development of this movement at the University of
Michigan, and a number of similar ones, presents a two-fold challenge to
socialist scholars who today, as Russell Jacoby reminds us in *The Last
Intellectuals* (1986), are largely socialist *faculty members.*

First, since such faculty members are often veterans of anti-racist, anti-
war, and feminist struggles of the 1960s radicalization, we have much to
offer the current movements. But this can only happen if we develop a
political strategy to overcome the disorienting and debilitating "culture of
professionalism" that saps the energy and the will to resist of many professors, preventing us from galvanizing our resources into militant action.

If we can do this, what socialist faculty can provide as activists in the
movement are political and cultural analyses of the social functions of the
university and of racism, and assistance in constructing a corresponding
program of action that is very much needed in the present situation.

This socialist analysis to which I refer, is derived from the view that the
primary function of the university is to dispense the culture of the society of
which it is a creation; that is, the university inculcates students with the
society's vision (or, within certain perimeters, visions) of history, literature,
art, philosophy, science, etc., in order to produce educated workers who
will allow the system to function under the current relations of power
and domination.

Thus, it is "no accident," as we doctrinaire Marxists are always pontificating, that the university claims to be objective and neutral, but actually promotes the prevailing socio-cultural prejudices in complex and sometimes devious ways.

This socialist analysis is also based on the view that U.S. racism, whatever its origins in the ancient world, is an ideology that evolved as an instrument of domination in the colonial era. Today, it continues to play a dynamic role in national and international politics, effectively preserving and extending the power of those who have held it historically.

Thus, socialist faculty must stand on the perspective that no program to eliminate racist practices at a university or anywhere else can avoid a confrontation with the material roots of domination sustained by racism. In fact, not only racism but also sexism, anti-Semitism, homophobia, and other forms of prejudice that can be found at every university are closely linked to the same phenomena in the larger society.

Hence, there is simply no reason to fundamentally revise the view many of us promoted in the 1960s. The university is *not* neutral, but comprised of a population that will have to make crucial decisions as to whether its purpose is to ratify, or maybe "critically support," the opprobrious values of the larger society, or to challenge those values and join with those seeking to change the structures of domination reinforced by those values.

In summary, the responsibility of socialist faculty is to help the anti-racist movement develop a political strategy that progressively drains the institutions of domination of their authority while simultaneously creating forms to assist the empowerment of those who have been the targets of domination.

There is, however, a second aspect of the challenge to socialist faculty that is equally important. Since socialist faculty are in a relatively privileged position, mostly white males, and usually not the initiators or the leaders of the current anti-racist efforts, we must proceed with some humility. We must recognize at the outset that we have at least as much to learn from the new activists, especially the students of color, as they have to learn from us. Most importantly, we must understand that one cannot rest on past laurels but must earn the honor of constructively criticizing and abetting this new movement through activist participation.

In my view, the University of Michigan anti-racist movement presents a provocative case study of how this two-fold challenge has been met by some left-wing faculty, with about an equal balance between success and failure. The assessments and proposals contained in this essay may be of special help to anti-racist activists on campuses similar to the University of Michigan, such as the University of Massachusetts at Amherst; the University of Wisconsin at Madison; and the University of California at Berkeley. (Socialist faculty at the so-called "non-elite" schools may be faced with substantially different issues.)

The Michigan movement is also intriguing to study for two other reasons.

First, the Michigan movement involves a confrontation with a sophisticated liberal administration very willing to make cosmetic concessions, and rather adept at countering student demands with its own ideological offensive. This offensive, referred to in the above remarks about the *University Record*, offers a clever alternative vocabulary to describe and effectively obscure the central political issues.

The administration's ideological offensive also promotes an alternative history of the struggle in which the administration is depicted in its public statements as having formulated *ex nihilo* a "six-point initiative" for a "diversity agenda," rather than admitting what really happened: which is that the administration only reacted in embarrassment to a virtual campus uprising that attracted the attention of the national media with its twelve (now thirteen) anti-racist "demands."

So, for those interested in studying how an elite group attempts to establish a hegemony—domination by consent to common assumptions— the functioning of the University of Michigan administration is a marvelously rich source.

The other reason for special interest is that Michigan is also an example of where a group of faculty, particularly those who established the organization "Concerned Faculty," was inspired and re-educated by an alliance with radical students, particularly those in the United Coalition Against Racism (UCAR).

This alliance has worked to the extent that it has because the faculty members were not motivated by guilt, compassion, a sense of noble mission, or even a sneering, self-righteous arrogance about the "incompetence" or venality of the administration—an attitude that exists among many faculty members for a variety of reasons, but does not necessarily lead to support of real changes.

Instead, these Left faculty understood from the outset that they themselves, as faculty, also benefit from such an alliance and from participation in the anti-racist struggle. Their view has been that, despite the expected imperfections of any such undertaking, the student movement has been basically accurate in its analysis and understanding. The perspective promoted by Concerned Faculty has been that faculty participation in the anti-racist struggle, a struggle to uproot the inequalities that obscure our understanding and warp our culture, improves the quality of our lives as scholars and people.

The issues with which Concerned Faculty has grappled, revealing strengths and weaknesses as well as providing some lessons from which to learn, have involved the need to respond directly to white supremacist actions; the need to develop a plausible yet radical critique of university administration policy; the need for a fresh and searching critique of the academic disciplines as themselves purveyors of racist assumptions; the need to intervene in debates over administration terminology; and the need to build an alliance with the grass-roots anti-racist movement.

2. RESPONSE TO WHITE SUPREMACIST ACTIONS

The explicitly racist acts, against which there have been outcries at the University of Michigan, include the following: the episodic distribution of unsigned leaflets—sometimes slipped under the door and other times posted—that present standard racist insults about Blacks and threaten violence; the destruction of shanties built by the Free South Africa Co-ordinating Committee to symbolize the oppression of Blacks in South Africa; a physical assault on a Black female student by white females accusing the Black student of hiding a "tail" under her skirt and demanding to see it; the harassment of a female Black union activist by the writing of racist and sexist obscenities on the mirrors of the rest-room she was assigned to clean, and plugging the toilets there with paper and excrement.

In most of these incidents that involve an explicitly racist atrocity of a white supremacist character, it was students of color and their allies who first raised a militant outcry along with a demand for action. However, after a moment of shock, pretty much everyone, from the liberal University of Michigan administration to the leading left-wing student group, UCAR, was in agreement that white supremacist actions, whether of physical violence or mere propagandistic nature, could not be tolerated on the campus.

As long as there is that first public outcry, most university administrations can be fairly easily persuaded to issue *pro forma* denunciations of racism and affirmations of pluralism.

One problem that came up, however, is that some administrators are delighted to go even farther and to seize upon the situation to find ways to strengthen their powers to punish and expel *more* than just students caught engaged in such racist actions. At Michigan, for example, administrators were soon attempting to extend their powers so as to be able to punish students for *any* form of what the administrators consider to be inappropriate behavior.

They did this by rushing to enforce a "code of conduct" for students, with which the administration had been unsuccessfully fooling around for some years. This is especially ominous in light of recent militant protests against CIA recruitment on campus, not to mention the blockading and takeovers of buildings by anti-racist activists.

The Left was divided at first, with some people insisting that no paralegal powers of punishment should be established, especially ones that used academic sanctions for non-academic misbehavior. Others felt that threatened and harrassed people of color, as well as women, should have some recourse for action other than the court system, where it is rather difficult to pursue complaints of racism and sexism on the campus.

In the end, most of the Left, including Concerned Faculty, opposed the "Code" and counter-posed, instead, the notion of sanctions solely against perpetrators of white supremacist and sexist actions, specifically excluding from punishment activists in anti-racist, anti-CIA recruitment and similar demonstrations. Most importantly, UCAR, Concerned Faculty, and others on the Left proposed to formulate controls that place the power to select incidents for investigation and to pass punitive judgment in the hands of the broader campus population, and fought the administration's efforts to exempt faculty and administrators from sanctions, insisting that those with the *most* power should be the *most* accountable.

Another aspect of the problems inherent in the struggle for an effective response to violence against and harrassment of people of color, is that, given the strength of the propaganda apparatus at a university like Michigan, and the past experience with the student Left that some administrators have had, there is always the danger that a disorientation might set in following a period of vigorous denunciations of racism and affirmations of pluralism by the administration.

If the anti-racist activists limit themselves to the issue of overt action only, and do not seize the opportunity to draw links between these symptoms and underlying causes, the result could be the establishment of a hegemony—that is, the locking of the administration and the anti-racist movement within a common set of assumptions about fighting racism through sanctions against students and by making pronouncements of virtue. The result would be a paralysis of the movement, which is the only force that can be relied upon for anti-racist vigilance. Leadership on the issue would be handed over to the administration, which has shown itself to be completely untrustworthy. But this commonality of perspective is unlikely to last very long, for two reasons.

First, it will not last because the objective situation in our society is such that one university cannot significantly cure the sickness of racism, especially by *pro forma* proclamations. The large liberal university cannot *be what it is* and admit substantially larger numbers of people of color or hire significantly larger numbers of faculty of color, or even start teaching in a substantial way the liberal arts, and social and physical sciences from a perspective that is not patriarchal, class-bound, or Euro-centric. Racism is endemic to the social structure that the university serves, legitimatizes, and reproduces.

Thus it happens that, once a sector of the student population becomes seriously concerned about the issue of race, even starting with the simple but important reaction to white supremacist threats, there is good reason to believe that it will become increasingly conscious of racism's broader and more subtle manifestations, and that the students will be dissatisfied with the superficiality of administration propaganda campaigns.

Here it may be worth mentioning something about the question of the "sincerity" or "lack of sincerity" of a liberal administration such as that at the University of Michigan. In my view, one must avoid limiting the political issues to personal attacks, which I suspect that the administration would prefer to a deeper critique of university practices. The problem is that, whatever the degree of personal racism or insensitivity of any particular administrator, a liberal administration is nevertheless sincerely anxious to quell the students as well as Afro-Americans and other people of color in the community and nationally who have become incensed. Also, most liberals genuinely would like to end explicit racism on the campus and are embarrassed by the degree to which people of color are absent from non-menial positions at the university. The problem is that they would like to do this without altering the fundamental structures of power that racism serves.

But the perspective of ending racism in an authentic manner while maintaining the present relations of power, institutional forms, and criteria for the judgment of academic achievement is a fantasy. Thus, the administration can only move forward in any anti-racist activity under the prodding of militant mass pressure from the bottom up, and, in any given situation, they use language and formulae for "solutions" that can be ambiguously interpreted and then gutted entirely of significance once the atmosphere has cooled.

Second, this hegemony will not last because there exists on many campuses a politically-conscious segment of the student population that has had political experience—off the campus, in other political struggles, through the inspiration of relatives and friends who were 1960s activists, or, in the case of older students, because they themselves were 1960s activists.

And here it must be emphasized that one of the most valuable aspects of the current campus radicalization is that the break between the 1960s and the 1980s is not nearly as complete as it was between the 1960s and the 1930s. Many present struggles are largely extensions of the 1960s New Left, not the beginnings of totally fresh movements that are hostile to their predecessors. Moreover, the politicized element on the campus is often already quite experienced, trained, and capable of seizing every possible opportunity to foment an ever-deepening understanding on the part of anti-racist activists of the profound, indeed almost overwhelming, racist nature of the culture and institutional structure of the university.

3. Developing a Critique of the Administration

In fact, at Michigan, the second area around which the anti-racist activists attempted to raise consciousness, following the response to white supremacist propaganda and violence, reaffirms this connection between the 1960s and 1980s. This second area was the development of a critique of University of Michigan administration policy that showed how that policy represents a direct line of continuity with the earlier administration policy and practice created in response to the issue of racism and ethnocentrism following the Black Action Movement (BAM) strike back in 1970.

This earlier struggle also caused a crisis in the university and resulted in the negotiation of a series of anti-racist demands. Yet the eighteen years in between have showed no lasting improvement in enrollment and faculty-level hiring of people of color; at present, Afro-American enrollment has actually *decreased* from 7.2% to 5%. The administration, of course, never bothered to offer a satisfactory explanation or self-criticism of this record of failure.

In retrospect, we could see that the approach of the University of Michigan administration in 1970 was to make concessions in order to quiet the campus uprising, after which it more or less dropped the matter. Thus Concerned Faculty felt it was on solid ground in making the charge that the administration was and is not driven by its own commitment and analysis to make the requisite fundamental changes. We could find no evidence that the administration in 1987–88 had formulated an approach that addressed the issue more effectively than its earlier policies did.

Another aspect of our unfolding critique of the university has concerned statements issued by the University of Michigan administration, insisting that the University of Michigan curriculum and faculty are already of superior "quality," and that our task in promoting "diversity" is to find "minority" faculty and "minority" students who measure up to this "quality."

Concerned Faculty responded that this approach places the onus on people of color for failing to be of adequate "quality" in significant numbers. Moreover, the perspective is erroneous and one that serves to perpetuate ideas and assumptions facilitating racial and ethnocentric domination. It promotes attitudes that even led to the now infamous statement of the Dean of the College that, "Our challenge is not to change this University into another kind of institution where minorities would naturally flock in much greater numbers. I need not remind you that there are such institutions—including Wayne State and Howard University. Our challenge is not to emulate them, but to make what is the essential quality of the University of Michigan available to more minorities."

In contrast to the view of this Dean, who believes that the university must not emulate whatever qualities cause minorities to "flock" to an institution, Concerned Faculty argued that the university must learn many things from institutions such as Wayne and Howard in order to offer programs and support systems that will dramatically increase the participation of people of color at every level at the University of Michigan.

A third axis of the ideological debate that the activists undertook was that the University of Michigan administration was not facing the issue of racism squarely. The administration's initial gambit was to reduce racism mainly to an attitudinal problem. Rather, UCAR and Concerned Faculty described racism as a complex of institutionalized assumptions that sustain economic, political, cultural, and social domination in complex ways. Therefore, we charged that it was not sufficient to call for a punitive code enabling extra-legal action against those students caught perpetrating explicit acts of bigotry. Nor did we feel was it sufficient to educate administrators, faculty, and students on the need for "diversity" through sensitivity training sessions, another early response. Instead, we sought ways to address the means by which racism is institutionalized in the everyday affairs of the university.

Of course, Concerned Faculty was not at all opposed to educational action, but we argued that racism cannot be understood without hearing the true stories of those against whom racism has been perpetrated—the rich, complex, and diverse stories of the histories and cultures of Blacks, Chicanos, Native American Indians, Chinese-Americans, Japanese-Americans, and others. In our view, UCAR effectively addressed this need through proposing orientation classes and required classes on racism, and, of course, through the demands for a dramatic increase in faculty of color, who can serve as role models and train a new generation of scholars in these areas. One of Concerned Faculty's major projects became the development of a course on racism in collaboration with UCAR and with members of a more liberal organization of faculty called Faculty Against Institutional Racism (FAIR).

But our thinking was also that these "stories" constitute such a large quantity of hitherto neglected and misunderstood material that even a required course is not enough—that the "stories" can ultimately be told only through a profound cultural transformation in the life of the university. This is something that will require a major re-allocation of resources. Disciplines must be rethought through and reorganized so that the role of people of color in the *making* of history, art, music, politics, literature, economics, and society itself is recognized as central, not an afterthought, and that appropriate methods for study—as well as trained scholars in these fields—are available. It is only in this context that a massive program for the recruitment and retention of students of color will have more than mere temporary consequences.

4. CRITIQUE OF THE ACADEMIC DISCIPLINES

But when it comes to the issue of recruitment of scholars of color, one runs into the problem of the administration saying, "Yes, we will hire scholars of color—as long as such scholars are 'excellent' so that we do not sacrifice 'quality.'" Such a statement appeals to liberals who, of course, would not like to have scholars of color stigmatized from the outset as "inferior" in quality, and who are opposed to any sort of "double standard" in hiring according to race. Nevertheless, to accede to such a formulation is once more to agree to assumptions that will only assist in undermining any serious program to transform the university.

The problem is that, culturally, universities are organized around models of "excellence" and "quality" in the humanities, social sciences, and physical sciences that are derived from European culture—more precisely, an elite European patriarchal culture. These models are usually presented as universal, providing the terms in which non-European cultures must be evaluated and thus be judged as inadequate or non-existent . . . if they are even seen!

In the field of literature, it is clear that the major categories of analysis (romance, realism, naturalism, modernism) are derived from the European experience; that the major categories for periodization in the study of U.S. literature (colonial period, revolutionary period, the winning of the West, etc.) derive from a Euro-American perspective; and that the notions of aesthetic value, to the extent that they are seriously theorized, stem from an historical body of criticism derived from the celebration of Shakespeare, the Greek dramatists, Dante, Tolstoy, etc.

Moreover, the University of Michigan English Department institutionalizes this selective patriarchal European indoctrination at the very center of the undergraduate major through a series of three "Great Books" courses and other requirements. Nowhere along the line is anyone given access to the history, culture, folklore, or even the terminology that might assist one in gaining a perspective on literature of the oral tradition or anything other than this selective patriarchal European-derived body of writing. As a result, non-European and women's literature have been forced to fit into the interstices of this program.

It was the view of Concerned Faculty that, without making this kind of profound challenge to the very nature of what is considered "excellent," an anti-racist movement can easily be disoriented. This is because, as long as the underlying models for who is "qualified" to teach and who is qualified to "learn" are not challenged, administrators can feel free to campaign as aggressively as they wish for either "color-blind" admissions and hiring, or even "affirmative action," knowing in advance that nothing much will change—especially as long as there are no time-tables for goals or quotas.

In sum, Concerned Faculty took the position that to agree to a notion of a "small pool" of qualified faculty or students of color was to participate in consent to assumptions that paralyzed the movement. It was more effective to challenge the desiderata of "excellence and diversity," which the administration never clearly defined.

5. TERMINOLOGY

Concerned Faculty also found in our analysis and debates that it was necessary for us to go on the offensive in regard to gaining precise information about what really had happened and was happening in affirmative action. Both the administration and the local press continually made confusing references to "Blacks" and "minorities" on the campus. One university publication announced the appointment of a new "vice provost for *minority* affairs," whose job was to "increase the number of *Black* students and faculty." Other statements would also switch back and forth among the terms, suggesting at times that Black and minority were synonymous, or else that, whatever other groups might exist on the campus, the issue was still mainly a Black one.

We also found that in reporting figures of Blacks and other groups, neither the administration nor the press ever explained what exactly constituted the categories used by the university administration to measure its racial composition. Did "Black" mean Afro-American (roughly 11% of the U.S. population), which is what most people assumed? Or was "Black" actually a category (as we suspected it was) that includes a much larger group—such as the entire African continent as well as those from other parts of the Black diaspora in the Western Hemisphere? Similar questions needed to be raised regarding the categories of "Asians" and "Hispanics," although we found this to be a delicate manner since there are sensitive debates going on in regard to the appropriateness of certain kinds of terminology.

Nevertheless, we feared that there were certain consequences that would inevitably result from the university administration's tendency to be vague about the composition of "minority" groups.

First, the number of people contained in a particular category is easily inflated when the category is amorphously defined. Second, such vague categories obscure the real issue at stake, which is not just skin pigmentation and language group, but also respect for cultural difference at the university. A specialist in Puerto Rican culture cannot be automatically expected to address the needs of Chicanos, even if both are classified as "Hispanic." Scholars from the continent of Africa are crucial, but their presence does not necessarily mean that the broad field of Afro-American studies will be covered with the requisite expertise.

6. ALLIANCE WITH THE GRASS-ROOTS ANTI-RACIST MOVEMENT

Finally, Concerned Faculty also tried to make it a point of principle that we were unequivocally on the side of the student activists, especially UCAR, and had no interest at all in counterposing ourselves as a more "reasonable" substitute who would mediate the issue in place of the "unruly" ones.

In fact, we stated our view many times that, of all the forces on the campus, it is clear that UCAR has earned the moral authority for raising the issue of racism and demanding concrete action. In particular, we observed that, from the onset, UCAR had correctly chosen not to rely on the University of Michigan administration, with its record of failure, to resolve the issue. Instead, UCAR called upon the population of the entire campus to mobilize and take steps to resolve the issue democratically, at the grass-roots level. Specifically, UCAR focused on concrete goals and called for decision-making bodies outside the domination of the University of Michigan administration.

Concerned Faculty also observed that UCAR had the virtue of recognizing that the issue of racism goes far beyond acts of overt bigotry—although these are crucial to oppose—and that the targets of racism are not just Afro-Americans but all people of color. Also, we thought it important that UCAR aggressively sought to ally with other sections of the community, and that UCAR has been clear in its opposition to sexism, anti-Semitism, and class prejudice. Finally, Concerned Faculty was enthusiastic that UCAR understood and promoted an understanding of the international dimensions of racist domination, which are crucially connected to domestic racism.

7. CONCLUSION

Any evaluation of the University of Michigan experience must acknowledge that Concerned Faculty had mainly propagandistic successes. The group has yet to succeed in breaking the "culture of professionalism"—in making participation in mass protest, arm-in-arm with students in outright defiance of the administration, an acceptable mode of behavior. The activist core never got beyond a dozen, with perhaps fifteen to thirty attending semi-monthly meetings, and perhaps another fifty to sixty known sympathizers of varying degrees. This is out of a faculty of nearly 3,000.

Consequently, Concerned Faculty has not yet been able to carry out many crucial tasks, such as serious research into the reality of affirmative action at the University, which would enable precise challenges to the administration's precise claims. It has not yet built an apparatus to monitor current administration efforts in a systematic way, nor has it even begun to analyze the financial realities of the university in terms of who is getting what kind of money for which projects.

With a small number of people, one's forte seems to be dramatic issues more than the nitty-gritty, tedious work; but at some point such work will have to be undertaken to back up Concerned Faculty's charges. Rhetoric is good for a starting point, but, as the struggle continues, effective alternative models must be proposed. And these must be ones that respond to real needs, while also facilitating the ongoing movement for even more pro-found changes.

Still, because Concerned Faculty spent time developing a relatively clear analysis of the causes and appropriate response to racism, the organization could respond more quickly and audaciously than any other group of faculty. This ability to move rapidly and act in solidarity with UCAR should not be underemphasized.

In fact, it may seem to some that the University of Michigan has been magically "blessed" with a cadre of articulate anti-racist spokespersons, a plethora of "perfect" issues by which to expose the nature of the university system, and an abundance of student activists boiling over with energy to continue the struggle day in and day out. Such an interpretation might suggest that socialist scholars at other universities are virtually paralyzed until similar "objective conditions" emerge on their campuses.

In truth, the events at the University of Michigan have not been so unique. They have unfolded in a familiar, almost classic pattern, and it has been largely the quality of the "subjective factor"—especially the strategy promoted by the UCAR activists—that has taken the movement as far as it has gone. The ability of Concerned Faculty to defend and bolster that "subjective factor" has been its modest but most crucial contribution to date.

13

Theorizing Cultural Difference: A Critique of the "Ethnicity School"

THE CRUCIBLE OF SOCIAL FERMENT

Moments of intense political, social, and cultural ferment sometimes give rise to liberating new paradigms for discussing and assessing literary practice. During and after those moments, the terrain of what constitutes "literature," and the related matter of what constitutes appropriate critical tools, become nothing less than battlegrounds that bear complex relations to conflicts elsewhere in the society. Moreover, contestations of *critical* practice also involve the promotion and reflection of *creative* practice—in fiction, poetry, drama, and in new and hybrid forms. While these creative practices most often ratify the associated critical tenets, they may outdistance those tenets as well.

One such fertile moment, the Great Depression of the 1930s, helped to overthrow previously dominant critical tendencies such as the New Humanism; it also helped to drive forward at least two paradigms that in turn have shaped our perception of cultural practice in the U.S. ever since. The first of these, the Marxist socio-cultural approach, extended in theoretical and creative writing the terrain of literature to that of the workplace; immigrant life (especially Jewish, Irish, and Italian); plebeian and poor rural existence; issues of gender and of gender and race;[1] and, in some exceptional moments—as in the work of Robert Hayden, Langston Hughes, and Richard Wright—to folk and Afro-American culture. The other approach was that of the formalist school, later known as the New Critics, which responded to the social crisis by redoubling efforts to promote a cultural theory favoring elite Modernist poetry's structural dynamism and technical features.[2]

I point to this example from the 1930s to call attention to the burden of this essay, which is to make a sharp distinction between two alternative tendencies in critical methodology that came into being thirty years later at

168

another "moment" of historico-cultural crisis. For it was under the impact of the socio-cultural crisis of the 1960s and 1970s that the "Ethnicity School," on the one hand, and what I call the "proponents of class, gender and race methodology," on the other, emerged with their own new paradigms and claims.

Today, the ethnicity school can boast at least three very recent, substantial books of coherent cultural analysis (within its own categories), all published by Oxford University Press. These are Werner Sollers' *Beyond Ethnicity: Consent and Descent in American Culture* (1986), Mary V. Dearborn's *Pocahantas's Daughters: Gender and Ethnicity in American Culture* (1986), and William Boelhower's *Through a Glass Darkly: Ethnic Semiosis in American Literature* (1987).

In contrast, the class, gender, and race approach is expressed by a much looser grouping with many internal disagreements. As a result it does not yet possess the same degree of coherency. Among the most stimulating writings are from critics such as Barbara Christian, Henry Louis Gates, Susan Willis, Barbara Foley, Deborah Rosenfelt, Ramon Saldivar, and Houston Baker; the inspirational "discourse of colonialism" stemming originally from Frantz Fanon and Amilcar Cabral; classic works of social theory such as Robert Blauner's *Racial Oppression in America* (1972) and some maverick works on Third World writers, such as Barbara Harlow's pathbreaking *Resistance Literature* (1987).[3]

What, then, are the defining characteristics, the strengths and weaknesses of each approach? What are the perspectives, possibilities for reconciliation, and future terrain of debate?

"ETHNICITY" VERSUS "INTERNAL COLONIALISM"

First, there is the issue of terminology. It is true that both schools employ the other's terminology. But the terms in themselves are not as significant as the ways in which they are utilized for a larger vision of U.S. culture, or the respective weight given to each term. The ethnicity school and the class, gender, and race approach are alike in confronting an obstinate although, I believe, moribund elite, patriarchal Eurocentric establishment, and both have complex interactions with critical theory as it has evolved primarily through structuralism and post-structuralism. Moreover, both agree that "ethnicity" and "race" are social constructions in the manner of gender or, for that matter, popular notions of "class"; ethnicity and race are decidedly *not* cultural or biological "essences." Therefore, it is not so much in the challenge to the mystifications of the prevailing cultural dominant that the two schools diverge, as in the equally important process of re-theorization. Here, I regard the distinctions as irreconcilable.

Most damaging for the ethnicity school has been the charge that, in theorizing cultural difference, it privileges the category of ethnicity, relegating "race" to a mere feature of some ethnic groups. In contrast, the class, gender, race approach follows W.E.B. Du Bois' view that the "color line" runs through our culture today in a central manner, and Du Bois' later qualification that, among other things, the color line serves to support and rationalize real, material, social domination.[4]

Critics of the ethnicity school further charge that use of the category of ethnicity, usually not very precisely defined, as the fundamental perspective, facilitates the erroneous view of immigration and assimilation as the primary modes by which groups of people enter and then rise in U.S. society, with a view of the cultural process appropriate to that perspective.

In contrast, the class, gender, and race approach is more or less based on the "internal colonialism" model that came to full force in the Black Arts movement of the 1960s. However, this model has since been appropriated by other theorists of cultures of people of color; it has engaged in complex ways with feminist criticism; and it has sometimes benefitted from close encounters with critical theory. The strength of this internal colonialist model lies in its internal colonialist perspective on cultural formation and difference, and the use by cultural critics of what is now called the "discourse of colonialism." One of its weaknesses is a tendency to focus on one colonized group at a time, rather than in comparative perspective. Another is a failure to address issues of class and gender in an integrated manner; that is, the practitioners tend to "add on" gender and class perspectives, rather than treating class, gender, and race as inextricably and mutually enmeshed.

But the central argument is valid: a powerful and valid affirmation of a profound distinction—never to be forgotten—between the experience of people of color and the European ethnic immigrants in the *mode and consequences* of their incorporation into the social formation, and their subsequent treatment. People of color were usually *forced* into the economy through an act of dramatic violence—most notably the kidnapping of one-half million Africans, conquering of Chicanos in the South West, and genocidal war against Native Peoples. Or else, people of color underwent other forms of *colonial-like* experiences such as the forced relocation of the Japanese-American population and the racist labor contracts imposed on Chinese-Americans.

The argument for internal colonialism does not stand or fall on whether these populations of people of color are actually "internal colonies" or "oppressed nations" in the classical sense—although, arguably, Afro-Americans, Chicanos, Puerto Ricans, and Native Peoples have in varying degrees and at various times been characterized by a common culture, language, economy, and territory apart from that of the European invaders of the continent. What renders the internal colonial model useful as an *analogy* is the similarity in the dynamic of cultural struggle, particularly the importance of resurrecting non-European and oral traditions, and the peculiar race-connected (more accurately, color-connected) forms of economic and cultural exploitation.

People of color tend to have their cultures assaulted, obscured, and misrepresented in ways very similar to that experienced by colonial people, and only superficially similar to European immigrants; and the status of people of color in the U.S. as slaves, inhabitants of reservations, stoop-laborers, and the very lowest category of domestic workers, also parallels the situation of colonized people. According to internal colonialist theorists, the occupational histories of people of color in relation to country and city are of a different kind than those experienced by European ethnic immigrant groups.

In fact, the treatment of people of color within the U.S. is intimately connected with the general rise of Western Colonialism in which a deviation in pigmentation from the "norm" of Western society was alleged to be a sign of inferiority, marking one out for super-exploitation.

Therefore, the *kind* of exploitation being theorized by internal colonialist scholars is not merely a function of economic success or lack thereof, although it is clear that Blacks, Chicanos, Puerto Ricans, and Native Peoples have not advanced economically—and probably will not advance—comparably to European immigrants under our present system. Likewise, the obscurity or notoriety of writers of color is not what is decisive, either; probably, more academics can name Black-American writers than can name Greek-American or Italian-American writers.

If internal colonialist theory could be effectively integrated into contemporary class and gender analysis—in effect, into a Marxism that treats not only the social construction of "race" but also "gender" as major categories; that does not such reduce non-class social divisions to some form of class division; and that foregrounds the recognition that the components of a class are produced historically and may be comprised of different genders and diverse races—I believe it would bring a perspective with superior explanatory potential to the study of the cultural practice of people of color and U.S. literature in general.[5] More than any other methodology of which I am aware, it presents cogent reasons for the distortion of the cultural practice of people of color even by those with liberal sympathies using the European-derived critical tools of the dominant culture. Moreover, especially when conjoined with a version of the theoretical work of critics such as Gates and Baker, it points the way to the creation of appropriate text-specific critical practice.[6]

Yet this method to date also contains at least one problematic area. It leaves the theorization of cultural practice of the European immigrant groups at the level of generality, as if "whites" were some homogenous European "other"; as if the category of "the invaders" were itself not a simplistic shorthand for the complex and diverse life experience of women and men of different classes and highly distinct subcultures; and as if the difference between European and non-European culture were reducible to one or another simplistic binary opposition (written versus oral; linear versus circular; technological versus natural).

The usual protest from the ethnicity school is that some European ethnic groups have also suffered from super-exploitation culturally and in forms of labor. This certainly is more true than generally acknowledged; a complex hierarchy of culture exists within the European immigrant groups by class, gender, complexion, and geographic region. But this complaint is by no means fatal to the internal colonialist argument, for, even if oppression among some European immigrants existed in a *degree* equivalent to that which was experienced by some people of color, did it exist in *kind*? The massive research of sociologists such as Stanley Lieberson indicates that the answer is unambiguously, "no."[7] And it is precisely in the area of "kind" that culture—which is formed by far more than just "oppression"— presents its distinctions.

In general, differences cited by the internal colonialist theorists would include the following six:

ORIGIN

Most European immigrants came in search of self-betterment, even if in a position of servitude. None experienced the kind of kidnapping, conquest, and genocide of people of color in the U.S. True, twentieth-century immigrants from Mexico superficially parallel the European groups; but it is much more significant to their fate in the U.S. that they are mestizo, products of a colonization process and, also, historically, migrating from one part of their own country to another (the northern part of which has been under occupation for the past 140 years).

Among Chinese- and Japanese-Americans, there are perhaps more similarities to the Europeans—but, still, the distinctions carry greater weight. The displacement of the Japanese-American population in World War II, and not the German-American and Italian-American population, is indicative of a qualitatively different status, just as are the nature of the restrictions on Chinese-American immigration.

OCCUPATION

Here, those who support the internal colony thesis claim that, not just occupation on the gross level (slaves, field laborers, and domestics), but treatment within occupations, including the professions, reveals distinct patterns where people of color face greater obstacles than European ethnics—not, of course, in every individual case, but generally.

AMERICAN APARTHEID

De facto segregation exists more intensively for people of color, especially Afro-American, Latino, and Native Peoples, under qualitatively worse conditions than for European ethnics—some of whom, in fact, may be demanding "ethnically pure" communities to defend racist privilege.

RELIGION

Most European ethnic groups have as their primary religion the Judeo-Christian traditions. Whatever differences exist, this commonality creates bonds around symbolism, vocabulary, frame of reference, view of the world, etc. In contrast, most people of color are non-Christian in origins and, if they have adopted a version of Christianity, they have transformed it in complex ways, most notably in Black Christianity, Latino Catholicism, and the Christianity of Native Peoples.

CULTURE

European immigrants share a relatively common folklore and view of history, compared to that of people of color. By and large the literary tradition of all European cultures derives from a valorization of Greek and Roman classical civilization, and certain figures, such as Shakespeare, Dante, and Tolstoy, are revered as models for artistic value in different cultures throughout the European continent. Central to the cultural institutions of the U.S. have been that European experience refracted through British history and adapted to the "New World" situation as seen through the eyes of the elite, patriarchal colonial class.[8]

HISTORY IN THE U.S.

In general, the trend of most European ethnic groups in the U.S. is toward assimilation or at least accommodation, deghettoization, and intermarriage. The main trend for people of color has varied from group to group, but the experience of racism and cultural Eurocentrism have rebounded against the need to reconstitute a sense of cultural identity and has episodically resulted in dynamic nationalist movements—such as Black Panthers, La Raza Unida, Asian-American Left groups, Puerto Rican nationalist groups, and the American Indian Movement. Usually, from a Marxist point of view, these have been left-wing and progressive, although not always.

But the progressive political content of the evolution of ethnic consciousness among the European immigrant groups is less clear by far. It is true that certain 1930s proletarian, immigrant ethnic novels promote an ideology of social solidarity. But studies such as Jonathan Reider's *Canarsie* (1985), indicate that a good part of the so-called "new ethnicity" among white ethnics was a backlash of resentment against the struggles of Blacks. Some of this backlash was simply on racist grounds; some was motivated by the mistaken view that, due to poverty programs and affirmative action, Blacks were getting unfair advantages, getting something for nothing, and similar myths.

THE ETHNICITY LITERARY SCHOOL

The booklength works of what I call the Ethnicity Literary School tend to exhibit the main weaknesses of ethnicity theory in various ways. Dearborn is the most distressing in her conflation of people of color into the immigrant ethnic experience. In an incisive critique of this book in the *Women's Review of Books*, Barbara Christian demonstrates that, methodologically, Dearborn does little more than expand Eurocentric critical categories. According to Christian, Dearborn's category of "ethnic women writers" results in a failure to focus on issues of greatest importance to people of color—most obviously, the history and present-day reality of racism. It also causes her to misinterpret the function of the "mulatto theme," so that Dearborn regards the primary concern of this literature as that of "incest" rather than recognizing that Afro-American writers usually depict the mulatto experience to explore power relations between the races and also the issue of "norms of beauty."[9]

Most astonishing is Dearborn's failure to explicitly define what she means by "ethnicity." Instead, she relies on the dubious statement that "Ethnicity has always been defined as otherness; the other is always ethnicity" (p. 16). This leads to all sorts of peculiarities such as defining "miscegenation" as "sexual relations between white men and ethnic [!] women" (p. 103). The breadth of her analytical terminology usually prevents her from writing with specificity about particular tribes of Native Peoples, instead too often conflating this diversity into the category of "Indian." Finally, there is a fundamental confusion in a study that defines all "ethnic" women as "Pocahontas's Daughters," when, in fact, Pocahontas was not herself a writer but an historical figure abused by writers.

There is, of course, much insight, sensitivity, and intelligence in the book, as well as the resurrection of little-known texts and the intriguing juxtaposition of others. This only renders the book more frustrating, underscoring the need to articulate theoretical methods carefully to avoid violation of the very subjects one intends to elucidate.

Werner Sollers' *Beyond Ethnicity* offers a new mode of analysis organized around the categories of "descent" and "consent"—by which he means determination by one's cultural heritage as opposed to self-determination in spite of it. In several sections of the book the meanings of "ethnicity" and "cultural pluralism" are interrogated etymologically and historically, with much wit and erudition.

It is clear that Sollers has brilliantly challenged the category of ethnicity, demonstrating many of the confusing and contradictory roles it has played as cultural myth. But Sollers' method of theorizing cultural difference is predicated on the serious error of trying to relegate race to an aspect of certain ethnicities. He acknowledges that: "I have here sided with Abramson's universalist interpretation according to which ethnicity includes dominant groups and in which race, while sometimes facilitating external identification, is merely one aspect of ethnicity."[10]

Yet the evidence is strong that, to people of color, in their writings as well as their lives, race, not ethnicity, is by far the more central category in American culture; and by race is not meant genuine biological features, but the social construction of racial types centering on a mythology of color, and the concomitant attempt to diminish, trivialize, displace, and distort the culture of those groups subsumed by those mythological categories through the hegemony of a select patriarchal European aesthetic purporting to be objective.

This is why Henry Louis Gates cries out in his 1986 essay, "Talkin' That Talk": "We must attack the racism of egalitarianism and universalism in as many languages as we can utter."[11] In 1988, the assertion of "cultural difference" is not the call of white supremacists but of non-Europeans who have learned that "assimilation" in the U.S. is nothing less than to assent to a process of domination.

A huge literature of major texts by Winthrop Jordan and others explains how the negative connotations of dark colors in Western Culture were mobilized into the ideology of racism to justify the slave system and conquest of non-Europeans on the grounds that their *skin color* betokened cultural inferiority. The results of this centuries-long process were and remain utterly profound; even among Europeans there is a hierachy of skin colors (from noble blonds to untrustworthy darker Mediterraneans), and among people of color there are instances of the internalization of color coding so that lighter-skinned members are favored over darker skinned.

In sum, Sollers' categories of descent and consent have some application to people of color as well as white ethnics, but they translate into qualitatively different phenomena when one is marked by skin color in a racist society. These categories also function in qualitatively different ways when the particular subculture from which one comes has far fewer economic resources and role models—for, in this society, racial and ethnic groups are linked to class power of different degrees. One striking example of the way in which Sollers has lost his bearings in this particular aspect of the book is his discussion of "Bluish" writing, in which he purports to demonstrate a common methodology for the treatment of Black and Jewish writing. But his method only focuses on the epiphenomenal conjunctures and parallels, missing the substantial differences in life experience and culture.[12]

CULTURE-SPECIFIC METHODOLOGY

Sollers' work contrasts dramatically with *Figures in Black*, a collection of essays by Gates, which represents a bold challenge to literary studies as conceived by the ethnicity school. Rather than starting from alleged universal methods (which may be regarded as a code phrase for unacknowledged domination), Gates' central theme is the need for a culture-specific methodology.

Gates' analysis derives from important precursors and predecessors. One aspect of his work is predicated on Black nationalist scholarship in the U.S.; this has its roots in nineteenth-century figures such as Martin Delaney, and can be seen vividly in a masterpiece such as W. E. B. Du Bois' *The Souls of Black Folks* (1903). In the twentieth century, the cultural counter-part of Black nationalist politics continued to establish itself as the primary school in literary theory and practice through the Harlem Renaissance, and especially the "Black Arts" movement of the 1960s. This last introduced very explicitly what is usually referred to as the "discourse of colonialism" into the literary analysis of the cultures of people of color in the U.S. Today, however, many components of the orientation promoted by the Black Arts movement are shared by cultural workers among other groups of people of color as well as by feminists.

In brief, the common view is that, since culture is based on life experience (such as history, folklore, and religion), cultural difference must be understood in the context of that specific life experience. Diverse cultures cannot be analyzed merely in terms of the models and categories of cultural achievement received from the dominant educational institutions; as Gates says, these models and categories are actually selective patriarchal European values *masquerading* as "universal, transcendant normative values."[13]

We know, of course, that Gates is not the only person or even the first to promote such a view. But he is particularly articulate in his insistence that methods of literary criticism do not emerge from a vacuum, but are "text specific."[14] That is, theories of analysis and evaluation evolve from the protracted study of a selected group of texts.

Thus, people of color in the U.S. are in a situation in which notions of literary value and tools for classifying literature are derived from and designed to ratify a relatively small group of European patriarchal literary practices. This narrow body of theory is the framework in which Afro-American and other quite different literary texts are expected to be treated.

The second body of predecessor material through which Gates has worked his way to his present position is comprised of two recent, highly-rarefied schools of literary criticism. One is structuralism, which focuses on the underlying rules of language; the other is post-structuralism, which privileges the act of writing above language systems and is skeptical of the truth-claims of all forms of linguistic or other structuration.

Gates admits that the application of these theories to literature is derived from a focus on European texts; but he also holds that the formalist and skeptical elements in these theories allow the possibility of a kind of critical distance from all local culture. Thus the Afro-American critic can eventually return to the task of developing "Black text-specific" critical theories the very terms of which are derived from the ordinary language of Afro-Americans.[15]

Gates' book also has implications that go much farther than the mere development of a new Black text-specific literary theory. Parts of his essays challenge assumptions at the very heart of the notion of "culture" that predominates in the Western world—a notion centered on the valorization of European-type literacy and writing. Gates' underlying theme is that the Europeans, through what began as an economic and political domination, also carried out a pernicious ideological domination that identified authentic "culture" with writing. Moreover, the ability to write was taken as a sign of whether one possessed "reason," and in the case of slaves was sometimes grounds for manumission.

Gates charges that the colonized person of color, within or without the borders of the U.S., has been placed in a terrible trap. Due to historic relations of power, the instrument of writing—the achievement of which was taken as proof of "civilization"—is one formed largely by the Western European oppressor. Eurocentric language and models inherently strive to shape the voice of the non-European writer—one of the reasons for the predominance of the signifying mode among Black writers. Unfortunately, this argument, though provocative, is left unfinished, allowing for many ambiguities and even for less radical interpretations than the one I have offered.

AGAINST PREMATURE METHODOLOGICAL UNITY

In summary, what, then, is meant by class, gender, and race methodology, and what is the promise of this new orientation?

From my own point of view, "class" means redirecting the study of U.S. cultural formation away from myths, themes, symbols, and elitist networks—which are symptomatic, not causal—and focusing more precisely on conquest and invasion, capital accumulation, urbanization, colonial and imperial expansion, and late capitalism, as the framework that nurtures and limits the context in which active agents create culture.

"Gender" means the perception of sex roles and sexuality itself as ideological creations within the above context, as well as within the traditions of so-called Western and non-Western Culture. As a result, use of the category may increase our understanding of how men and women are "made" through the linguistic construction of sexual difference, and it may point to the need to reconceptualize our scholarly as well as "common-sense" notions about identity and language.

Use of this category also promotes a focus on culture in terms of the relations of dominance between men and women in productive sites such as the workplace and the family. Such patterned differences in life experience may produce semi-autonomous cultural traditions. Moreover, the category motivates us toward a commitment to the views and values of women artists and the female audience, as well as to a defense of the political interests of women in society.

"Race," of course, has nothing to do with "race" in a biological sense. This complex category refers, on the one hand, to an understanding of the ideology of racism through which people of color—primarily people of non-European origin—have been marked for special forms of super-exploitation. But it is also, on the other hand, a means of recognizing that people of color have forged new and complex cultures, many with distinct national features, blending and transforming elements of the dominant culture with elements of their indigenous cultures under precise conditions of exploitation.

The result has been the production of new forms of Christianity, folk traditions, family structures, linguistic patterns, literature, etc., which can not even be recognized—let alone understood—by the mere liberal expansion of the Euro-American analytical techniques we have seen to date.

In the end we must recognize that there is no such thing as "American Culture"; any attempt to *force a methodological unity* (in terms of critical terms and "aesthetic value") at this point will only reinforce the present relations of domination by new means. The complex social formation known as the U.S. is the home of many subcultures—each internally riven by class, gender, region, and in some cases color stratification—and each with a reservoir of widely varying social and economic power to defend its interests.

Therefore, theorizing cultural difference needs to proceed from the ground up, as according to the Gates methodology. Just as Eurocentric criticism evolved from a massive study and debate about European texts, so the study of the cultures of people of color will derive from the protracted study and teaching of texts from those cultures. Our primary task now is not to declare by fiat a precise "universal" methodology, but to deepen our familiarity with the distinctive features of the texts themselves.

Notes

I am grateful to a number of friends who gave me suggestions and criticisms after reading an earlier version of this paper: Michael Awkward, Lauren Berlant, Paul Buhle, Barbara Harlow, Lemuel Johnson, Townsend Luddington, Richard Meisler, Patrick Quinn, Paula Rabinowitz, David Roediger, and Kate Vangen. But I alone am responsible for the opinions expressed and any errors.

1. See the extraordinary new collection edited by Charlotte Nekola and Paula Rabinowitz, *Writing Red* (New York: Feminist Press, 1987).
2. I cite here only two broad tendencies, one associated with the Communist-led *New Masses* and John Reed Clubs of the early 1930s; the other with Southern Agrarian publications and the New England-based *Hound and Horn*. In between there were some remarkable but incomplete efforts at reconciliation, especially that of *Partisan Review*. For further details on efforts to synthesize Marxism and Modernism in the 1930s, see my books, *The Revolutionary Imagination* (Chapel Hill, N.C.: University of North Carolina Press, 1983), and *The New York Intellectuals* (Chapel Hill, N.C.: University of North Carolina Press, 1987).
3. See the following: Barbara Christian, *Black Women Novelists* (Westport, Conn.: Greenwood, 1987); Henry Louis Gates, Jr., *Figures in Black* (New York: Oxford University Press); Ramon Saldivar, "A Dialectic of Difference," MELUS 6, no. 3 (Fall 1979): 73–92; Barbara Foley, *Telling the Truth* (Ithaca, N.Y.: Cornell University Press, 1986); Susan Willis, *Specifyin'* (Madison, Wis.: University of Wisconsin Press, 1986); Houston Baker, *Blues, Ideology and Afro-American Literature* (Chicago: University of Chicago, 1984); Frantz Fanon, *The Wretched of the Earth* (New York: Grove, 1963); Amilcar Cabral, *Return to the Source* (New York: Monthly Review, 1973); Robert Blauner, *Racial Oppression in America* (New York: Harper and Row, 1972); Judith Newton and Deborah Rosenfelt, *Feminism and Social Change* (New York: Metheun, 1985); Barbara Harlow, *Resistance Literature* (New York: Metheun, 1987).
4. Manning Marable, *Blackwater* (Dayton, Ohio: Black Praxis Press, 1981), 61.
5. I am influenced here by two recent, provocative efforts to consider feminist theory from class and race perspectives: Floya Anthias and Nira Yuval-Davis, "Contextualizing Feminism—Gender, Ethnic and Class Divisions," *Feminist Review* 15 (Winter 1985): 62–85; and June Howard, "Feminist Differings: Recent Surveys of Feminist Literary Theory and Criticism," *Feminist Studies* 14, no. 1 (Spring 1988): 167–89.
6. For a compelling argument for the extension of a critical assimilation of the traditions of the Black Arts movement through a dialogue with post-structuralism and feminism, see Michael Awkward's "Race, Gender, and the Politics of Reading," *Black American Literature Forum* 22, no. 1 (Spring 1988): 5–27.
7. Stanley Lieberson, *A Piece of the Pie* (Berkeley: University of California Press, 1980).
8. For an informative discussion of some of the specific carry-overs from the

English literary heritage to early colonial culture, see "English Literature at the American Moment" by Barbara Kiefer Lewalski, in Emory Elliot, ed., *Columbia Literary History of the United States* (New York: Columbia University Press, 1988), 33–44.

9. Barbara Christian, review of Mary Dearborn, *Pocahontas' Daughters*, and Susan Willis, *Specifyin'*, *Women's Review of Books*, 4, nos. 10–11 (July–August 1987): 25.

10. Werner Sollers, *Beyond Ethnicity* (New York: Oxford University Press, 1986), 36.

11. Henry Louis Gates, Jr., ed., *"Race," Writing and Difference* (Chicago: University of Chicago Press, 1986), 409.

12. In any event, Sollers' attempt to find Black-Jewish parallels is so brief that he may have exaggerated his assertions just to draw attention to the cleverness of "Bluish." See *Beyond Ethnicity*, 163–65.

13. Gates, *"Race," Writing and Difference*, xx.

14. Ibid., p. xix.

15. Ibid., p. xxi.

14

Free Speech and the Campus Anti-Racist Movement: The Need for Immediate Response and Long-term Transformation

RAMPANT RACISM

The national press is slowly acknowledging what the radical press has warned for some time: The end of the 20th century is characterized by a dramatic increase in the reported number of racist assaults on people of color in the United States, a fact confirmed by police surveys and documented by research foundations.[2] For the Left, this has meant a general recrudescence and re-orientation of anti-racist movements during the past several years—a further movement away from the early demands simply for "civil rights" for African-Americans, and more toward a campaign "against racism" that affects all people of color. The change is quite noticeable on university campuses where vile racist attacks appear to many people to be incongruous with the ethos of "liberal education," and where the tradition of political activism remains stronger than elsewhere in society.

In the initial phase of the campus anti-racist actions—from Massachusetts to Michigan to Wisconsin to Berkeley—the demands of the student movement focused on two issues. One was the demand that administrators take dramatic action in the form of curriculum renovation (such as implementing less-Eurocentric courses and hiring faculty qualified to teach them). The other was the formulation of punitive policies against explicitly racist—as well as sometimes sexist, anti-Semitic, and homophobic—behavior. During the past two years, however, there has been a backlash during which conservatives have denounced curriculum reform as "political indoctrination." Some liberals have joined conservatives in charging that punitive policies to curb racist hate-epithets are a violation of First Amendment

181

rights.[3] What strategies might be promoted by socialists who wish to participate in these struggles, responding with decisive immediate action yet also pushing long-term emancipatory possibilities to the limit?[4]

While I think that most activists would hold that, in the long run, *the broader struggles to fundamentally change the culture of the university are more significant than punitive action*, the mainstream as well as liberal news media (such as the *New York Times*, ABC's "Nightline," and the *Nation*) have focused debate on the legalistic aspect of the issue of "Free Speech." This may be partly because debates over "Free Speech" lend themselves to more simplified and sensationalistic reporting. But I also suspect that some news media see the "Free Speech" angle as attractive because it is a divisive sore point. The question of whether and how to ban epithets that demoralize and may lead to violence aimed at students of color has tended to split anti-racist activists from civil libertarian and faculty allies in such a way as to make "good copy" suggesting that even the components of the Left are so disunited that they can't find agreement with one another. And the Right wing has falsely painted efforts of the Left to democratize the university atmosphere as if they were repressive attacks on "Free Speech' and "Academic Freedom."

Among the most publicized of such "Free Speech" cases has been that at the University of Michigan. There, in May 1988, in response to explicit racist incidents that had occurred on campus in 1987, an anti-harassment and anti-discrimination policy was put in place by administrators, only to be struck down by a U.S. District Court in September 1989. The American Civil Liberties Union (ACLU) was the group that took on the University, on behalf of a student who is now feted by right-wing academic networks; the judge ruled that such a university policy violated the guarantee of "Free Speech" provided by the First Amendment. Since that time the University of Michigan has revamped its regulations on harassing and discriminatory speech, vastly limiting the areas of applicability. University of Michigan radical students, who tended in the past to be sympathetic to the banning of violence-producing epithets while they adamantly opposed all "codes" to monitor any other aspect of speech and behavior, are now confused about the matter. A number of other universities considering such policies have also come under scrutiny and criticism.[5]

THE DYNAMIC OF THE STRUGGLE

The issues complicating the debate over "Free Speech" and the anti-racist movement are many. First, the general dynamic of these struggles provides an important context for assessing certain aspects of the various proposals. The issue usually arises when student activists, often students of color, respond angrily to a racist attack of some sort on campus, mobilizing a constituency to demand action through demonstrations, press conferences, the seizing of a building, etc. Then the administration, embarrassed by local and national publicity that might hurt its reputation and thereby endanger admissions and financial stability, looks for the quickest and the least painful fix. Of all the options raised by the students—which usually include a call for a dramatic increase in enrollment, support, and financial aid for students of color, and the hiring of faculty of color and specialists in the complex issues of racism and ethnocentrism—the administrators are most agreeable to institutionalizing some sort of authoritarian "code" of behavior against students. Their impulse is to make it broader than many of the protestors intended, and to ignore demands that anti-racist activists and students who are the targets of racist assault participate in formulating and applying the policy. (Here we should also point out that neither the University of Michigan anti-discriminatory policy, nor any of the others I have seen, make faculty or administrators accountable.)

At this point in the struggle, some civil libertarians, both in the legal profession itself and among the university population, have entered the picture. They accurately warn that policies that prohibit certain kinds of speech, even vilifying epithets, will establish a dangerous precedent. After all, once the university administration has power to limit speech in one area, it can move more easily into other areas.

In addition, since it is very difficult to determine in advance how a prohibitive policy will be interpreted, there is every reason to fear that punishment will be exacted primarily against the students of color themselves and the Left—for example, against Nation of Islam students who may want to hold a meeting for Louis Farakhan (who has made anti-Semitic statements); against critics of Zionism (who are frequently slandered as anti-Semitic); and against radical anti-CIA protesters (who have been accused of "harassing" and of "discriminating" against the rights of U.S. government representatives). Beyond that, critics of anti-discrimination policies concerning speech charge that a focus on restricting individual behavior diverts energy to a symptom without addressing the real, underlying, social causes of racism.

From my experience, the events at the University of Michigan indicate that the fears raised by the civil libertarians *must be taken seriously.* The University authorities have a much stronger record of moving against protesters on the Left—such as participants in anti-CIA demonstrations and editors of the *Michigan Daily* who criticize Israeli state policy—than they have against right-wing racist activists. With the single exception of a campus radio station employee who was tape recorded (by African-American students) when he aired racist jokes, racists have never been seriously impeded in their activities. These include violent acts such as destroying the symbolic shanties built on campus by the United Coalition Against Racism, the Free South Africa Co-ordinating Committee, and the Palestine Solidarity Committee, as well as the distribution of racist fliers that physically threaten people of color with execution.

The central problem here, then, is a familiar one: Those who have been the targets of oppression and hence the quickest to decry racism and militantly mobilize against it, want *immediate relief*. Of course, their first response, which socialists fully support, is to mobilize the largest possible demonstrations on the campus and in the community to try to educate people and change the climate of the university. But one cannot expect people to mobilize day in and day out. Nor can one place the burden on people of color, or their allies, to find time to prepare a mobilization in response to every episode of racism. It is in this context, that of institution-alizing sentiments expressed from the bottom up, that many activists feel that a response, even in the form of administrative sanctions against racist verbal behavior, will be a victory, provide legitimacy, and encourage further fight-back.[6]

What Are "Free Speech" and "Academic Freedom"?

Of course, the civil liberties argument cannot be dismissed merely because of its frequent origin as part of the sideline commentary on the struggle. More problematic is that this approach, while presenting truths that have a kind of general validity, simply does not respond to the issue of demanding immediate relief from outrageous language, threats, and other forms of verbal behavior that interfere with a student of color's Fourteenth Amend-ment right to a hypothetically equal education. In particular, the ACLU spokespersons in the University of Michigan case, when calling on students to focus instead on the "real" problems of racism, offered little but plati-tudes. When a local ACLU Board member commented on the complex cultural issue of racism, he revealed only a superficial grasp of the debate.[7]

Moreover, even socialists who adhere to a general civil libertarian orien-tation but who have been part of the anti-racist struggle, among whom I count myself, have not really come up with satisfactory short-term re-sponses to the demand for immediate relief following the important first step of building mass mobilizations against the racism that prevents free-dom of expression on the part of its targets. Among the more substantial problems currently faced by the campus anti-racist movement are the following:

• There is still a simplistic reliance by some activists on very abstractly-defined categories of "Free Speech" and "Academic Freedom"; this is a dubious concession to the perpetuation of concepts lending themselves to a variety of contradictory interpretations depending upon relations of power. The problem is that both liberals and conservatives tend to throw these terms about as if they described conditions already extant and now in danger of being overthrown if radicals succeed in making people account- able for racist and sexist behavior. But the fact is that the speech and academic work of students, faculty, and staff, as well as the general culture of the university, are shaped, determined, limited, and unconsciously cen- sored by a host of legal restrictions (for example, against slander, obscenity, death threats), customs, material resources, and the dubious "norms" of various academic disciplines.

At most universities, there are real, material reasons why students do *not* have the "Freedom" to study Chicano History as seriously as that of European elites; to concentrate on the Native American Indian novel without first going through required indoctrination courses in Shakespeare, Milton, et al.; to major in Socialist Revolution; etc. In bourgeois society, "Free Speech" and "Academic Freedom" provide important openings for the Left but also function as the means by which the dominant ideology is naturalized. Of course, the task of socialists is *not at all to abandon the call for "Free Speech" and "Academic Freedom,"* which also have historical connota- tions and emotional weight in our culture that are favorable to the Left, but one must not passively accept their conventional usage, either. *Instead, socialists should struggle to redefine the content of "free speech" and "academic freedom" so that they change from unchallenged weights of domination, basically ratifying the status quo (and readily curtailed in time of war), to active instruments that give voice to exploited people in society who are shut out by the present relations of power.* The use of racist hate-words should not be equated with the expression of "Free Speech," but, rather, understood as creating a situation in which "free" expression is impossible for those who have the most impediments to gaining expression in the institutions of our society.

Moreover, in the history of U.S. universities, socialists have fought to interpret "Academic Freedom" as the right of dissident scholars to maintain their teaching positions in spite of the fact that their political views are at odds with the rulers of the society and sometimes of the university (regents, trustees, wealthy backers, etc.). So far as I know, the issue of "Academic Freedom" for faculty first became a national concern when professors opposed to U.S. policy in World War I were fired from schools like the Wharton School of Business (Scott Nearing) and Columbia University (from which Charles Beard resigned in protest). The issue was raised a few times in the 1930s when pro-Communist or merely pro-labor faculty came under attack, and then with greater force in the period of the McCarthyite witch-hunt when U.S. government committees collaborated with university administrators across the country to cast out academics who would not "name names" and serve as stool pigeons.[8]

In the 1960s and 1970s there were also a series of "Academic Freedom" cases, such as the one at the University of Maryland where Bertell Ollman was denied an appointment as chair of the Political Science Department due to his Marxist views, and the one at Boston University where the prominent radical pedagogist Henry Giroux was denied tenure. In addition, there continue to be "Academic Freedom" cases where women and people of color have received unfair treatment due to institutional racism and sexism by administrators.

It is true that, in some cases, right-wing faculty have claimed to be persecuted in ways that violate their "Academic Freedom" to propagandize for imperialism and carry out research for various death machines, just as several decades ago there were Cold War liberals who claimed their freedoms were being limited by student protest movements. Moreover, it is true that, in the 1960s, some portions of the Left fell for a popularized version of Herbert Marcuse's idea of "Repressive Tolerance" (against "anti-social" forces) while others cited Stalin, Mao, and even Trotsky to justify the banning of reactionary speakers and films through mobilizations to "stop fascism." But, for the most part, due to relationships of power, I feel that, historically and in the future, "Academic Freedom" is a cause that ought to be associated with the Left and the anti-racist movement (although it will have to be reconceptualized to some extent to deal more precisely with racism, sexism, and homophobia). This is because these groups stand for the empowerment of the economically and otherwise disenfranchised in opposition to the ruling elite. Therefore, rather than defend and celebrate such abstract ideas as conditions that already exist and must thus be defended, we ought to assiduously strive to *impart to them contents consistent with anti-racism and empowerment of the population.*

THE "FIGHTING WORDS" ARGUMENT

• Another problem with some approaches to the issue of racist hate-words is the separation that some believe can be clearly drawn between fascist/racist "actions," which may be suppressed by law, and fascist/racist "speech," which must be tolerated as a necessary evil to prevent suppression of our own controversial speech. Unfortunately, racist ideology is so deep, ugly, and intertwined with the dominant culture of the United States, that in some contexts certain epithets and types of speech are triggers to action. In other words, due to the concrete features of U.S. history, there does not exist a formal "equality" of epithets.

In the case of most groups of people of color in the United States, there is an historical past that somewhat resembles a "colonization" process in which the epithet/violence connection played a central role. An intensive indoctrination of the white population with the view of people of color as objects and barbaric was necessary to rationalize kidnapping, invasion, conquest, enslavement, massive land theft, and the outlawing of indigenous language, religion, and culture. Vile epithets were institutionalized along with the punitive techniques of branding, castration, and mutilation. Four centuries ago as well as today, real or threatened violence ineluctably appears when invoked by cultural symbols and verbal expressions. Whereas the original verbal levers of such violent oppression inhered in the imputation of sub-human qualities to people of color, today the associations are more along the lines of connecting people of color to a permanently degenerate "underclass" of gangs, prostitutes, and drug addicts.

A residue of this remains even when we move into the realm of academic discourse. For example, when a Yale University English Professor was cited by critics for characterizing accused African-American rapists as "uneducated monkeys who aren't ready for civilization," and a University of Michigan Professor of Sociology was alleged to have characterized Malcolm X in his classroom as a "red-haired pimp," it is hard not to feel that the choices of words were especially upsetting to students of color because the signals they touched off are associated with horrendous patterns of oppression and exclusion.[9]

On the other hand, racist expressions against whites, such as that of the City University of New York Chair of Black Studies who characterized whites as "ice people," materialistic and intent on domination, in contrast to Black "sun people," who are humanistic, seem in the context of U.S. history to be tragic and disorienting, but not the ideological counterpart of systematic discrimination against and violent physical assaults on Euro-Americans.[10] Even the more dangerous Nation of Islam expressions of anti-Semitism are still in the category of the deluded frustrations of a beleaguered group, not the excrescence of centuries of entrenched patterns of horrendous domination of Jews by African-Americans within the United States.

Thus, whatever abstractions may be offered about the need to be "color blind" and to judge all ethnocentric talk "equally," the fact is that racist epithets in the United States concerning people of color have a *specificity* about them that requires somewhat separate categories of analysis, evaluation, and response from other forms of ugly prejudice. Moreover, it is hard to take into account these specificities with the abstract civil liberties language of "rights," which often relies to a large degree on notions of formal equivalence, reciprocity, and universality. At the least, the use of certain epithets on the part of white students that has been documented in the university incidents that have received national attention—"Coon. Nigger. Porchmonkey."—is so intimately linked to violent suppression in our society that a student of color who is exposed to these epithets may understandably feel fear, demoralization, or anger that is a major block to his or her realizing an education. The designation by some legal experts of certain words in certain contexts as "Fighting Words" (words that inflict injury or incite immediate breach of peace) or "Words That Wound" (language interfering with the ability to function), and the banning of these epithets from the university community, has a measure of validity as a strategy that is not so easily countervailed by the argument that this action undermines "Free Speech" in the same way as the banning of other, merely disgusting and repulsive, offensive speech.

THE CAMPUS AND THE STATE

• Another confusing argument is that some activists blur significant distinctions between the situation on a university campus and what one finds when directly confronting the capitalist state—a state that socialists, of course, never trust. While any notion that the university is an ivory tower, apart from the mainstream of society, is ridiculous—and disproven at once by the presence of virulent racism at universities, in spite of all the official propaganda against it—important differences between the campus and the state are worth considering.

For example, since the university is a workplace of a very specific type, it has considerable potential for becoming the site of "liberated space." In particular, students are relatively freed up from nine-to-five work hours and direct parental supervision, so that they can devote more time to the work of organizing, mobilizing, and demonstrating. Faculty are sometimes veterans of the student activist movement themselves and may have special areas of expertise and material resources that can aid student anti-racist struggles. Campus facilities exist for student-controlled meetings, news reportage, cultural publications, political speakers, and educational events.

Moreover, while one can not forget the murders at Jackson State and Kent State in 1970, the conventions of university life may still act as a buffer against the use of armed force and other direct repressive measures as readily on the campus as elsewhere in society. The reason for this is partly because the university still functions *in loco parentis* with undergraduate students regarded more as children (whose parents are paying the university to "care" for them) than employees (to be fired and replaced at the university's convenience), and also because of the popular idea that debate and controversy are more acceptable at universities. Thus it is reasonable to consider that mobilized students, faculty, and staff may be able to devise procedures for insuring that the banning of "Fighting Words" occurs more democratically and with fewer dangers to other rights than is currently possible when dealing directly with the state and its own legal system.

SOME STRATEGIC OPTIONS

The experience of the last few years suggests to me a number of tactical and strategic points that socialists ought to take into account and perhaps promote as participants in current anti-racist struggles on university and college campuses:

• Socialist anti-racist activists should *not* become the allies, against the activist movement, of the particular kinds of professional civil libertarians, armchair academics, and sideline critics who only seem to step into the struggle in order to raise objections at the moment when immediate action is demanded by students of color for relief from racist abuse. However, simultaneously, socialist activists should base their support for immediate relief on an awareness of the *double-edged* nature of any repressive legislation—whether it is aimed against merely action or against racist hate-speech itself—when the power of interpreting that legislation is mainly in the hands of administrators who identify their self-interest with the corporate world and not with the general population. Some University of Michigan radicals have suggested that, as a result of administration claims that it wishes to provide better "protection" through an anti-discriminatory policy and the deputization of a university police force, the environment has become far less free for the Left.

• If the demand of the activists of color is for immediate relief from harassing and intimidating language, the concept of "Fighting Words," if it can be *defined so as to be restricted to racist epithets against people of color* in a context threatening violence, demoralization, or exclusion, provides a legitimate starting point for a policy. Despite dangers, such a policy may be necessary because of (1) the special nature of racist oppression of people of color in the United States; (2) the fact that violent racist speech perpetuates an environment in which "Free Speech" is anything but a reality and inhibits rather than promotes alternative perspectives; and (3) the need to support the right of anti-racist activists of color to set their own agenda. (In other words, the Euro-American component of the anti-racist movement should not try to make the banning of racist hate-speech a demand *for* the anti-racist activists of color, but should accept it as a demand when it arises naturally, from the anti-racist activists of color themselves. Of course, it does not follow that socialists automatically support any and every demand raised by victims of racism; principles of class solidarity, internationalism, opposition to sexism and homophobia, etc., must also be taken into account.)

Moreover, the precise application and limitations of even the "Fighting Words" argument remain in question, which is why I am *unenthusiastic about raising it unless under duress*. For example, the Constitutional Law expert at Stanford University Law School, Thomas Gray, insisted to *Nation* correspondent Jon Weiner that the use of "Nigger" constitutes "Fighting Words," but that "'Black son of a bitch' won't do"![11]

In another variant of an attempt to restrict punishment to personally-harassing language, the most recent version of the University of Michigan anti-discrimination guidelines gives four examples of racist discourse, the first three of which are now deemed to be *acceptable* at the University: a student announces in class that cranium size is an indicator of intelligence; a student praises in class the holocaust on the grounds that it destroyed "an inferior religion"; a student tells a racist joke during a class discussion; and a white student uses a racial epithet to tell an African-American student just before an exam that she should "go home and stop using a white person's space." According to the new University of Michigan policy, *only* the *fourth* example can be considered for disciplinary action because the goal of the epithet was not exchanging an opinion but "affecting a particular student's performance on an exam. . . ."[12] But it seems to me that a much wider range of behavior than that exemplified by the fourth example might affect a student's performance on an exam, and also that it would be a highly unusual occurance for a student to decide to spew out racist filth with such a precise focus in mind. However, I do hold the opinion that, if a student believes such outrageous ideas about cranium size or the holocaust, it is far better to allow him or her to express the views openly where they can be thoroughly refuted, rather than intimidate them into private conversations among friends who may reinforce them.

• The ambiguities of even the "Fighting Words" approach to prohibiting violent verbal abuse underscores the *frailty* of the whole strategy of calling on institutional regulation. "Immediate relief" from racist verbal harassment simply can't be the primary axis of the whole anti-racist struggle, but only an emergency stop-gap that serves largely as a *symbol* of a willingness to see the seriousness of the whole matter of racist culture—a life and death matter for people of color in this society. Regulation is one way of registering the anti-racist opinion expressed through anti-racist mobilization, given the impossibility of most people to re-mobilize day in and day out, whenever a damaging episode occurs.

The problem here is not an abstract moral one—that one must protect the right even of bigots if one is to protect everyone else's rights—but that the methods of the short-term immediate response approach are foreign to the socialist project as a whole. That is, relying on university administrators to "catch" somebody in an explicit act of a certain kind is simply not an expression of the dynamic of "socialism from below." The latter is more accurately defined as empowering in a liberatory fashion the targets of racism and their allies by garnering numbers and material resources. These are the means to giving power and legitimacy to anti-racist (or, from another angle, internationalist) views on the campus. And here we must *affirm as a general policy* that the route to liberation will come through "*using,* not *curtailing* free speech."[13]

Toward this end we have to look more seriously, albeit critically, at the experiences of anti-racist centers or counter-institutions, such as the Ella Baker/Nelson Mandela Anti-Racist Center at the University of Michigan, and the Third College at the University of California at San Diego. Certain features of these counter-institutions may point toward the eventual creation of alternative centers of real power on the campus. But this will only happen if such centers can develop so that, in contrast to the universities themselves, their functioning is under the democratic control of students, faculty, and staff, with strong representation from people of color and a clear commitment to a liberatory culture that is opposed to authoritarianism.

• We must also take into account that, while explicit racism periodically erupts on many campuses, several recent studies suggest that the real axis of campus racism may rotate around far more subtle issues. We know that the preponderance of racist physical attacks occur not at the university at all but when a person of color accidently enters neighborhood turf controlled by gangs of young white males (as in the now famous cases in Queens and Bensonhurst). In contrast to that urban pattern, a recent study conducted by the University of Michigan School of Public Health claims that the most pressing preoccupation of many students of color is the classroom situation in which an issue of race and racism is clearly implied by the material under discussion, but where no one is willing to raise and confront the issue except students of color. A second preoccupation of respondents was that, when an issue of race did come up, the students of color were then looked upon to provide expert testimony on "the Black experience," etc., which in the eyes of the Euro-Americans seemed to be exclusively equated with poverty and deprivation.[14]

This suggests that, for all the theoretical advances that have been made by scholars of color and others in regard to various aspects of sociological, anthropological, cultural, and literary research, the bottom line is still a profound ignorance on the part of most Euro-American students and faculty. For all of the administrators' glib talk about "tolerance" and "diversity," for all of the insistence that the majority of the university is anti-racist and the bigots are a tiny minority with "bad ideas," the fact remains that misconceptions remain widespread that prevent the university community from appropriating the vocabulary and analytical perspectives necessary to discuss racism in an atmosphere conducive to productive exchange.

In my view, this is largely because the explanation for modern racism—as an ideology elaborated to rationalize super-exploitation of people in those parts of the world conquered by European elites—requires a basically radical critique. If the analysis is carried out consistently, it threatens the view of U.S. capitalist society and the role of Europe in world history that is the basis of the academic ideology of the university. *Hence, any expectation that top-down administrative solutions to racism are going to be crucial to eradicating racist practices is misguided.* The prime focus for socialists must be on developing a sort of cultural revolution *from below*, in the sense that material forces must be gathered, organized, and set in motion to progressively alter the culture of the university at its roots. This alteration should include every aspect—the decor, names of buildings and physical locations, relation to the community, composition of faculty and staff, nature of the curriculum at the foundation (organization of disciplines, models of "academic excellence"), how knowledge is validated (including the abstract/formal approach to "Free Speech"), etc.

Moreover, the strategy and tactics for such a momentous undertaking, which ultimately cannot proceed to fulfillment without major changes outside the university as well as in the center/periphery relations of the capitalist world, can best be characterized as "liberatory," not "repressive." This is in spite of the fact that the goal, from Day One, is to disempower racist behavior.

For example, while there is a sound case to be made for demanding that the entire university community participate in required courses that take up the complexities of racism, socialist activists should fight against the insinuation that the sole object of such courses is to force students to face up to the horrors of racist oppression and deprivation. On the contrary, such courses should be presented as an opportunity to expand the participants' grasp of the forces that shape their own lives and possibilities of experience. The "required" aspect of such courses is only a necessary concession, and hopefully a temporary one, to the fact that the university is permeated by a system in which (1) making a course a "requirement" is a necessary qualification to gain serious attention and appropriate resources, and (2) numerous existing "requirements," fundamentally based on Eurocentric notions (often most pernicious where least acknowledged because the subject matters are allegedly "value-free," as in the teaching of composition skills or the hard sciences), are already firmly in place and will therefore take precedence over non-required courses in a student's schedule.

In summary, *the strategy of mass militant mobilization and formulating demands to prioritize a human culture on the campuses remain the foundation* of any movement that hopes to defend learning, understanding, and freedom in the concrete. In my view, racism against people of color constitutes a special and horrendous category of assault. Therefore *if activists of color themselves* raise the demand to provide immediate relief by banning certain violence-provoking epithets—the unique verbal instigators, facilitators, and allies of material oppression—socialists should be supportive and suggest ways in which the university population as a whole, especially the targets of racism, can play the major role in monitoring and interpreting such restrictions against wounding epithets. However, the *main concern* of socialists must be to mobilize forces to strike at the unequal resources that empower the racist conceptual foundations of the culture of the university. To that end, we should also work toward the creation of counter-cultural centers under control of those who have been targets of racist assault and ideological domination, animated by the kind of thinking that for some has been roughly symbolized by books such as Samir Amin's *Eurocentrism* (Monthly Review, 1987) and Martin Bernal's *Black Athena* (Rutgers, 1987).

Notes

I am grateful to the editorial board of *Against the Current* for criticisms of an earlier draft of this article, and to Ann Arbor Solidarity members Matthew Schultz and Ellen Poteet for a number of specific suggestions. However, I alone am responsible for the argument and analysis. Following the completion of the essay, I was given a copy of "If He Hollers Let Him Go: Regulating Racist Speech on Campus," by Stanford Law Professor Charles R. Lawrence III, which appeared in the *Duke Law Journal* (Spring 1990): 901–52. This thorough study, by an African-American specialist in First Amendment rights, provides a number of useful legal arguments for the view of this essay that racist hate-speech is not a legitimate expression of "Free Speech," but rather an activity that denies constitutional rights to the targets of such racist vilification.

1. Daniel Goleman, "As Bias Crime Seems to Rise, Scientists Study Roots of Racism," *New York Times*, 29 May 1990, B5–7.
2. See "Dean Delays Changes in Disputed Civil-Rights Course," *New York Times*, 30 July 1990, B4; and Jon Weiner, "Free Speech for Campus Bigots?," *Nation* (26 February 1990), 272–76.
3. Space restriction, as well as limitations on available information, require me to focus this article exclusively on racism against people of color. However, struggles against sexism, homophobia, anti-Semitism, and other forms of prejudice and bigotry have obvious parallels.
4. See Weiner, "Free Speech for Campus Bigots?," *Nation* (26 February 1990), 272–76; see "University of Michigan Interim Policy on Discrimination and Discriminatory Conduct by Students in the University Environment," available from the Office of the President, University of Michigan.
5. Of course, if one happens to live in an environment where regular mobilizations are feasible, or where only a relatively few mobilizations can be a successful

means of eliminating racist activity, there is no need to go further. However, most of the places where I have witnessed anti-racist actions are in the long run subject to the weight of the larger culture, so that, following even the biggest anti-racist mobilizations, racist patterns gradually reassert themselves.

6. In his essay, "Should the University Punish Discriminatory Behavior? Code Misses the Point," local ACLU Board member James S. Johnson argues that the issue is "bigotry" rooted in "ignorance," a view similar to that of the University of Michigan administration, which treats racism as a form of intolerance that can be overcome through sensitivity workshops, etc. In contrast, the anti-racist movement at the University of Michigan has been arguing that racism is rooted in material conditions of exploitation with historic, ongoing, and international dimensions. See *Consider* (Summer 1990): 2.

7. See Ellen Schrecker, *No Ivory Tower* (New York: Oxford, 1987).

8. See Nina Morrison, "Poison Pen," *The New Journal* (20 October 1989), 12–14.

9. See "The Self-Defeating Ideologies of Racism and Anti-Semitism," *In These Times* (2–8 May 1990): 14.

10. See Weiner, "Free Speech for Campus Bigots?"

11. See "University of Michigan Interim Policy."

12. James Lafferty, letter to the editor, *Guardian*, 29 August 1990, 2.

13. *A Report of Student Concerns about Issues of Race and Racism in the School of Public Health at the University of Michigan* (April 1990).

15

Chicano Radicalism

Carlos Muñoz, Jr. *Youth, Identity, Power: The Chicano Movement*. (New York: Verso, 1989). 16 pp. $17.95 (paperback).

Carlos Muñoz's bold and compelling new study of the Chicano radical movement is a striking intervention into U.S. political culture in at least three areas. First and foremost, *Youth, Identity, Power* clarifies the complex interaction between the older Mexican-American struggle for equal rights and the student upsurge of the 1960s. With careful documentation and theoretical acumen, Muñoz demonstrates how that cross-fertilization advanced the Chicano Left to a program of national rights and a *sui generis* form of "self-determination" that remain indispensable parts of the socialist agenda to this day.

Second, Muñoz provides an enormously helpful institutional history and collective biography of the Chicano radical movement in all its phases from the 1930s to the 1980s. While the scope of this effort is so broad that he probably treats a number of organizations and individuals in ways that will not satisfy all his critics, the skill with which he "maps" the political terrain and periodizes pivotal moments provides a sound foundation for further research and analysis.

Finally, Muñoz offers a cogent survey of the history, and a critical examination of principles, of efforts in the Southwest and on the West Coast to establish community-based Chicano Studies Programs in universities. A chief consideration here is the search for an appropriate paradigm, one usually based on some version of the "internal colonialism" model of Chicanos as an invaded and conquered non-European nationality. A related preoccupation is the ongoing ordeal of Chicano activist-intellectuals who seek to realize the historic mandate of *El Plan de Santa Barbara*, a stirring 1969 manifesto of political commitment reprinted in full as the appendix to *Youth, Identity, Power*.

Muñoz's study is incisively structured in a way that allows maximum accessibility to novices who need to gain a preliminary familiarity with the political struggle of this specific and complex population—a population that

195

still remains part of the "hidden history" of the U.S. At the same time, the work is informed by a sophisticated political perspective enabling Muñoz to dialectically develop a series of potent themes with which the U.S. Left as a whole must come to terms if we are going to make any headway in the development of effective anti-racist and revolutionary socialist movements in the 1990s.

One of these is the "politics of identity." Mexican-American radicals, from their earliest awareness of "difference" and racist discrimination, sought to forge an image of themselves and their history to explain their position in U.S. society and to suggest a way out. The forms of this expression varied not only according to historical contexts, but also according to the political and religious structures of thought available to the activists for self-expression. Muñoz's book is exciting for the manner in which it encourages us to put aside our own preconceptions about this subject and to follow the ways in which activists in the movement themselves have theorized the issue.

In the 1930s, for example, the Young Men's Christian Association (YMCA) sought to "Protestantize" and "Americanize" European immigrants and then Mexican-Americans through the sponsorship of youth organizations. In a telling episode, the young Mexican-American leaders of the YMCA-initiated boys' clubs and annual Mexican Youth Conference independently began to use YMCA institutions to affirm a unique identity. In the pages of *The Mexican Voice*, UCLA student Félix Gutiérrez (known by the pen name "Manuel De La Raza") rejected his identification as "Spanish" or "Spanish-American," affirming instead a pride in Mexican ancestry within the context of the U.S. By 1942, the YMCA-promoted leaders opted for organizational independence, forming the Mexican American Movement, Inc.

Muñoz refers to these and later activists in the 1950s as "The Mexican-American Generation." Although Gutiérrez and others were propelled by the logic of their "different" status (a status due not only to racism but to a unique and complex cultural heritage and history) toward autonomous organization, they were ideologically wedded to the myth of assimilation. Most were also procapitalist and antisocialist as a result of the widespread delusion that the gains of the New Deal and the post–World War II G.I. Bill would eventually equalize the economic status of Mexican-Americans with Euro-Americans. However, this perspective collapsed at the same time that the Southern Civil Rights movement emerged, setting the stage for a newer and higher expression of identity politics.

Muñoz uses an impressive method that shuttles among historical summary, biographical portraits, extensive quotation from documentary sources, cultural critique, and theoretical generalization. This approach proves especially effective in demonstrating the inspiring role played by the rise of the African-American struggle in the 1960s without reducing the "Chicano Power" movement to a mere imitation. The "Chicano Generation" had its roots among students whose first political awakening tended to be the Viva [John F.] Kennedy Clubs, the Student Non-Violent Coordinating Committee, the 1963 March on Washington, and the Cuban Revolution.

Yet it was probably the 1963 takeover of the city government of Crystal City, Texas, that led to the creation of one of the most dynamic—and telling—features of the Chicano movement of the 1960s. This was the creation of La Raza Unida Party, an independent electoral apparatus to which Muñoz devotes one of his most exciting chapters. The party was inaugurated shortly after the Crystal City victory by a radical former student at St. Mary's University in San Antonio named José Angel Gutiérrez.

Shortly afterwards, a Democratic Party activist named Rodolfo "Corky" Gonzales, one of a few members of the Mexican-American Generation to make the switch to the Chicano Generation, resigned from the Democrats to form a militant civil rights organization in Colorado, called the Crusade for Justice. Two years later, in June 1967, the New Mexico activist Reies López Tijerina led an armed action to regain lands that had been illegally removed from the communal status to which they had been consigned in the treaty following the U.S. conquest of Northern Mexico.

Within a short time, new political organizations sprang up on campuses throughout the Southwest called the Mexican American Youth Organization (MAYO), United Mexican American Students (UMAS), and Mexican American Student Federation (MASC). Along with support for Gonzales and Tijerina, these student groups promoted the United Farm Workers campaign led by Cesar Chávez. The campus-based movements also promoted the cultural writings of playwright Luis Valdez, who emphasized the nonwhite and proletarian elements of Chicano identity. At this time *El Grito*, the first Chicano scholarly journal, was launched as a forum for "Mexican American self definition."

These developments were central among the factors comprising the background to the March 1968 "Blow Out" of East Los Angeles High School students—an act of protest for which the author of this book was charged with "conspiracy" to disrupt the city of Los Angeles and its schools. If continuing protests had not resulted in acquittal, Muñoz and the twelve others who were charged would have faced a possible sixty-six years each in prison. Instead, the case of the "L.A. Thirteen" inspired actions such as the first Chicano college student uprising, at San Jose State College. In November of that year, Chicano students for the first time united in the broader "Third World Liberation Front" to wage a six-month strike at San Francisco State

College for demands that included a Department of La Raza Studies.

From 1968 on, the Chicano struggle proliferated in the high schools, colleges, and barrios across the West Coast and Southwest, retaining distinctive features yet also playing a catalytic role along with the other components of the national and international youth radicalization of that time. Among the most notable efforts to co-ordinate and consolidate this movement was a week-long National Chicano Youth Liberation Conference called by the Crusade for Justice in March 1969. More than a thousand participants announced support for *El Plan Espiritual de Aztlán*—the Spiritual Plan of Aztlán ("Aztlán" is the Aztec term for a legendary northern homeland that came to be identified with the area of Mexico stolen by the U.S. in the mid-nineteenth century).

This famous program, penned by the poet Alurista, expressed a revolutionary nationalist ideology that rejected the dominant culture of the U.S. and called for a cross-class alliance of all Chicanos to win control of Mexican-American communities. However, among the unique features of this nationalism was that its culture was decidedly anti-bourgeois, derived instead from the streets (including the gang values of "brotherhood"). Moreover, the economic program was one of promoting people's co-operatives to replace capitalist institutions in a head-on struggle against the two-party system.

Among the most influential resolutions of the Denver conference were those calling for community control of public schools and radical anti-assimilationist Chicano Studies departments in the universities. A similar concern inspired Chicano students, faculty, and staff in the California state university system to call a conference at Santa Barbara that ended up trying to implement El Plan Espiritual de Aztlán and that folded all existing student organizations into a new one called the Chicano Student Movement of Aztlán(MEChA). This name not only valorized the key terms "Chicano" (affirming a unique identity intransigently opposed to the assimilationist philosophy of "uplifting" those of Mexican ancestry, a perspective that was now identified with the term "Mexican-American") and "Aztlán," but it also translated as "match," connoting political militancy.

MEChA, along with the Brown Berets, a paramilitary community defense organization, helped to spearhead the first Chicano demonstration against the Vietnam war. In August 1970, over 20,000 people poured into a park in East Los Angeles. As a result of the ensuing police riot, three Mexican-Americans were killed and thousands of demonstrators retaliated by destroying businesses and cars on a main thoroughfare.

Muñoz's book continues the story of the Chicano movement from this high point through the twenty years until the second Jesse Jackson presidential campaign of 1988. In his effort to account for the considerable decline of Chicano radicalism in these decades, Muñoz convincingly treats the phenomenon as distinct and yet within the problematic of the decline of the 1960s movement as a whole. Here, as elsewhere in the left-wing movement, earlier leaders defaulted; police repression took its toll; internal ideological disagreements assisted dissolution; student activism, although briefly rekindled over issues such as U.S. intervention in Central America, failed to regain its earlier strength; the ascendancy of Reaganism boosted more traditional establishment organizations and middle-class Chicano mayors; and even Luis Valdez, following his success as the Hollywood director of *La Bamba*, attenuated his cultural militancy.

MEChA has continued to be among the few important reservoirs of the earlier Chicano radicalism, along with the National Association for Chicano Studies(NACS), in which a cadre of 1960s activists continue to promote left-oriented scholarship. Among the most exciting developments in this milieu has been the emergence of Chicana feminists, some of whom initiated the journal *The Third Woman*. Still, there is disturbing evidence that among Chicanos in academe, as elsewhere on the Left, the decline of the mass social protest movements of the 1960s has caused a kind of "degeneration" on the part of some of the radical scholars who got their jobs mainly because of the space created by those mass social movements and the vision promoted by those movements.

In this regard, it is certainly worth emphasizing that Muñoz's book demonstrates in practice precisely the kind of scholarship envisioned by the still-inspiring Plan de Santa Barbara. *Youth, Identity, Power*, which was completed on the twentieth anniversary of the Los Angeles "Blow Outs" and the author's own indictment for "conspiracy," is a book that emanates many of the strengths that flow from scholarship bonded to social purpose. Muñoz knows that there are important stakes in the story he tells for the larger community; this sense of purpose fuels his drive toward accuracy, his refusal to romanticize, and his impressive interdisciplinary approach.

Moreover, it is clearly "no accident" that, among all the autobiographical portraits in the book, the haunting one to which Muñoz most frequently turns is that of the late Ernesto Galarza. Galarza, born in 1905, was a student radical who became a skilled intellectual and author of books such as *Merchants of Labor* (1964). His devotion to the Chicano working class and community, fueled by a militant anticapitalism and pro-unionism, kept him apart from academe altogether. In Muñoz's affinity for the model represented by Galarza, we can already see the seeds of yet another remarkable book-length contribution to Chicano history. But such contributions are equally important for the politics and culture of the entire U.S. Left, if we are to understand our authentic sources of power and inspiration.

In this regard, I want to comment on just a few of the issues that this book and a subsequent article by Muñoz ("Mexican Americans and the Socialist Crisis," *Crossroads* [October 1990]: 2–6) pose for those of us committed to transforming our brutal, racist, capitalist society into a system democratically self-managed by the producers with an internationalist culture.

• First and foremost, the socialist movement has no future until its theoretical and practical relation to the Chicano movement is elevated qualitatively above the status of publishing an occasional article in its press or episodically including Chicanos as a sub-category in discussions of racism or the labor movement. The most obvious pattern that needs to be broken is the subsumption of all struggles of people of color into groups of "others" that are dwarfed by the African-American movement.

It is true, of course, that, as in the case of Asian Americans and Native American Indians, the visibility of the Chicano population is far greater in the Southwest and on the West Coast than in the Midwest or on the East Coast, where many socialist groups produce their publications and have their national offices. Nevertheless, blind provincialism in regard to the centrality and urgency of the Chicano movement will ultimately be as disempowering as would be a blind U.S. nationalism that occluded from view the centrality of the South African or Latin American struggles for the fate of world socialism. It is out of self-interest, in terms of understanding the dynamics of our own social formation (and the richness of its diverse history and culture) that the Left must expand, enrich, and complicate its ways of thinking in regard to all people of color.

• Second, socialist movements must recognize the dangers of "tokenism" in regard to the Chicano and other populations of people of color. Female and male activists from these movements must be aggressively welcomed to play *central* and decision-making roles on leading bodies of socialist groups and in their publications. This means, on the one hand, making technical skills and support available to such activists, but, on the other hand, recognizing that an initiate in the socialist movement from such a community may in certain respects be more knowledgeable and insightful about these and other struggles than many long-time socialist functionaries and "theoreticians."

In this regard, it is crucial that books such as Muñoz's be studied and discussed among socialists in order to understand the complex and unique features of Chicano history and culture. While most Chicanos may have some common overall historical features rooted in the conquest of Mexico, it would be a mistake to ignore crucial differences according to region and occupation, not to mention variations by class, gender, and culture. The imposition of simplistic class-reductive or vulgar nationalist (or anti-nationalist) schemas on this population must be avoided.

• Third, socialist groups must develop ways of supporting Chicano struggles that do not interfere with the autonomous character of such struggles. Here is where I find Muñoz's book to be weakest in providing guidelines and models, although he may well hold the view that "answers" in this area can only come through the protracted process of self-critically examining many experiences.

Nevertheless, I feel that there may be much more to be learned about the concrete experiences of socialist groups in relation to the earlier Mexican-American and later Chicano movements. The claim that Marxist groups have been manipulative, dogmatic, opportunist, sectarian, and even "racist" may have a general kind of validity. But most often the attacks I have read are predicated on "horror stories" (which may well have occurred, but which may not be representative of a general practice) or appear in virulent critiques (sometimes vulgar and other times scholastic to the point of tedium) mainly designed to "smash" a rival perspective.

What we lack are detailed studies of policies and practices. My own research into the history of the U.S. Communist Party, and my personal experiences in a West Coast branch of the Socialist Workers Party, suggest to me that, in fact, there is a great deal, positive and negative, that can be learned for the politics and organization of the Left if we can find an appropriate method.

A final, somewhat related, concern of mine has to do with two of Muñoz's excellent discussions of various controversies. One of these is the debate over the term "Hispanic" to designate not only Chicanos but other diverse Latino populations. The other is his review of the ups and downs of the "internal colonialism model."

Muñoz's case for the superiority of the term "Chicano" seems convincing. Yet the fact remains that in some regions of the country the general population as well as leading radical political groups prefer other terms—Mexicanos, Hispanos, etc. I do not see how socialists, who both respect the necessity of "politically correct" designations, and yet also respect the right of self-determination, can easily resolve this or similar issues. As in the case of gender attitudes, we neither want to adapt to backwardness nor do we want to try to impose values and perspectives from the outside that might play a divisive role.

Similarly, the internal colonialism model has been interpreted by some people as viewing the Chicano population as an existing nation or nation-in-formation, a political analysis that Muñoz rejects. On the other hand, opposition to the internal colonialism model has just as frequently led to an economist view of Chicanos as merely a racially oppressed group, to a downplaying of unique features of its history and culture that can only be expressed by "national" demands in regard to bilingualism, community control of schools, the return of communal lands, etc. My own view is that the explanatory power of the internal colonialism metaphor is too great to abandon merely because of the dangers of a bourgeois-nationalist misappropriation, or because of the polemical edge that ambiguities in this metaphor might give to anti-nationalist dogmatists.

Muñoz argues convincingly that there is a great deal of uniqueness and specificity in the U.S. social formation in regard to the incorporation and exploitation of diverse populations, especially non-European people of color. This suggests to me that concepts of nationalism, self-determination, and internal colonialism can and should be applied—but in a creative manner, based on, and modified in light of, extensive empirical research. In any event, the end question of whether the Chicano population will in its majority move toward some form of national autonomy or semi-autonomy, or define itself in some other manner, will ultimately be determined by the actions and consciousness of that population itself through its continuing struggle against capitalist exploitation and racism.

Socialists must be alert to changing sentiments and perspectives, and must seek to support those that seem most compatible with the internationalization and democratization of the struggle. Of course, this is a process that would be enormously facilitated by the presence as leaders of numerous Chicano militants within the socialist Left itself. However, what we must reject is the notion of a small group deciding on a "line," nationalist or anti-nationalist, and then "fighting" for the hegemony of that line to "lead" the Chicano movement. That approach is part of the elitist vanguardism that has now been discredited in the Chicano movement as well as elsewhere on the Left.

PART IV
Commitment

16

In Tribute to
Burger's Daughter

Burger's Daughter (1979), the sixth novel by the white South African writer
Nadine Gordimer, blends political subtlety with compelling insight into the
psychology of radical activists in the contemporary anti-apartheid movement. With acute sensitivity, Gordimer focuses on the dilemma of Rosa
Burger, the rebellious daughter of a martyred South African Communist of
Afrikaner descent, who initially abandons and then resumes commitment to
the anti-racist struggle of her father. Technically and thematically, the novel
has many complex origins. What is especially striking is the manner in
which Gordimer, whose vision is partly animated by a modern socialist and
feminist consciousness, surpasses many of the achievements of her more
famous male European predecessors who have written in the tradition of
the "political novel."

In her setting, Gordimer depicts the "real, existing totalitarianism" of
Johannesburg and Soweto, not a fantasy world of the future, as in George
Orwell's ambiguous *1984*, or a tendentious blend of imagination and
historical fact, as in Arthur Koestler's anti-communist *Darkness at Noon*.
Moreover, in contrast to Alexander Solzhenitsyn's early socialist novels,
The First Circle and *Cancer Ward*, Gordimer explores the multifaceted effects
of political and social repression in a broad, natural way; she never relies on
contrived mechanisms such as Solzhenitsyn's technique of assembling a
group of "representative" figures in a prison for political dissidents or a
cancer ward.

Burger's Daughter is remarkably faithful to the historical background of
the movement for social emancipation in South Africa. Indeed, it has a
certain non-fiction, almost documentary component. Many of the background characters and events are factual. Even the life of Rosa's father,
Dr. Lionel Burger, resembles that of the South African lawyer Abram
Fischer, also a member of a noted Afrikaner family who became a Communist in his youth and died in prison in the 1960s. A leaflet from the Soweto

uprising of 1976 is reprinted just a few chapters before the end of the novel, which terminates when Rosemarie Burger (named for both the Polish revolutionary Rosa Luxemburg and her own Afrikaner grandmother) is incarcerated in 1977.

Despite the authentic recreation in the novel of much of the social and political reality of South Africa, *Burger's Daughter* is also an experimental work with a modernist sensibility echoing James Joyce and Virginia Woolf. Sometimes the plot is narrated in the first person, by Rosa; other times in the third, by an omniscient voice. Several chapters are addressed by Rosa to "you," referring to Conrad, her former lover; other times "you" refers to her father, and occasionally to Zwelinzima Vulindlela (called by the nickname "Baasie"), a Black African youth who lived for a while with the Burger family when his own father was imprisoned for anti-apartheid activity. The reader is not always immediately informed of the identity of the "you" to whom Rosa addresses her interior monologue. Moreover, the punctuation of the novel is eccentric; there are no quotation marks around the dialogue. The plot is non-linear, constructed by flashbacks and flash-forwards.

Despite all this, *Burger's Daughter* is characterized by a high degree of unity between Rosa's internal reflections and the external reality. As the critic Robert Boyers observed in an unusually perceptive commentary ("Public and Private: On *Burger's Daughter*," *Salmagundi* [Winter 1984]), the novel probes to a large degree the "personal," especially the disruption and reorientation of Rosa's social consciousness, and also the ambiguous family bonds that can exist between an overwhelming father and an independent-minded and sensitive daughter. Yet rarely have we been more powerfully reminded of the profundity of the feminist movement's observation that "the personal is political."

Gordimer's exceptional skill as a political artist is most evident in her characterizations. Gordimer intends to dramatize political themes through her protagonists, but avoids the vulgarity that Karl Marx called "Schillerizing," in reference to the German poet Johann von Schiller (1759–1805), whose characters Marx believed to serve as merely mouthpieces for ideologies. The main characters in *Burger's Daughter* are memorable, human, and complex, distinguished by a blend of foibles and virtues that render the choices made by political activists in real life far from simple and self-evident.

Dr. Lionel Burger, for example, is a man who from moral conviction abandons a successful career to become an outcast and die in prison. He comes from a wealthy family of the white ruling minority of South Africa; he has had such a first-class education and possesses such enormous personal talents that even his enemies regard his defection to the side of the Black majority as a terrible loss. And he undertakes his struggle to overthrow the racist apartheid system with no illusions about what will happen to him, adhering to that struggle to the end, which is death in prison. Unforgettable is his courtroom speech during his trial for subversion, which he knows will bring him a life sentence:

> My covenant is with the victims of apartheid. The situation in which I find myself changes nothing . . . there will always be those who cannot live with themselves at the expense of fulness of life for others. They know "world history would be very easy to make if the struggle were taken up only on condition of infallibly favorable chances."
> . . . this court has found me guilty on all counts. If I have ever been certain of anything in my life, it is that I acted according to my conscience on all counts. I would be guilty only if I were innocent of working to destroy racism in my country.

We do not sense in these and other statements of Lionel Burger a power-hungry person, as Communists are often depicted by their enemies; only a man with a vision of a better world for which he is willing to sacrifice. Yet, at the same time that Gordimer unambiguously acknowledges the heroic qualities of Dr. Burger, she also shows his blindness and insensitivity. For example, although Lionel in his courtroom speech defends the record of the Communist Party, we are reminded in other episodes that being a party member has meant supporting some unconscionable acts by his foreign and domestic comrades. Rosa's world-weary lover, Conrad, points out to her early in the book that being a loyal party member may have meant fighting totalitarianism in South Africa, but it also meant supporting in the USSR and Eastern Europe a system that enforced its own brand of "totalitarianism" by imprisoning its own dissident Lionel Burgers: "There were the Moscow trials and there was Stalin—before you and I were even born—there was the East Berlin uprising and there was Czechoslovakia, there're the prisons and asylums filled with people there like your father here." We are also presented with a list of some of the bizarre twists and turns in Communist policy in South Africa, which Lionel had apparently endorsed, even at the price of having to vote for the expulsion of Sidney Bunting (an historical figure who was a central party leader until 1930), the Communist he most admired:

> After the shame of the red banner, "Workers of the world unite and fight for a white South Africa," flown in 1914 [*sic*; this is apparently a reference to the 1922 miners' strike on the Rand], had been erased in the 1920s by the acceptance of Lenin's thesis on the national and colonial questions, after the purges when Lionel Burger . . . voted for the expulsion of his mentor Bunting, after the Party in South Africa turned right and then left again, after it refused to support the war that South Africa

was fighting against racialism in Europe while herself practicing racialism at home, after the Soviet Union was attacked and this policy of opposition to the war effort was reversed . . . .

Moreover, it is suggested that Lionel, out of the best of convictions, *uses* people; that is, he draws others into the struggle who may not understand fully the price they might have to pay. He has no hesitation in involving his daughter from a very young age. It is in fact her sense of having been used, almost created, by her father that inspires Rosa's anti-political rebellion and flight from South Africa. The broken health of Rosa's mother, Cathy, which results in her own death after a long period of detention in prison, is likely a result of the excessive pressures of the political struggle which she has carried out side-by-side with her husband even as she has raised a family. There is also the woman who testifies against Lionel in the subversion trial, claiming that she was ignorant of the full scope of the dangerous anti-government activities to which he had recruited her.

Lionel's disturbingly familiar combination of utter devotion to an idealistic cause with a frightening emotional toughness is also dramatized in the poignant episode of the death of his son, Tony, in the swimming pool. The Burger family swimming pool is a symbol of Burger's anti-racist politics. It is the only pool where whites and people of color come together, and he personally teaches the children to swim. In a certain sense the communal life he establishes at the pool is a prefiguration of the non-racist society he hopes to establish.

Yet one day Tony decides to show off his diving when his father isn't around, cracks his head on the bottom of the pool, and drowns. The emotional response of most parents to that situation would likely be to shut the pool down for a long time, perhaps forever. But Burger knows that the pool is more than a private possession; it is a symbol of anti-racism. Within a few days he throws his daughter back into the water and the pool is open for the Black and white neighbors again. We see here effectively dramatized a useful point about the relationship of politics and character—character in the psychological, not moral, sense. Burger's toughness in standing up against the apartheid dictatorship is not without major consequences for his emotional and personal life.

Other characters, both major and minor, show the same convincing and authentic pattern of a *mix* of motives and qualities, no matter with which side they are allied. The Communist friends of the Burgers, Dick and Ivy Treblanches, are devoted to anti-racism but quite conformist within the norms of Communist Party behavior. Their own daughter, Clare, is a conformist counterpart to Rosa. The journalist Orde Greer is an unattractive man with a drinking problem. His political commitment seems questionable, almost parasitic. Early in the book he embarrasses Rosa, exploiting her situation insensitively in a debate with Black activists. When challenged as to whether whites can play a role in the struggles, he simply points to Rosa and reminds them of her father's death in prison. Yet at the end of the book when he, too, is tried for subversion, there is a kind of modest dignity in his statement quoted in the papers:

> I've spent many years being proud of hob-nobbing with the people who were brave enough to risk their lives in action. I spent too many years looking on, writing about it; I would rather go to prison now for acting against evil than have waited to be detained without even having done anything.

It would be a perverse violation of the best traditions of Marxist literary criticism to attempt to translate the ideas and events in *Burger's Daughter* into a "political line," judging it according to precise policies and organizational allegiances which the book may or may not imply. Indeed, by emphasizing and ignoring certain elements, one might interpret Gordimer's concluding stance as either a critical endorsement of the South African Communist Party or a call for a new kind of post-Marxist commitment! But it would also be a disservice to the social commitment at the core of Gordimer's work to fail to recognize that there *is* an important political argument in the novel, one that has a far broader relevance than to the situation in South Africa alone.

Gordimer appears to have written her novel as a response to the complexities of political engagement in the modern world: a world in which the sophisticated person knows that most political struggles do not lead to the promised land; that many individuals who appear to be moral and righteous, whether religious leaders or social activists, can be just as neurotic and self-seeking as anyone else; that the racially and economically oppressed can be tragically imperfect; that all members of the oppressing group are neither fools nor conscious villains; that life is short and the moulding of one's behavior to please someone else, be it parents or society, can result in personal bitterness and a stunted existence. To this end, she presents us with the odyssey of Rosa Burger, a woman of our time, seeking freedom and personal fulfillment, in a social order in which the contending forces of Afrikaner ideology and her parents' Communist subculture deny her free choice and shape her destiny against her will.

Rosa has grown up as a dutiful daughter. What is unusual is that her duty was to a devout Communist, a father to whom she was utterly loyal and whose wishes she automatically carried out. When Dr. Burger dies after serving sixteen months of his life-term imprisonment for violating South Africa's anti-subversive laws, everyone, from the police to family friends, assumes that Rosa will simply take her father's place and carry on his work. Yet she is already in the process of rebelling—rebelling against what appears to her to be a predestined role of conforming to the behavior of a man who was regarded in his own society as a nonconformist. Thus she is drawn into an affair with Conrad, an aimless young man who first hangs around the fringes of the Burger's community swimming pool, and later attends Dr. Burger's trial; Conrad assumes the role of an observer who refuses to commit himself to the cause although he is clearly not a supporter of apartheid.

To some extent Conrad may be a projection of Rosa's own psychological uncertainties. Indeed, before long she halts sexual relations with him, feeling they are "incestuous." If Rosa has experienced the world through the prism of politics, Conrad's viewpoint is distinctly psychological. She has been shaped by the social strife of race and class struggle; he has been shaped by the psycho-sexual trauma of having witnessed his mother copulating with a strange man in his father's absence.

While Conrad assists Rosa in breaking free of the conformity of her family—by questioning Dr. Berger's real motives and the efficacy of his actions—it eventually becomes clear that Conrad himself presents no viable alternative. He imagines he is freer than Rosa because he eschews social commitment, but he remains a prisoner of his own egoism and self-centeredness.

This insight, however, only comes late in Rosa's development. Soon after meeting Conrad, she becomes increasingly detached from the memory of her father and his way of life. She concludes that his social concern, his political commitment to ending suffering, was itself a form of neurosis: "Even animals have the instinct to turn away from suffering. The sense to run away."

Several subsequent encounters with the stark brutality of life convince her to abandon political struggle altogether, assuming a more or less stoic philosophy. At one point, she witnesses a man die on a park bench; at another, she sees a Black African brutally beating a donkey. In the face of the inevitability of death and of the imperfectability of humanity, she concludes that the effort to remake the world is futile. Consequently she seeks out her father's first wife, Madame Bagnelli, now in France, because Rosa wants to learn from her how to break away from the emotional grip of Lionel and his world of austere political commitment.

A subtheme in the novel is the ambiguous role played by "sexual freedom," in the sense of casual, non-marital sexual relations. Because sex is primarily self-centered, it can be an avenue to detachment from an environment or way of life in which one is unthinkingly imprisoned; in that sense it is a positive, liberatory factor, as in Kate Chopin's classic novel, *The*

Awakening. Madame Bagnelli had wanted to be a dancer and felt unsuited to the Communist movement; her break with Lionel was prefigured by her affair with his comrade, Dick Treblanches. Rosa uses sexual relations with Conrad and also a Swedish filmmaker to distance herself from her father's world as well.

But sexual liberation in and of itself seems to lead nowhere. Thus, while visiting Madam Bagnelli in southern France, Rosa finds herself in an environment that is depicted as one of sexual decadence. The milieu in which she lives for a while is replete with heterosexual and homosexual seducers immersed in their personal lives, which go on aimlessly and meaninglessly, oblivious to the world of social strife that lies beyond. Rosa naively falls into what is certain to be a frustrating dead-end affair with a married schoolteacher, Bernard Chabelier, working on his Ph. D. He will not leave his wife, so Rosa must be content to share him, and she will have to forsake the idea of having her own family, should she desire one.

But Rosa's adaptation to this new way of life is only superficial. Visiting London, she is drawn to an anti-apartheid gathering, and, recognized by the participants as the daughter of the legendary South African Communist martyr, she again becomes "Burger's Daughter." To her surprise, she encounters Zwelinzima Vulindlela at the event, and is deeply affected by her interaction with him. He does not plead for her to return to the struggle; such a moralistic approach would have been unsuccessful, since part of her new-found cynicism is a skepticism of people's moral pretenses. Rather, he denounces her and her father as frauds who are totally useless to the struggle, and who, in fact, have personally benefitted from it. He points out the all too painful truth that many Blacks, including his own father, had died just as nobly as Lionel Burger, yet no one had sung *their* praises; no one had treated *them* as martyrs; and no one had celebrated *their* children.

The *New Republic* (29 September 1979) criticized *Burger's Daughter* on the grounds that this encounter with Vulindlela provides insufficient motivation for her decision to break her relationship with Chabelier and return to South Africa to work as a nurse in a Black hospital, protest apartheid, and ultimately and inevitably assume her place in prison. I strongly disagree with this view. It is true that her change, her switch after Vulindlela's explosion, is not explained to us in ideological or intellectual terms. Her response is emotional, indeed, physical; Rosa goes into the bathroom and vomits.

But from the beginning, Gordimer has been demonstrating to us that politics is not mere ideology—not pure logic, reason, or rhetoric. Political commitment is based on personally felt experience. Rosa's father was a Communist not simply because he read logically-convincing documents, but because he genuinely wanted to see the harmonious existence of whites and people of color, as demonstrated by the interracial community he created at the family swimming pool. True, the intensity of his vision caused him to embrace a doctrine by which to explain and combat the oppressive social reality, and this doctrine, like all doctrines, had its limitations. But such failings only indicate that Burger is human and therefore defective; they do not negate the fact that, given his social context, he was on the "right" side in a situation where right and wrong are clearly demarcated.

Thus Vulindlela's harsh words are quite plausible as the catalyst of her change, precisely because they strike her at an emotional and personal level. At once she sees that his words are true: even as a martyr, Lionel Burger, being white, received privileges; and, even as a martyr's daughter, Rosa Burger, being white, received privileges. What is it, then, that affects her so strongly? Some would say "guilt," an explanation often proffered condescendingly by nonactivists to discredit the behavior of politically active people who themselves are not especially oppressed. But a careful reading of the novel shows that Rosa's decision is more likely due to a clearer sense of how she can affirm her dignity as an independent woman, not from a neurotic need for atonement.

Rosa's return to South Africa is a consequence of her enhanced understanding of social reality, and new insight into the dialectical relation between freedom and determinism. When she acted only as her father's daughter, carrying out her political obligations the way a Catholic or Jewish daughter carries out her Catholic or Jewish duties, she was more a determined function of external forces acting upon her than an agent of her own desire. Yet it has become evident to her that the momentary happiness she achieved with Bernard in France was in its own way equally imprisoning and artificial.

Moreover, this attempt to find "freedom" by establishing an existence far removed from the intense, daily social struggle she had known when she was still "Burger's Daughter" is such a fragile illusion that it is easily shattered by Vulindlela's powerful expression of emotion, his bitter truths. In one instant she repudiates the subjectivism of Conrad, the view that one creates reality through one's state of mind. A dose of that kind of solipsism was perhaps liberating at a certain stage of her development, but, as a mode of life, it is fraudulent.

Rosa's ultimate evolution is foreshadowed in an earlier exchange with Clare Treblanches. Clare, like Rosa, is the daughter of Communists, and has taken up her parents' struggle in what Conrad had characterized as a conformist manner. In many ways she is a less impressive version of Burger's daughter: her appearance less attractive than Rosa's; her father, a laboring man, less prepossessing than Rosa's; her affair with a married man less romantic than Rosa's. And yet, in her simple way, she sees much earlier a truth that Rosa had tried to evade. When Rosa complains that the two of them had been impressed into radical political activity by their parents, and asks, "were you given a choice?", Clare replies: "Yes . . . I suppose if you want to look at it like that . . . But no! Rosa! What choice? Rosa? In this country, under this system, looking at the way blacks live—what has the choice to do with parents? What else could you choose?"

Thus Nadine Gordimer communicates to us more or less what Frederick Engels said in the last century when he wrote, "Freedom is the recognition of necessity." In other words, Freedom is not a subjective abstraction; it can not be equated with a retreat from social pressure into pure intellect or fantasy, or the artistic construction of an imaginary life that "liberates" us from objective reality. Freedom comes from taking appropriate action to control one's life by first recognizing the authentic dynamics of one's environment.

This perception is what may be intended by the epigraph to the novel from the structuralist-anthropologist Claude Levi-Strauss: "I am the place in which something has occurred." We are created by the world around us—the environment in which we are born and in which we grow up. What is required to achieve the maximum autonomy available to self-conscious humans is to *challenge* what is oppressive in that environment. After all, one diminishes one's freedom not only by retreating to an imaginary world devoid of the social strife that still continues to affect one, but also by unthinkingly and unquestioningly conforming to the moral, religious, and cultural beliefs and practices of the family or society into which one is born.

Rosa may be partly intended as a role model for the generation of young people in the late 1970s and early 1980s, a generation that has in some respects evidenced a waning of political commitment in comparison to that of the 1960s—although the book may also be a plea to lapsed radicals of the 1960s to abandon Yuppie hedonism and return to their best instincts. But *Burger's Daughter* is certainly *not* an argument for the predestination of the children of political parents. Rosa in *essence* returns to her father's position, but her return is by choice, not from conformity; she is well aware of some of the weaknesses and even hypocrisies of revolutionary commitment by white South Africans. Yet she has also observed the even greater weaknesses and hypocrises residing in the illusion that one becomes "free" by eschewing politics, by wishing away the maelstrom of class forces so central to the making of the world today.

Gordimer's incisive dramatization of the superiority of a *conscious* political choice is heightened by her socialist and feminist awareness of the *problematic* nature of commitment itself. Thus *Burger's Daughter* not only transforms the conventions of the political and modernist novel in a stunning artistic achievement, but her book also deserves recognition as a moral pharos for the anti-racist movement of our time.

17

Jacoby's Complaint

Russell Jacoby. *The Last Intellectuals: American Culture in the Age of Academe* (New York: Basic, 1987). 290 pp. $18.95.

Russell Jacoby, an intellectual historian trained under Christopher Lasch, has been an editorial associate of the journal *Telos* since the early 1970s. Best-known for several critical studies of the psychoanalytic profession and a pole-mical survey of Western Marxism, a feature of his work over the past two decades has been the regular publication of jeremiads for his generation.

The burden of these laments is the endless failings of New Left intellectu-als, mostly those born in the 1940s and coming of age in the 1960s and 1970s. Among the most memorable are a diptych published in *Telos* at the beginning and end of the 1970s: "The Politics of Subjectivity" (#9, Fall 1971) and "The Politics of Objectivity" (#34, Winter 1977–78). Here, young Leftists of all types are taken to task for the alternate blunders of voluntarism and dogmatic Marxism.

There is considerable truth in these and other complaints of Jacoby about the New Left in those years. Moreover, such complaints were made with a combination of panache and Frankfurt School erudition imparting an aura of brilliance to his critique, even when his alternatives were never very clear. Jacoby also had the saving grace of wit; one commentary on class consciousness and economic theory was called, "A Falling Rate of Intelli-gence?" (*Telos* #27, Spring 1976).

But his new book, *The Last Intellectuals*, recalls the defects more than the virtues of these earlier tropes of lamentation. The feistiness is still there, as well as the warnings and castigations. Still, despite his turn toward a less-convoluted prose style—something adroitly carried out in practice while advocated in theory—the argumentation is more abstract and the political perspective more dubious than ever.

The strength of *The Last Intellectuals*, which has been remarkably effective in capturing the attention of left-wing and intellectual publications, lies in the important truth of one of Jacoby's central observations. A large percent-age of New Left activists has ended up in universities; the result is a

214

proliferation of Marxist and radical caucuses, but the price extracted may have been too great. In particular, the language of much of this new scholarship is highly specialized, narrowing the audience to whom the work is addressed.

Beyond this, many of Jacoby's claims are in the category of preliminary speculations; they remain to be verified by evidence beyond his selective quotations and scathing characterizations. Unfortunately, Jacoby tends to assert such speculations as if they are "facts" established beyond doubt.

Among his provocative but unproven hypotheses are the following:

1) At one time there existed a category of "public intellectuals," which he defines mainly by incanting the name of C. Wright Mills, as well as an odd lot of others such as Lionel Trilling, Dwight Macdonald, Paul Sweezy, Edmund Wilson, Harold Rosenberg, and Irving Howe. This dying breed (the "last" intellectuals of the book's title) allegedly possessed an independence from institutions, even when they taught for a living. They addressed not merely other academics but an educated public. Jacoby's contention is that such a category is entirely "missing" from the generation now in its thirties and forties.

2) The primary factor responsible for the "disappeared" younger intellectuals is the post-war expansion of higher education, absorbing and transforming them. Simultaneously, there was the elimination of inexpensive Bohemian urban enclaves that had nurtured the public intellectuals.

3) Younger intellectuals have been housebroken by the new academic professionalization process. New Left professors working under the tenure system have succumbed to depoliticization for careerist reasons.

Despite denials, Jacoby clearly idealizes the earlier generation of "Public Intellectuals." He provides no means of demonstrating that they reached a broader audience numerically, percentage-wise, or in any other measurable way, than contemporary figures such as Stephen J. Gould, Ellen Willis, Barbara Ehrenreich, and Manning Marable—just a few examples of the many living refutations to Jacoby's claim about a "missing generation," and who are never mentioned in his book.

Moreover, Jacoby seems to contradict himself in praising the "public idiom" of someone like Lionel Trilling. Trilling's fetishization of terms such as "moral realism," "modulation," and "the imagination of disaster," not to mention "anti-anti-communism," was part of an in-group vocabulary also reflected in his use of the royal "we." Likewise, the rarefied rhetoric of Harold Rosenberg must have struck many readers as the academic jargon of his day, and still mystifies many students in ours.

Moreover, if "radicalism" in thought and practice is prized by Jacoby (there is some ambiguity about this, considering his models), the superiority of the good old days to the present seems even less convincing. Mills certainly had a radical personal style; the case for a profoundly radical political and sociological theory is never made.

In contrast, the younger Left intellectuals have made uneven but significant advances over their predecessors in many areas. Jacoby never mentions the major assault—largely inspired by the Black Arts and feminist movements—against the domination of elite European patriarchal culture in literary studies. Nor does he discuss the challenge of younger social historians to the reigning paradigms of the profession. The snobbism and high culture delusions of the previous generation, typified by the pseudo-radicalism of *Partisan Review* in the 1950s, did as much harm as good.

A special villain in Jacoby's morality play is the Marxist literary theorist Fredric Jameson, who is accused, on the basis of various quotations, of surplus jargon, insularity, and of essentially making much ado about nothing. There is no question that a good deal of what is being written in the name of "Marxist theory" today is superfluous and pretentious, but the approach here of shooting from the hip is a poor substitute for careful refutation.

In fact, the space created by Jameson in literary studies has been crucial to the increasing opportunities to teach Marxist cultural theory openly and regularly. While I am not familiar with Jameson's overall record of activism, I do recall that he made an appearance at a University of Michigan literary conference several years ago conditional on the university also arranging for him to give a public address on Palestine, where he defended the right of self-determination with force and clarity. He has also traveled to Nicaragua, and in published material has addressed central issues in the revolutionary process.

The point is not that Jameson is a model revolutionary, or that his own work is beyond abuse. It is, alas, that Jacoby has not significantly researched his subject. Jacoby signals him out for special attack, but bases his case on imputation, not facts.

Such a shoddy method is then elevated from an individual case to assess entire groups. Is it true that tenure has destroyed a generation of young scholars, or has it enabled a remnant of the New Left to go forward under difficult circumstances? Can we really make categorical judgments of this type, or might there be considerable variation from situation to situation? Haven't many who never received tenure abrogated their political and intellectual responsibilities as well? Shouldn't people be judged by their authentic practice?

Jacoby's absolutism has gotten him into trouble before. At the end of 1980, he presented an argument that can now be seen as the premise for his present resurrection of intellectual models from the 1950s: "Today you do not need a weatherman to know the revolutionary storm is over. The 80s will be as close to the 60s as the Black Hundreds are to the Red Guards. . . .

The murder of John Lennon is a sign of the times; nor should we forget Allard Lowenstein, and the others. The lesson is clear: the 60s will not be ignored but annihilated" (*Telos* #46, Winter 1981).

Admittedly, times have been tough in comparison with some of the more heady days of the 1960s. But universities across the country have been aflame for the past several years over issues very similar to those animating the earlier radicalization. Continuity with the 1960s is sometimes manifest in surprising ways. At the University of Michigan, the grandson of Herbert Marcuse was assaulted and arrested by the campus police at an anti-CIA protest in the fall of 1987, and the most widely attended lecture of the Winter term was that given by 1960s activist Angela Davis—and attended by 2,000 cheering students.

The point is not that capitalism is finally through at last, but that Jacoby has an inadequate grip on fundamental problems that face the intellectual Left in the 1980s. His central theme, that there has appeared no C. Wright Mills of the New Left generation, is as about as relevant to the present situation as the common complaint of the upholders of the traditional U.S. white male literary canon: "Where is the female equivalent of *Moby Dick*? Or Black equivalent of *The Waste Land*?"

Instead, the central issue for radical intellectuals should be their relationship to oppositional social movements—not only the labor movement, but also movements of women, oppressed minorities, ecologists, anti-interventionists, and anti-nuclear weapons activists.

Finally, I am far less sanguine than Jacoby about demanding that intellectuals conform to a certain "more popular" mode of discourse; efforts at homogenization of Left intellectuals, especially on the grounds that they are too inward-looking, have been disastrous in the past. Such calls have in fact become instruments for populist authoritarianism, Left and Right, harboring perhaps unanticipated but nonetheless profoundly anti-intellectual sentiments.

18

Radical Pedagogy

Paulo Freire. *The Politics of Education: Culture, Power, Liberation*, trans. Donaldo Macedo, Introduction by Henry A. Giroux. (S. Hadley, Mass.: Bergin and Garvey, 1985). xxv + 209 pp. $9.95 (paperback); $24.95 (cloth).

The Left Academy: Marxist Scholarship on American Campuses, ed. Bertell Ollman and Edward Vernoff. Volume 2. (New York: Praeger, 1984). xvii + 182 pp. $10.95 (paperback); $23.95 (cloth).

Ira Shor. *Culture Wars: School and Society in the Conservative Restoration 1969–1984*, foreword by Paulo Freire. Critical Social Thought Series. (Boston: Routledge and Kegan Paul, 1986). xvii + 238 pp. $9.95 (paperback); $29.95 (cloth).

For the past twenty years, leftwing students and faculty inspired by the political and cultural upheaval of the late 1960s have been writing intensively about the nature of the educational system in late capitalist society. Now that many veterans of the radical movement of those years have completed graduate school and commenced academic careers, increasing attention is also being directed to the achievements and dilemmas of Marxist scholars working in the university environment.

By 1987, there exists a rather large body of literature on these subjects. Recurrent topics include the elaboration of techniques of radical pedagogy, usually inspired by the writings of Brazilian educator Paulo Freire; calls to advance Marxist theory, especially regarding the complexities of class, gender, and race; and arguments for a more subtle dissection of the dynamics of domination and resistance that characterize the conditions of working and learning in U.S. educational institutions.

These three recent books by Ira Shor, Bertell Ollman and Edward Vernoff, and Paulo Freire are characteristic of contributions to the ongoing debate over these and other issues. All are exemplary in the manner in which they fill in gaps in our knowledge of pedagogy, theoretical developments, and life in the U.S. educational system. But strangely lacking in each case is a substantive consideration of the problem of implementation: the

218

precise means by which our cultural work—whether in the form of scholarly writing or in the creation of critical consciousness among students—expresses itself in organized collective political activity that concretely leads to the restructuring of the U.S. social and economic order.

In September 1968, the Columbia University chapter of Students for a Democratic Society sponsored an address by the Belgian Marxist theoretician Ernest Mandel on "The Revolutionary Student Movement: Theory and Practice." The packed auditorium of more than 600 people burst out in thunderous applause when Mandel declared: "We must maintain as a general rule that there are no good theoreticians if they are not capable of participating in action, and that there are no good activists if they are not capable of assimilating, strengthening and developing theory" (Ernest Mandel, *The Revolutionary Student Movement* [New York: Merit, 1969], p. 12). Although the social, cultural, and economic conditions in which we function today are markedly different from those of 1968, nothing has occurred during the past nineteen years to refute this "general rule" for socialist students, teachers, and scholars.

Most radical critics of the educational system and most Marxist academics would probably agree in a general sense that it is necessary for teachers and scholars to become allies of oppressed groups and to participate in the political movements required to organize and cohere struggles for the self-emancipation of humanity. But nowhere in these three books is there a consideration of the forms through which that alliance and political unity should occur, and the unique problems faced by teachers and scholars who attempt to realize their beliefs through such collective social practice.

Traditionally, socialist political commitment translates into attempts to unify the diverse elements in the revolutionary process in a manner that promotes the interests of the working class without reducing other important struggles to merely the "class struggle." Toward this end, a rigorous internationalist political perspective is worked out through study, discussion, and debate. Activities are then developed promoting the self-confidence of the population through collective self-organization and mass mobilization. Special attention is devoted to creating truly democratic processes for the meetings that are held and committees that are formed. An extra emphasis is placed on the needs of groups who have undergone special oppression in our society—people of color, women, gays. Finally, the most committed socialists also assist in the creation of longer-term organizations that study the experiences of the present as well as past history in order to put forward the most effective longterm strategy. The significant absence of this whole issue of realizing the socialist goals championed by our scholarship and implicitly animating our radical pedagogy is not without consequences for the books under discussion.

Ira Shor's *Culture Wars* presents an overview of a profound transformation in the U.S. educational system engineered by conservative forces over the past two decades. Most of us recall the various catchwords of this counter-revolution in education, such as "back-to-basics." But the unique contribution of Shor's book is that he provides, for the first time, an important periodization that allows a clearer perspective on the experience we have been undergoing and the lessons that must be learned.

Shor's central argument is that, in response to the leftist challenge of the 1960s, the Nixon and then Reagan administrations launched a three-phase political counter-attack masking itself as concern over educational issues. This assault has been victorious temporarily, but, in the long run provides unsatisfactory solutions. Thus the stage has been set for the subsequent struggles that may result in a more salutary outcome. The heart of Shor's book is a thorough, relentless, and cogent documentation of this analysis.

According to Shor, the first phase of the counter-attack was the educational system's emphasis on "career education" between 1971 and 1975. The second phase was the claim that a crisis in "literacy" had occurred, requiring a return to "basic education" between 1975 and 1982. Most recently, conservative policies have been instituted under the guise of a war for "excellence" against mediocrity. The result has been an ideological war waged continuously in the educational system. On one side have been educational radicals loosely united by the egalitarian themes of peace, justice, and community; on the other have been those seeking to enforce the business-oriented values of authority, competition, and elitism.

In the interstices of this compelling overall argumentation, Shor offers many fascinating observations. For example, at one point he examines the strategical problems of the cultural counter-revolution from the point of view of the counter-revolutionaries themselves. At the outset of their offensive the rightwingers found that they were in something of a bind because the political character of the New Left did not allow the conservatives to raise the traditional bogey of "communism" as the enemy. Thus a search for the appropriate way to opprobriously "name" the new educational radicals ensued. One group on the Right decided to denounce "secular humanism" as the source of all evil; but this choice in turn disturbed another faction of the conservative camp. Eventually the conservatives learned that a consensus could be reached only around the promotion of abstractions such as "excellence," "standards," "accountability," and "quality," which meant all things to all people.

Shor ends his study with an admirable "opposition agenda" of demands, that, if implemented, would undeniably enhance education in the United States considerably. Much of this agenda could in a certain context lead logically toward a humane, nonracist, nonsexist, nonexploitative society, controlled by the free association of producers themselves—socialism. Yet the issue of the implementation of these demands is never seriously addressed. I find this particularly frustrating because, after teaching for twelve years at the University of Michigan, I have come to realize that significant advances in the struggle against institutionalized racism have never come from the classroom methods championed by Shor, although a number of faculty members explicitly try to follow them. Instead, advances have only occurred when hundreds of students and faculty have banned together to organize mass demonstrations, protests, sit-ins, and militant confrontations that have forced the university to grant specific demands. Many of Shor's demands are the same as those raised in recent anti-racist struggles at the University Michigan; but his book leaves activists primarily with the moral injunction to promote critical consciousness which in turn will eventually bring about the necessary change.

The failure to seriously address the implementation of political objectives is also a distressing defect in the impressive series edited by Bertell Ollman and Edward Vernoff, *The Left Academy*. In Volume One (1983), the editors frankly admit that the bonding of Marxist scholarship to political practice in the United States is a problematic area: "without a clear, ongoing link to working class politics, there is the constant danger of Marxist ideas breaking down into a patchwork of synonyms, reworked, relabeled and married off to one of the many ideological suitors that inhabit the corridors of any university. Revolutionaries as well as revolutionary ideas get tamed in this way" (*The Left Academy*, Vol. 1, p. 3).

Unfortunately, the essays in Volume Two of the series ignore this activist aspect of being "left" just as blithely as do those in Volume One, although the contributions certainly expand our knowledge considerably about what has been happening in university scholarship concerning Marxist approaches to literature, art history, classical antiquity, education, geography, biology, and law. On the whole I would say that this book, like the series itself, is more useful in informing us of the existence of work by lesser-known Marxist scholars than for fresh evaluations of the work of the famous and influential.

However, from the perspective of political practice, there is a most striking defect in the essays about the disciplines with which I have greatest familiarity. It appears that the implicit disparagement of activist Marxism results in some cases in depoliticization of the historiography of Marxist scholarship in the area of considering the connections between the cultural and political practice of the theorists described.

For instance, Alan Wallach provides a chapter on "Marxism and Art History" that is really quite excellent in its contrast of the Marxist and "bourgeois" approaches. Yet his survey of the work of the Marxist theorists themselves is characterized by a limited political perspective as well as a lack of interest in political precision that can be quite misleading.

One example of this is that the political trajectory of Meyer Schapiro is depicted by Wallach as coinciding with the general trend of avant-garde artists and writers of the period who suffered "political disillusionment after the Hitler-Stalin pact" and who subsequently rejected Marxism (p. 36). In fact, Schapiro was a relatively idiosyncratic figure in that he broke with official Communism very early in the 1930s and was under the influence of Trotskyism when he published the three crucial essays that are cited by Wallach. Moreover, Schapiro was almost alone in remaining a Leninist throughout the entire World War II period. Thus the Hitler-Stalin pact was merely an opportunity for Schapiro to more aggressively promote his anti-Stalinist Marxism. What eventually moved him from revolutionary Marxism to social democracy was the failure of revolutionary movements to transform Western Europe in the wake of World War II.

In my judgment, the inclusion of some precise information about the political activities and associations of some of the scholars whose work is reviewed would be enormously helpful in gaining insight into the relation of different kinds of Marxist scholarship to different kinds of political practice. It is, of course, quite proper and important that the volume has the ecumenical approach of accepting "many Marxisms" and casting a wide net. Yet such an approach need not require one to abstain from comparing and contrasting different aspects of these competing tendencies in scholarship in terms of their relation to different kinds of political practice, nor should it obligate one to depoliticize the scholars to the extent of neglecting altogether any political activities.

One exception to this depoliticization of cultural practice occurs in the chapter on "Marxism in Literary Studies." This area of scholarship is described by coauthors James Kavanagh and Fredric Jameson as "The Weakest Link." By this phrase from Lenin, they mean that literary studies is furthest removed from "bourgeois ideological domination," rendering it a site in which Marxism may "find the opportunity for its most daring advances" (p. 1).

In this chapter, two literary critics of the Communist Party—the largest organized Marxist movement to have existed in the United States—are mentioned, but simply as a negative foil: "[Mike] Gold and Granville Hicks were the most prominent critics closely associated with the American Communist Party in the thirties. Their writing, in journals like *The New Masses*, was strongly influenced by Zdhanovite prescriptions for 'socialist realism,' and relied heavily on evaluating writers on the basis of their class background or immediate class-political allegiance" (4).

The statement is accurate, but it is only a partial—and wholly derogatory—assessment of an achievement by a large number of pro-Communist writers and critics that may not appear to be so mean after a full-scale reconsideration. This negative statement also comes at the only time that the coauthors raise directly the question of the relation of culture to collective and activist political practice. (To be fair, one should note that the coauthors themselves are quite politically active. Also, they do call for a reevaluation of the 1930s, but their reference appears to be primarily to non-Communist writers such as Philip Rahv, Edmund Wilson, and F. O. Matthiessen.)

Another defect of the three-volume series is the failure to treat the autonomous cultural movements of women, Chicanos, Afro-Americans, Native Americans, Asian Americans, and other racial minorities—despite the appearance of entire chapters on "Black Studies," "Puerto Rican Studies," "Chicano Studies," "Asian American Studies," and "Feminist Scholarship" in Volume 3. Much of this work—as well as the general study of colonial discourse—is being carried out today with a Marxist orientation and is of great interest to Marxists.

That Volume Two engages important theoretical concern is without doubt; this is especially true in matters such as the subtleties of base and superstructure, and of Hegelian influences. But commitment is never engaged.

The theme of commitment, however, is clearly part of the pedagogy of the Brazilian educator Paulo Freire, who has been a major figure in radical education throughout North and South America. In the United States he is a central inspiration for Ira Shor, Henry Giroux, and other theorists of left pedagogy. In Nicaragua, some of Freire's ideas were adapted to Nicaraguan conditions by the government-sponsored literacy crusade following the 1979 revolution. It is also well known that Freire promotes the unity of theory and practice as a central concern in his writing and life; yet, the peculiar way in which he does this may help explain why his influence in the United States does not result in the kind of political practice one normally expects from committed Marxists in advanced industrial societies.

As Martin Carnoy observes about Freire in his contribution on "Marxism and Education" to *The Left Academy*: "All pedagogy, for him, is a political and social issue, all politics is pedagogy, and all educational theories are political theories. In Freire's method, teaching and learning are inseparable from the social and political context of the educational process. Learning to read, for example, is a political act. . . ." (Vol. 2, p. 84). One problem with this approach is that, if virtually every instance of teaching and learning represents "political action," then there seems to be no distinct category of political practice that distinguishes revolutionary socialist commitment (as described at the outset of this review) from other forms of political action.

The Politics of Education, of course, is derived from a political and cultural experience far removed from that of advanced industrial capitalism. Yet even taken in its own terms, Freire's collected writings seem to be more inspirational work than writings with clear practical implications. Like *Pedagogy of the Oppressed* (1973), it is brilliantly suggestive and highly partisan on behalf of social liberation. Yet much is highly redundant of itself and earlier books. Also, it is organized around a series of vague concepts, making it appear at times that Freire's contribution is reducible to a set of admirable but abstract maxims: one must respect the poor; illiteracy is not a disease but a social condition; speech and work are transformative acts; "critical consciousness" must be opposed to "banking education"; etc.

In other words, what we have here are only the preliminary stimulae for a revolutionary practice; there is no clear route for effective transformation into an emancipatory practice in the United States, especially without the elaboration of a mode of implementation. In a favorable but not uncritical study of Freire's methodology, Henry Giroux actually cites a *New York Times* report that Consolidated Edison was using Freire's methods "to teach 'skills' to the uneducated so they might become 'employable and promotable'" (*Ideology, Culture and the Process of Schooling* [Philadelphia: Temple University Press, 1981], p. 140).

The "missing link" in the three books—that of activist and collective implementation—is by no means an abstract desideratum of the future. Throughout this century we have seen radical educators and scholars participate in the formation of unions of professionals, educators, journalists, and teachers. We have also seen them work for the transformation of these and other unions into instruments of genuine social reform; for the construction of revolutionary political organizations uniting workers and intellectuals in the common task of preserving the legacy of the struggles of oppressed groups and elaborating programs for social transformation; and toward the development of publications and other cultural forms expressing the vision of these unions and organizations; etc.

Since the 1930s traditional socialist political organizations have justifiably come under considerable attack—for top-down bureaucratization and the stifling of intellectual freedom, not to mention racist and sexist practices. Unfortunately, the tendency of New Left academics in recent years has been more to junk this legacy entirely, without the semblance of an alternative, than to build upon what is viable in that legacy and create safeguards against the repetition of past errors.

19

Continuity in Working-Class Literary Movements

In 1935, in an introduction to the anthology *Proletarian Literature in the United States*, the prominent Communist critic Joseph Freeman declared: "Art, an instrument in the class struggle, must be developed by the proletariat as one of its weapons." In 1978, the publishers of Singlejack Press, a small operation featuring a series of "Little Books" by workers about the work experience, observed: "We are all starved for images of ourselves, for identity and for aids to communicate the condition of our lives and the good in them. But the millions who do the so-called 'unskilled,' 'semi-skilled,' 'craft,' and even professional jobs in American workplaces are seldom, if ever, represented fairly in the popular literature and media of the nation." It would be useful to probe the relationship between these two statements on the nature of working-class literature, formulated nearly forty years apart.

An examination of the short stories and reportage included in *Proletarian Literature in the United States* reveals only a few selections that actually depict the work process in the manner advocated by the Singlejack Press publishers, Robert Miles and Stan Weir.* Moreover, the Singlejack focus is entirely absent from a recent compilation of radical writings from the Great Depression, *Writers in Revolt: The Anvil Anthology, 1933–40* (Lawrence Hill and Co., 1973). Conversely, those Singlejack "Little Books" published to date rarely offer worker-writers dramatizing militant class struggles or exhorting readers to engage in revolutionary politics, two themes that dominated much working-class literature published during the 1930s. Although Miles and Weir have initiated one of the most successful worker-writer projects of the last decade, one might justifiably ask whether they are

---

* In January 1983 Miles left Singlejack to devote all his time to a separate publishing venture. However, since this essay is concerned with Singlejack's history prior to that time, Miles will be treated as one of the publishers throughout.

building upon or rejecting the achievements of one of their most important literary antecedents. The answer is necessarily complex.

The primary difference between the organized working-class literary movements of the thirties and today is that the former were mostly channeled through the institutions of a single political organization, the Communist Party (CP). The CP had far outstripped its rivals, the faction-ridden Socialist Party and the miniscule Trotskyist and Lovestoneite groups, to achieve hegemony on the U.S. Left. This hegemony went unchallenged during the early 1930s when the CP cultural wing called for a distinctly "proletarian literature," and CP strategy was only challenged on the Left by a small group of New York–based Trotskyist-influenced intellectuals when, after 1935, under the impetus of the Popular Front, the CP's cultural orientation began to emphasize liberal, patriotic, and anti-fascist themes.

There are, of course, other important differences affecting the creation of working-class literature during the thirties and today. For example, during the Great Depression, not only were millions out of work, but social welfare programs, if they existed at all, were even less effective than they are now. Consequently, a good deal of writing during the thirties was devoted to "bottom-dog" life, depicting down-and-out, demoralized victims of unemployment. Furthermore, inspiring international developments such as the struggle against fascism in Spain and the steps toward socialism that many imagined were being taken in the Soviet Union, affected the consciousness of the radicalizing workers in a manner that has no contemporary analogy.

One of the most pressing tasks facing the present generation of radical scholars is the need to develop a substantial reassessment of the left-wing literary achievements of the 1930s, advancing beyond the several academic studies that were published in the 1960s and early 1970s. This task must be carried out in the context of two new developments. The first is the more subtle appreciation of Marxist cultural theory that exists today, in contrast to the narrow orthodox "Marxism-Leninism-Stalinism" that shaped much of the criticism of the past. Far less dogmatic and mechanical than its counterpart in the thirties, the new Marxist literary theory is distinguished by pioneering explorations in materialist culture and ideology by Raymond Williams and Terry Eagleton, the rediscovery of the "Mediation Theory" of the Frankfurt School, the assertion of the category of gender and of national cultures in feminist and ThirdWorld writings, and the emergence of a dialectical notion of mass culture that allows for a subversive content to counter the manipulative intentions of "the consciousness industry."

The second development is the appearance of a new school of historians of U.S. Communism, especially the writings of Paul Buhle, Maurice Isserman, and Mark Naison. These scholars, while critical of Stalinism, nonetheless have retained a compassion that acknowledges and embraces the heroic commitment of thousands of rank-and-file Party members. Moreover, their work explores the Party's relative heterogeneity, community ties, and ethnic dimensions.

Such a reassessment of Great Depression writing, of course, cannot change the fact established by previous scholars that only a handful of radical novels have had major influence on our culture. I, nevertheless, believe that a reexamination will disclose that many more than is currently imagined may be discussed on the level of artistic seriousness now given only to European "classics" of political literature such as André Malraux's *Man's Fate* and Ignazio Silone's *Bread and Wine*, or, more recently, Nadine Gordimer's *Burger's Daughter*. However, more important will be the necessary recognition that the left-wing cultural achievement as a whole was so large, diverse, and contemporary in its concerns that it deserves a far more important place in the history of U.S. culture than it has been given. Still, the pioneers who carry out this project will not be able to avoid at least two particularly troubling aspects of the predecessor movement: the unrealistic pretensions of some of the left-wing literary critical proclamations of the thirties and the artificial character of some aspects of the poetry, fiction, and drama. In my view, one way of appreciating the contribution of Singlejack Press is to see how its publications have tried to overcome these historic problems.

As stated, the first problematic aspect of the thirties legacy involves the exaggerated expectations and considerable arrogance marking a good deal of the critical claims of the Communist Left. It is not my intention here to add to the unfair caricatures of the radical literary movement as a whole that have dominated U.S. literary history for so long; however, intermixed with and sometimes overshadowing some cogent and prophetic insights of Marxist critics of the time were a number of absurd claims. Michael Gold declared in 1930, for example, that the proletarian literary movement would produce "a hundred Shakespeares" in the next ten years. When Clifford Odets launched his career by writing several radical plays, Communist critics compared him to Chekhov, O'Casey, O'Neill, Tolstoy, Dreiser, and Wolfe. Non-Communist writers who had produced universally recognized masterpieces—such as Joyce, Proust, James, Eliot, and Pound—were sometimes dismissed with vile invective. Other writers, including Archibald MacLeish, were said to reflect a "fascist unconscious" in their work. Such unscientific and contemptuous attitudes not only helped to misdirect the creative effort of some radical writers into avenues that were not very productive; they also provided a skewed frame of reference for evaluating literary achievement.

To what extent can we excuse such hyperbole as braggadocio or as well-meaning but poorly formulated attempts to encourage young and "outsider" writers from the non-elite classes? The problem is that such claims tend to reflect the theory, promoted by Gold and others, that the duty of revolutionary criticism was to promote an autonomous "proletarian culture." This view, first articulated by Gold in the early 1920s, received the imprimatur of a number of increasingly Stalinized literary and political organizations in the Soviet Union over the next decade. An unresolved debate ensued in the pages of the Communist-sponsored *New Masses* and John Reed Club organs throughout the early thirties as to exactly what constituted "proletarian culture." Did the concept mean writing by workers? Did it encompass writing about working-class life? Did it include writing that expressed political ideas that aided the class struggle?

The confusion underlying this debate stems largely from a desire to analogize artistic creation and articulated political ideology by arguing that both are reducible to contending poles aligned with antagonistic classes. In 1923 Leon Trotsky's *Literature and Revolution* criticized the theoretical shallowness of the notion that a full-blown proletarian culture could develop during a turbulent period in which the working class was, in fact, battling to abolish itself as well as the ruling class and create a classless society and a classless culture. While Trotsky advocated the promotion of cultural activities by workers and urged them to exercise their creative talent on working-class themes, he believed that those who proclaimed that an entirely new culture would be created in the process—a task in his view that would require centuries to realize—were violating historical proportion. He predicted that such a policy would result in the creation of mediocre works. The novelist James T. Farrell augmented Trotsky's arguments in his 1936 polemic, *A Note on Literary Criticism*. Moreover, the whole notion of two or more autonomous cultures in a single social formation is very much at odds with Antonio Gramsci's theory of organic culture in which particular elements can be articulated for diverse ends.

This tendency to reductively conflate art and political ideology also explains a second troublesome feature of the literary legacy of the thirties: the inauthenticity of aspects of the writers' movement, at least insofar as political criteria for judging texts were sometimes concocted in response to the larger objectives of the Soviet-led Communist movement. For example, when the proletarian cultural theory was precipitously abandoned in 1935, together with the John Reed Clubs and the promotion of the unknown working-class writers, the lack of a serious critique of the strengths and weaknesses of this whole project suggests that its "real" purpose was only to bolster the Party itself at a certain conjuncture. Now the Party was engaged in a new Popular Front strategy and thus a new cultural orientation was set in place, one that was directed more to the cultivation of the sympathies of "big-name" authors and significantly less to the plebeian revolutionary ones. A different kind of cultural organization, the League of American Writers, with its star-studded conferences, was now promoted to accommodate the new turn. The unity of liberals and Communists on the basis of liberal politics became a cultural as well as a political objective. Harsh Communist criticism of anti-Marxist authors, such as MacLeish and Hemingway, was now transformed into praise, while Marxist writers, such as James T. Farrell, who committed the unpardonable sin of condemning the Moscow Purge Trials were denounced as "gangsters of the pen."

From this perspective, it appears that Weir and Miles' Singlejack Book series has managed to shunt aside this legacy of arrogance and manipulation in order to connect with the positive core of the radical cultural movement of the 1930s: workers transforming their life and work experience into literature. Singlejack's project of providing a natural, organically evolving forum by which workers can explore their lives through creative writing and reportage derives from the origin of the publishing house. Singlejack's genesis can be traced back to a series of personal connections among three West Coast workers who had a common background as longshoremen. The catalyst was Stan Weir, a longtime socialist and labor radical, who has spent twenty-five years performing blue-collar work as a merchant seaman, auto assembly-line worker, construction worker, teamster, and longshoreman. His original intention had been to raise the spirits of a depressed former partner on the San Francisco waterfront, George Benet. Benet had published a Mickey Spillane–type thriller, *The Hoodlums*, in 1953, but since then had only accumulated a trunkful of rejected manuscripts. In 1976 Weir made the acquaintance of Robert Miles, a second generation longshoreman in Southern California who ran a 1,100-member book club featuring best-sellers of the small press. Miles and Weir read Benet's manuscripts and discussed the feasibility of publishing a book by him on their own. Of the three, only Weir had a background in the Marxist movement, having been a leader of Max Shachtman's Workers Party from the early 1940s until the late 1950s. Miles is a class-conscious trade union militant. Benet is a fast-talking former barroom performer who affects the pose of a right-wing Catholic, male chauvinist, and bigot, although he acknowledges that his best friends are radicals.

Weir managed to raise $500 and in 1978 he and Miles published a collection of Benet's stories and poems called *A Place in Colusa* as a one-shot effort and personal favor to a friend. In the wake of very favorable reviews and numerous orders, Miles and Weir decided to publish a second book, *Quilts: The Great American Art* by Patricia Mainardi, a New York art critic. *Quilts* was followed by the first of the "Little Book Series," *Labor Law for the Rank and File* by Staughton Lynd, which was very favorably received by union militants. Miles and Weir then decided to give a special focus to their press: henceforth they would publish "how-to" books telling workers what they needed to know to fight back against the bosses, and books depicting the work experience itself.

The location and administration of the press is also indicative of the character of the worker-writer movement of the 1970s and 1980s. The Singlejack office is not in New York or Chicago—centers of the proletarian literary movement during the 1930s—but three blocks off the waterfront at 395 West 6th Street in San Pedro, Port of Los Angeles, the largest port on the West Coast. From there the Singlejack books are shipped to customers and the correspondence answered. Occasionally longshoremen and writers stop by for a chat. The building in which the office is located abounds with marginal small businesses, and is surrounded by cafés and places where longshoremen, merchant seamen, and ship scalers dine. Across the street is the seventy-year-old City Fish Market, a hangout for local fishermen.

Miles and Weir volunteer their time to the press, with each contributing twenty-four hours a week. While the norm in publishing is to charge eight times the production cost when determining the retail price of a book, Miles and Weir compute the retail price at about three-and-a-half to four times the production cost in order to keep the prices of the books reasonable. Singlejack does all the editing and designing; authors, typesetters, and printers are the only ones who get paid.

Miles and Weir do not adhere to any program or theory in selecting manuscripts, beyond the necessity that the manuscript stand on its own as "good writing" that illuminates the nature of a particular kind of work. Ultimately, the criteria for selection are rather personal: Miles and Weir will not publish anything about which they themselves aren't excited, believing that they must be personally enthusiastic about a book in order to communicate their excitement to others. They also believe that they are well qualified to make all decisions on accepting manuscripts: both have worked extensively, and Miles has had experience selling books through his book club. They do consult with their wives, both of whom have degrees in English literature, and they have established a network of readers for submitted manuscripts that includes blacks, women, unionists, lawyers, writers, and a former publisher. In addition, Miles continues carefully to follow the contemporary small press, and both have a fairly strong background in classics. Weir was raised with a great-grandfather he remembers as "a working stiff into Shakespeare." Both are aficionados of humor as represented not only in classics but also in working-class life.

Thus, in contrast to the fairly programmatic and frequently orchestrated radical literary movements of the thirties, it seems that, almost happenstantially, and yet as a natural consequence of their love of literature and sense of solidarity with other workers, Miles and Weir found themselves operating a publishing house with a unique function. To some extent they have developed their mode of operating on a pragmatic basis, guided by a desire to foster a good self-image among fellow workers. It would be a mistake, however, to conclude that Miles and Weir are without strong views as to the political stance of their press vis-à-vis the workers' movement both today and in the past. Indeed, the negative aspects of the literary experiences of the thirties weigh heavily on Weir's mind. His primary objection to some of the manuscripts that Singlejack rejects is that they are dominated by an explicit and sectarian class-struggle program, one that demands that workers engage in revolutionary action according to someone else's short calendar. In contrast, Weir believes that, "If the work people do can become visible, there's no need for a program for the initial radicalization. This is because in the process of becoming visible, looking at the work one does and work like it, one becomes conscious of one's own values and gets a better self-image. And without a better self-image one will never try to change the world."

Steve Turner's *Night Shift in a Pickle Factory* (1980) is a representative "Little Book." The story tells the experiences of a laid-off mill worker in a small New England town who is in desperate financial straits and takes a minimum-wage job in a pickle cannery. While the narrative is infused with an understandable political consciousness, the author focuses on small episodes in the life of the factory, giving the reader a sense of how it feels to do the work. This approach contrasts dramatically with stories in *Proletarian Literature of the United States* such as "Strike" by William Rollins and "A Class in English" by Louis Lehrman which, along with other stories, depict lovers split apart when they take opposing sides in the class struggle, a baby dying from malnutrition because its parents are unemployed, club-swinging cops, placards with Communist slogans, and the singing of "The Internationale."

Turner's work is arguably just as political if not more so than are Rollins' and Lehrman's stories. From the outset he manages to subtly interweave a number of Marxist economic concepts, including various strategies used by capitalists to increase their profits, and the elementary workings of surplus value. In the closing pages he introduces the intertwined theme of the necessity of unions and the failure of contemporary union leadership. His most effective device is his careful literary construction of a factory that dominates and shapes the lives of individual workers, so long as they remain individuals. It is unlikely that one will come away from this story without a strong sense of the seething rebelliousness that lies beneath the surface of the U.S. work force, a rebelliousness awaiting leadership and focus. Turner is a skilled craftsman, as are most of the "Little Book" authors, which is certainly a reason why they have found a place in a number of university-level sociology classes.

The main strategy of the "Little Books" dealing with work experience—the "how-to" variety of "Little Books" and the large-sized Singlejack publications are another matter—seems to be the communication of political and sociological ideas by implication. Clearly this contrasts favorably with the trend in literature of the Great Depression that gave the impression of artificially manipulating form and content to communicate an immediate political "message." Yet, a variety of strategies are necessary to create memorable art that captures the essence of experience in all its complexity, and here there are signs that the "Little Books" still retain features of apprentice works. For example, as explorations of neglected or caricatured elements of contemporary life experience, they lack the social vision, narrative dynamism, cultural allusiveness, and striking imagery of fiction of the same era by Afro-American writers such as Toni Morrison and Native American writers such as Leslie Silko.

Moreover, a glance through *Proletarian Literature in the United States* will reveal a few extraordinary pieces such as Ben Field's "Cow." Shorter than any of the Singlejack "Little Books," but embodying more complexity, power, and potential for affecting a wider range of readers, Field depicts a fat Jewish radical from the city who comes to work on a farm. Turning every prejudice against him to his own advantage (when another worker calls him a "cow" he embraces the epithet as his nickname), his altruism and love of life gradually transform the consciousness of those with whom he works. "Cow" is a multi-dimensional work of art, an imaginative rendering of the work experience also filled with dramatic tension. It is also strong in an area that the Singlejack "Little Books" have yet to even enter, for the center of "Cow" is its remarkable characterization of the radical. Ultimately of heroic stature, he is not without flaws, contradictions, and mysteries; one would like to read more about him. That the "Little Books" are weak in such characterization is surprising, for one of the complaints of Miles and Weir is that workers in the United States are usually depicted in popular literature and media as "clowns and culprits, near-apes or gum-smacking hollow-heads."

One might speculate whether Field's ability to characterize the radical so powerfully is connected with the explicitness of his own radicalism in the story, or even with the visionary zeal of the thirties movement as a whole, elements that are considerably tempered in the Singlejack books. But the important point is perhaps that the appearance of stories of this type in collections of thirties writing ought to remind us of the unevenness and unpredictability of all literary ventures, and of the fact that memorable art can still triumph over dubious programs, while even the most compelling theorization of culture cannot guarantee the creation of rich and enduring texts.

Thus we see that the elements of continuity and discontinuity in working-class movements are complex and ambiguous. As one expression of the contemporary worker-writer movement, Singlejack is linked to its ancestors through a pattern of acceptance and rejection. Although the Singlejack project is in certain ways more authentic as a natural expression of the need for workers to write, the publishing house has yet to make a mark with a memorable work of drama, vision, and especially characterization, although readers who have worked at the same or similar jobs as those depicted in the "Little Books" will undoubtedly experience a shock of recognition and find the series memorable for that reason. But a more positive development in the Singlejack project is by no means excluded, even though the editors have wisely refrained from indulging in pretensions about what they have achieved or expect to accomplish in coming years. Both Singlejack and its thirties predecessors testify to the fragmentation and unevenness of the workers' literary movement across the decades to the present. This fragmentation can be overcome only through dialogue, criticism, a dispassionate study of past models, a deepening of literary skill through practice, and a growth in our understanding of the history, culture, and current activities of the class that may hold the future of our society in its hands.

20

Remembering
George Breitman

An abridged version of this talk was given at a memorial meeting for George Breitman (1916–1986) in June 1986 in New York City. For over five decades Breitman was an activist and writer in the U.S. Trotskyist movement, best-known as the author of The Last Year of Malcolm X *and chief editor of the fourteen-volume series* Writings of Leon Trotsky (1929–1940).

Those of us who had the privilege of collaborating on scholarly and historical projects with our dear friend George Breitman, have an incalculable debt to repay to the socialist and working-class movement. For it was this movement that gave George his theme and vision, and so many of his skills. In turn, George passed these on to us through countless hours devoted to personal correspondence, the reading of our manuscripts, the examination of historical documents, and those many memorable periods of intense discussion.

I did not know George personally until April 1976, when he wrote a letter volunteering to help in my work of reconstructing the lives and activities of several long-deceased and largely forgotten Trotskyist writers and intellectuals.

From the moment we met in person, a few weeks later, I was overwhelmed by the extraordinary intensity of this man whose health appeared so fragile, and who worked with so many physical handicaps. For example, even though George shifted among three different kinds of eyeglasses as he labored, none would allow him to see the paper when he typed; this forced him to lean forward, which in turn produced excruciating pains in his neck and spine.

Yet George's working environments at that time—a small office at Pathfinder Press and a modest apartment on East Eleventh Street—were bursting with the paraphernalia of numerous scholarly projects. Prior to 1975, George had been a popularizer and educator in his writing. But in the mid-1970s he shifted his emphasis more directly to the membership of the

Socialist Workers Party (SWP) and Young Socialist Alliance (YSA), so that a good deal of his work took on a more historical, theoretical, and internal character.

What astonished me most in meeting George was that he had far more precise information about the literary and intellectual figures with whom I was preoccupied than even their closest friends and relatives. This was the case even when he had hardly known or never actually met the people under discussion! Moreover, as George marshaled what researchers call the "primary evidence" into view—that is, documentation not dependent on memory—it soon became clear that many of those who claimed to know people the best, including the figures themselves (through autobiographical recollections and statements in later years), actually knew them least.

With considerable ease, George demonstrated how one intellectual, who wrote in a personal letter to me that he had broken completely with the Trotskyist movement at news of the assassination of Trotsky, was still publishing regularly in the Trotskyist newspaper under a pseudonym several years later. He also documented for me how another figure, who had claimed to launch a business career only after his disillusionment with revolutionary socialist politics, had misremembered the dates of certain conventions and conferences so that, once put in their proper order, the chronology was actually the reverse: the business career was launched in advance of the political rupture.

In his historical research, I think, George lived closer to the world of "fact" than anyone else I had ever met. And one of the things he taught, from his ruthless criticizing of my own research as well as the putatively scholarly books and monographs of others, was relevant to life as well as to work. It had to do with the human and subjective factor, which is always present, and which we can control only to the extent that we understand the subtle ways in which we ourselves fall victim to it.

Methodologically, this meant for George the uncompromising interrogation of all empirical data, something he carried out in practice long before Louis Althusser theorized its necessity in *Reading Capital*. And let me add that no one was exempt from this interrogation, including Trotsky and James P. Cannon. George was possessed of one of the most critical intelligences I think I have ever known.

This, I believe, is quite extraordinary, because so many people, in order to sustain themselves for decades as advocates of an unpopular cause, to carry on day in and day out with considerable amounts of self-sacrifice, need a balm. Sometimes this balm is the idealization of some infallible leader or some country where the promised land of socialism is already in view, or a habit of mind that sees everything in the most positive light, with a socialist transformation "just around the corner." To survive as a critical intelligence, always questioning, always rethinking in light of the harsh realities and disappointments of life, is a rarity.

It was George's combination of a ruthless skepticism with the demand for thorough and precise documentation that made me feel that the highest praise I ever got from George was a statement that "I admire your ability to report things accurately and objectively."

Finally, after seven years of collaboration, when George completed a review of a 500-page manuscript of mine and reported that "I found only a dozen errors, so minor that they are not worth listing," I was in Marxist heaven. This was because, if one knew George at all, one knew that any error he found too small to be "not worth listing" must be truly microscopic.

Of course, when George expressed his admiration for accuracy and objectivity, this did not mean for him the absence of partisanship. Rather, it meant rhetorical restraint and a sense of fair play in the treatment of data, and, where possible, a distinction between the interpretation and the description of events, insofar as these can be differentiated.

But there was a personal flipside to George's research method, too. Since George was so acutely aware of the distortions rendered by the subjectivity of others, he struggled to force himself to be doubly on guard against the distortions that might be wrought by his own psychological needs and unintentional bias. Moreover, George was never satisfied; never for a moment did he sit back with smug satisfaction and trumpet the illusion that past achievements betoken superior wisdom.

Exactly the opposite was the case, for George's own research had taught him quite well what may be one of the most painful lessons of life: that age and experience guarantee nothing. He felt this most acutely, of course, when during the last few years of his life he and many of his comrades had to in a certain sense begin building their political lives anew, from scratch.* George observed sadly that "One of the by-products of old age is for some of us a loss of restraint and diminution of discretion," and that he now found he had to "more consciously control myself, guard against exaggeration and simplification, etc., much more than I had to just a few years ago."

Yet, that being said, I can't think of anyone who was better prepared for that difficult situation than was George Breitman. George had lived his whole life without illusion; he had studied more circumspectly than anyone else of whom I am aware the lives and political patterns of radicals so that he was fully conscious of the ambiguities and sudden turn-abouts inherent in any situation; and, most of all, he tried to avoid the mistake of confusing

---

* In early 1984 Breitman and many other founders of the Socialist Workers Party were expelled on charges of "disloyalty" as the organization consolidated its move toward Castroism. At the time of his death Breitman was a member of an organization called Fourth Internationalist Tendency.

loyalty to ideas with "loyalty" to charismatic personalities and cozy institutions. If that remark I quoted appears to express some self-reproach, it was only because George was twice as hard on himself as he was on anyone else . . . and, to be frank, he *was* quite hard on others.

It doesn't follow from this analysis that I feel George was correct and convincing in all his judgments about historical matters; indeed, if one knew George, nothing would more effectively cause his stomach to turn, would cause him to depart from this very room, than some sort of hagiographical or martyrological eulogy that made no effort to critically assess his life's work. Indeed, that is why I believe our collaboration was so full and continuous over a ten-year period, despite our differing views on the history of the SWP, Leninism, and Trotskyism. It was because, as George put it rather delicately, after one horrendous row, he much appreciated the "frankness we both feel in expressing our opinions."

We argued back and forth about how to interpret the policy followed by the SWP in World War II. We disagreed in our assessments of the comparative impact of Trotskyism in the U.S. and Britain during the 1960s and after. We had heated exchanges over George's writings on French Trotskyism between the wars that were contained in his essay "The Rocky Road of the Fourth International" and more obliquely in his edited collection on *The Crisis of the French Section.*

In fact, the last instance was one where I did part company with George on a methodological level, believing that the simple presentation of what appeared to be "facts" along with one's own interpretation was inadequate for the task. I argued that there are instances where the Marxist scholar, especially when dealing with rather remote, obscure, as well as complex, episodes, has an obligation to at least make an attempt to offer a plausible case for his or her opponent's point of view. I recalled an interview with an old Trotskyist, Milton Alvin, where he emphatically narrated how the Trotskyist leader James P. Cannon had told him that in every factional dispute one's opponent had some strong element of truth, and that one's responsibility was to reach out and critically assimilate that element. I thought that George did not appreciate that necessity in some of his work; he, in turn, held that what I saw as a dialectical method of critical incorporation and transcendence was actually closer to a feigned neutrality.

In considering the final phase of George's life and work, we have to ask ourselves why it was that George had this passion for historical reconstruction. Why was it that, while so many other political veterans are content to reminisce, to recreate history as they imagined it (and often with themselves assuming a far more central role than was the case), George turned relentlessly back to primary materials, something that can be quite unsettling and disconcerting in regard to long-held convictions?

There was, I think, one particular episode that gives some insight into this drive on the part of George. In 1983 the collection of writings called *Fighting Racism in World War II* appeared. George had played a central role in preparing the volume, and by all rights should have been credited as editor of the volume and author of its introduction.

But when George discovered, to his dismay and horror, that the editors at Pathfinder Press had deleted certain portions of a pamphlet they reprinted by C. L. R. James, without clearly indicating these deletions, because they now disagreed with what James had said on behalf of the SWP forty years ago, George insisted that his name be removed from any sort of editorial responsibility for the book.

In discussing this incident by mail, I was quick to label the act of the Pathfinder staff a venal example of "tampering with history." George, who saw more subtleties in the situation, replied that, yes, there may have been an element of such tampering, but the incident mainly showed the Pathfinder editors' "utter lack of interest in the past except insofar as it resembled what they say now."

In other words, George's fascination with history went far beyond functional purposes; his laborious research was not undertaken in the service of proving a political line, smashing a factional opponent, or establishing certain credentials for himself. The inner-directed nature of his research was part of the reason why he complained to me in February 1980 that "virtually no one is interested in the main things I want to write."

Of course, George was a revolutionary socialist, so historical inquiry was hardly an idle exercise, either. But I do believe that George's passion for history had a sort of aesthetic dimension to it. Like a novelist in the realist and naturalist tradition, who is driven to reconstruct the authentic life experience of his or her times, George was engaged in a struggle to reconstruct the political world of Trotskyism over the past five decades, as he knew it.

Yes, George was the consummate self-educated scholar. But he was also in his own way an artist, the practitioner of a highly skilled craft. In these last years, Trotskyist historiography was George's forté. He was not a biographer, although he collaborated with myself and others in preparing biographical portraits of John G. Wright, Duncan Ferguson, and Carl Skoglund. Through careful documentation he made it possible to bring back to life the central political issues preoccupying those predecessor comrades who loved, argued, fought, and suffered, just as he had himself. George, more than anyone else, gave us tools so that we might then reclaim our own history, warts and all.

I use the cliché "warts and all" quite deliberately, because I will never forget George's extreme sobriety, a sobriety that I think must have grated against some of his associates.

Often at memorial meetings for much-loved socialists, such as George Breitman certainly was, there is a good deal of talk about the comrade's "optimism," "joy of life," and even of turning the memorial into a "celebration" of his or her life. Now, I am not saying that George was a pessimist, and I am not saying that George was joyless or humorless, by any means: but his was a *critical* intelligence. His devotion to socialism was, I believe, an act of will, not faith, a scientifically-derived moral response to the otherwise meaningless and ephemeral nature of human existence.

What other person has faced the conundrums, ambiguities, and embarrassing errors in his or her own political movement so carefully as did George Breitman in his arduous research? And what is impressive to me is that that confrontation, which must have been painful at times, only strengthened George's resolve to go forward in constructing a socialist organization to help guide the infinitely complex struggle toward a better world.

Among other things, it is that critical intelligence that we are here to honor, to commemorate, and perhaps even to try to begin to assimilate, in this memorial for our friend, our comrade, our teacher, and, in some respects, our father, George Breitman.

INDEX

parties, Social Democracy), xiv, 3, 49, 76
Socialist Register, xix
Socialist Workers Party, 4, 19–36 passim, 44, 46, 49, 69, 73–82 passim, 124, 201, 229, 234–39
Solidarnosc (Polish Solidarity), 71
Sollers, Werner: *Beyond Ethnicity*, 169–79 passim
Solow, Herbert, 45
Solzhenitsyn, Alexander: *The First Circle*, 205; *Cancer Ward*, 205
South Africa, 207–13
Spanish Civil War, 92, 95, 118, 226
Spector, Maurice, 43
Stalinism, xv, 41, 46–52 passim, 57, 58, 87–90, 104, 108, 112–14 passim, 207–13 passim
Stalin, Joseph, 42, 45, 50, 69, 70, 76, 89, 112, 186, 207
State Capitalism (theory of the USSR), 68, 70
Steinberg, Stephen: *The Ethnic Myth*, 62
Steiner, Ralph, 87
Stewart, Donald Ogden, 93, 124
Stone, Ben: *Memoirs of a Radical Rank and Filer*, 82 n. 1
Stout, Rex, 93
Strand, Paul, 87
Structuralism, 177
Struppeck, Jules, 14, 16, 29
Student Non-Violent Co-ordinating Committee, 197
Students for a Democratic Society (SDS), xi–xiv, 219
Susman, Warren, "The 1930s," 64
Swados, Harvey, 75, 93
Sweezy, Paul, 215

Telos, 214, 217
Third College (U.C. San Diego), 191
Third Woman, The, 199
Thirties, xiii, 138, 161, 168, 224, 225–33 passim
Thompson, E.P., 57
Tijerina, Reies López, 197
Tito, Josip, 50
Tolstoy, Leo, 164, 173, 227
Transition, 118

Tresca, Carlo, 48
Trilling, Diana, 42
Trilling, Lionel, xvii, 42, 56, 57, 75; *The Middle of the Journey*, 62, 215
Trotskyism, xiv, xvi, xvii, 3, 4, 19–36 passim, 39–52 passim, 56–66 passim, 67–71 passim, 111, 124, 222, 226, 234–39
Trotsky, Leon, xvii, xviii, 24, 30, 45, 47, 48, 56, 65, 67, 71, 74, 76, 80, 186, 235; *The Revolution Betrayed*, 43; "The Moralists and Sycophants Against Marxism," 44; *Literature and Revolution*, 228
Trotsky, Natalia Sedova, 23
Troubadour, 104
Tsiang, H.T., 129
Turner, Steve: *Night Shift in a Pickle Factory*, 231
Tynan, Kenneth, 91

Ultraleftism, 77
United Coalition Against Racism (University of Michigan), xix, 158–67, 184, 221
United Farm Workers campaign, 197
University of Michigan, 155–67 passim
USSR, xiii, 226

Valdez, Luis, 197, 199
Vernoff, Edward: *The Left Academy*, 218–24 passim
Vietnam War. *See* Anti-Vietnam war movement
Viva Kennedy Clubs, 197

Wald, Alan M.: political biography, xi–xv, 78–81; Jewish identity, xii, xiv; as teacher, xiv; research interests, xv–xix; books by, xvi; friendship with James T. Farrell, xvii; political objectives, xvii–xviii; attends Antioch and Berkeley, vi–viii, 78; relations with Students for a Democratic Society and Economic Research and Action Project, xi–xiii; relations with Young Socialist Alliance and Socialist Workers Party, xi–xiii, 78–81; friendship with